THE PRESIDENTIAL CAMPAIGN OF 1860

THE
PRESIDENTIAL CAMPAIGN
OF 1860

BY

EMERSON DAVID FITE, Ph.D.

KENNIKAT PRESS, INC./PORT WASHINGTON, N.Y.

CONTENTS

PREFACE

PRESIDENTIAL campaigns in the United States are great popular debates, in which different sections of the country and different political parties join in discussing concrete propositions of national policy from various points of view, and sometimes pass judgments of far-reaching importance; almost invariably, the contests, with their divergent moods and appeals, well merit close study. Yet, strangely enough, they have hitherto been neglected as subjects for historical investigation, so that the present volume, as far as the author's knowledge extends, is the first serious work done in the field. My attention was first directed to the war elections by Professor Edward Channing, to whom I am glad to render cordial thanks.

The publication of the party platforms in the Appendix is self-explanatory; the four typical campaign speeches, hitherto not readily accessible, are printed because of the valuable light which they throw on the arguments offered to the people in the crisis.

EMERSON DAVID FITE.

NEW HAVEN, CONNECTICUT,
    October, 1910.

INTRODUCTION

THERE have been more exciting and enthusiastic political campaigns in the history of the country than that of 1860, such as those of 1840 and of 1856; one at least has involved equally important issues, that of 1864; but never has a campaign been waged in which the people of the whole nation have taken a more calm, serious, and intelligent interest.

The most characteristic feature of this campaign was the strong control over the political situation in the North exercised by the masses of the people; in the South it was more of a battle of leaders. From the moment of John Brown's raid and the dramatic importance suddenly given in the House of Representatives to Hinton Rowan Helper's *Impending Crisis* to the day of the election, there was no moment when politics were not under popular domination; compared with the point of view of the people, and their words and deeds, the platforms and utterances of leaders were of minor importance. The Harper's Ferry raid was not "a mere episode, a spectacular incident, without consequence"; everything would not "have happened just as, in fact, it did happen, if Brown had never lived, and never been hung."[1] The tide of the "irrepressible conflict" had, indeed, by that time already set in, but the Charlestown drama further agitated the fury of its currents, added to their volume, and immeasurably accelerated their speed. The resulting popular reaction against slavery far

[1] This quotation is an opinion expressed in the *Atlantic Monthly*, November, 1910, p. 667, by John T. Morse, Jr., in a review of *John Brown: A Biography Fifty Years After*, by Oswald Garrison Villard, Boston, 1910.

exceeded any ever before known. Herein, and not in the mere trial and execution, must be sought the real significance of the event. The South now with new hatred expelled from its midst suspected Northerners, and the stories of the victims aroused new animosities in the North against the South; by countless fresh aggressions, one following closely upon another, and persisting throughout the canvass, the flames of sectional hatred were fanned brighter and brighter.

Homely, almost unnoticed events among the people reveal the full influence of the speakership contest and of Helper's *Crisis.* With suddenness and amid unusual excitement political parties were led to commit themselves to opinions from which there could be no retraction, with the nominating conventions and the summer's campaign close at hand. Conservatives stiffened in their conservatism, the radicals became more sturdy and uncompromising, while between the two surging currents William H. Seward, not knowing which way to turn, trembled and fell, and lost the prize of a presidential nomination. This was but one of the effects of Brown's raid, wrought through an aroused people.

The popular judgment of slavery dictated the party platforms, and later, when the deceptions and evasions of these documents became apparent, practically determined the issues of the campaign itself, "slavery" or "no slavery," "union" or "secession." As if to recognize this control of the people and helplessness of the leaders, the Republicans held their convention in a large hall before ten thousand spectators, and welcomed the active interference of the crowd in that body's proceedings, unconsciously setting a precedent pregnant with evil for the future; significant, too, is the fact that the most unique demonstration of the campaign, the activities of the Republican marching clubs, the Wide-Awakes, arose spontaneously from the people.

With their supreme control the people were serious-minded ; physical violence and offensive personalities, as a rule, were conspicuously absent ; campaign speeches far exceeded in number those delivered in any previous contest, and were characterized by an intellectual tone and historical breadth of view that were remarkable. The whole history of the country, and its social, legal, and governmental institutions, were searched for proof and refutation ; contemporary society, manners, and customs were rigorously held up to view, analyzed, and judged. Rarely has the nation taken a broader view of itself.

Heckling of speakers on the stump, the natural expression of a serious-minded electorate and at the present day common in English political life, although lacking in the United States, was now prominent. Douglas' frank answers on secession and coercion, Breckenridge's evasive answers on the same topics, Yancey's evasions on secession, and Douglas' on the morality of slavery were marked and influential features of the struggle.

Every party was guilty of hedging on some subject. Both Republicans, and Breckenridgeites to some extent, kept clear of the subject of secession, the latter because their desire to secede was better concealed for the moment, the former because while opposing secession they did not care to enhance the timeliness of the subject by discussing it. Republicans, too, generally refused to meet Douglas in the open on popular sovereignty ; Douglasites would not commit themselves on the morality of slavery, while the Bell-Everetts hardly knew what they believed on any topic. Except for their Border state leader, who was forced to trim in order to carry his home communities with him, the Breckenridgeites were the most open of all the parties.

Commercial considerations, although not usually recognized as one of the factors that went to make up the popular judgment of 1860, were yet of considerable weight. Northerners, following the lead of Helper, expressed in the *Crisis*, and of Senator Sumner in his speech on "The Barbarism of Slavery," were fond of boasting of their own commercial prosperity and of taunting the South with commercial inferiority; only rarely did a Southerner attempt an answer, and then with sorry results, as witness William L. Yancey, in his New York speech. Yet the single crop of cotton, although it could not stand in comparison with the diversified industries and pursuits of the North, was sufficient cause for boasting. But it is almost pathetic to behold the strange infatuation that prompted Southerners to stake their hopes of European intervention, and through this, their hopes of an independent Southern nation, so largely upon the world's dependence on King Cotton.

In the last analysis the one complete justification of secession was the imperative necessity of saving the vast property of slavery from destruction; secession was a commercial necessity, designed to make these billions secure from outside interference. Viewed in this light, secession was right, for any people, prompted by the commonest motives of self-respect and self-defense, and with no moral scruples against slavery, would have followed the same course. The present generation of Northerners, born and reared after the war, must shake off .their inherited political passions and prejudices, and pronounce the verdict of justification for the South. Believing slavery right, it was the duty of the South to defend it. It is time that the words "traitors," "conspirators," "rebels," and "rebellion" be discarded. But the North was no less right in opposing slavery, for theirs was a course springing from the natural promptings of morality. History, then, must adjudge that both sides in the controversy were right, and that the war was bound to come when the opposing sides conscientiously held, the one to the wrong, the other to the right, of slavery.

How the two sections came to hold opposite views on

slavery is a problem hard to solve, though Douglas' famous dictum would seem convincing. "Slavery, therefore, does not depend on the law. It is governed by climate, soil, and productions, by political economy."

Commercial factors, in this early day of the Republican party, when moral principles have generally been reckoned its sole stock in trade, had a determining influence on the dominant party. The tariff, internal improvements, a Pacific railroad, a Pacific telegraph, and a Homestead Act, were not mere subterfuges to cover up offensive tendencies of anti-slavery; they were as well a recognition of the industrial needs of the country. The West, after a decade of rapid expansion, now loomed large in the public eye; already the way was prepared for that diversion of markets and transportation routes to the new section that characterized the succeeding war period. Develop the West was the cry, fill it with antislavery immigrants from the East and from Europe, pass the Homestead Act, and the slavery question will be settled.

The interested student of political science finds much to attract him in the year's happenings; indeed, his is the best point of view from which to study the national conventions, the principle of availability and of the dark horse in the Republican convention, which gave the nation its greatest president, not for his own known qualities but for the conscious purpose of defeating another, and the wrangling of the Democrats over the unit rule, the two-thirds rule, convention representation, bolting, and the powers of convention committees, presiding officers, and national committees. He may study fusion in its practical workings, the customary powers of presidential electors, the possibilities involved in a presidential election in the House of Representatives, and the working of the spoils system at the height of its power.

PRESIDENTIAL CAMPAIGN

CHAPTER I

JOHN BROWN

ON the morning of Tuesday, the eighteenth of October, 1859, the leading New York papers and a few in other cities printed vague rumors of an uprising of slaves at Harper's Ferry, Virginia, and almost immediately full confirmation of the story followed the first dispatch, as detail after detail was laid before the country. On the preceding Sunday night, the sixteenth of October, between eleven and twelve o'clock, a band of twenty-two men, each armed with a rifle and pistols, rushed across the Potomac River from the opposite Maryland shore and took forcible possession of the little Virginia village of Harper's Ferry, first of the streets, then of the engine house and the government arsenal itself, and finally of the armory a half mile away. In an immediate attempt to liberate slaves, armed parties of the raiders scoured the surrounding regions and still under the cover of darkness brought in as prisoners three or four gentleman slaveholders with their slaves

Within two hours a passenger train, arriving on the Baltimore and Ohio Railroad, was arrested at the bridge, but was soon allowed to go on its way, — the bearer of the first intelligence of trouble to the outside world; in the darkness and confusion at the bridge a negro porter in the employ of the railroad was killed, although the village itself was not disturbed. When the villagers stirred at daybreak, workmen coming to the government works were fallen upon and imprisoned, until the number of prisoners in the hands of the attacking party totalled over forty. Even then, Monday morning was far advanced before the real situation was well known to all the citizens. From the nearby towns of Charlestown and Martinsburg, ten and twenty miles away, armed relief parties set out, but before their arrival the inhabitants of Harper's Ferry recaptured the outlying armory after bloody fighting and forced the surrender of many prisoners at the arsenal. Ten leading hostages, however, still remained in the engine house under the close guard of eight or nine of the invaders, and were not released until this stronghold was carried by storm by United States marines under the command of Robert E. Lee, troops sent posthaste from Washington by President Buchanan at the urgent request of the Governor of Virginia. In the entire encounter, from the midnight attack until the final surrender, four of the inhabitants of the town were killed and ten of the conspirators, while seven of the latter suffered arrest and five escaped. Not a slave left his master.[1]

The leader of this ill-fated expedition, John Brown of Ossawatomie, and all his followers, were militant antislavery crusaders, who had but recently arrived from the war-ridden territory of Kansas, where in the support of their principles they had been guilty of many dastardly crimes, including robbery and murder; it was there in the West, in fact, that they had planned the Virginia raid, which was to be simply a repetition of the nigger-stealing raids which the band had carried on from Kansas into Missouri.

Despite his record Brown proved to be a remarkable man, as even his enemies admitted. An unsympathetic Ohio Congressman, who visited him in prison before his trial and while his wounds were still fresh, reported: "It is vain

---

[1] *U. S. Senate Reports*, 36 Cong., 1 Sess., No. 278.

to underestimate either the man or the conspiracy. Captain John Brown is as brave and resolute a man as ever headed an insurrection, and in a good cause and with a sufficient force would have made a consummate partisan commander. He has coolness, daring, persistence, the stoic faith and patience, and a firmness of will and purpose unconquerable. He is the furthest removed from the ordinary ruffian, fanatic, or madman."[1] Governor Wise of Virginia said: "They are mistaken who take him for a madman. He is a man of clear head, courageous fortitude, and simple ingenuousness. He is cool, collected, indomitable; and it is but just to him to say that he was humane to his prisoners; and he inspired all with great trust in his integrity and as a man of truth. He is a fanatic, vain and garrulous, but firm, truthful, intelligent."[2]

In an interview with a reporter of the *New York Herald* and others, Brown himself explained his purposes in words the simple grandeur of which went straight to the Northern heart. "*Mr. Mason.* How do you justify your acts? *Mr. Brown.* I think, my friend, you are guilty of a great wrong against God and humanity. I say it without wishing to be offensive, and it would be perfectly right for any one to interfere with you, so far as to free those you wickedly and willfully hold in bondage. I do not say this insultingly. *Mr. Mason.* I understand that. *Mr. Brown.* I think I did right and that others will do right who interfere with you at any and at all times; I hold that the Golden Rule, 'Do unto others as you would that others should do unto you,' applies to all that would help others to gain their liberty. *A Bystander.* Do you consider this a religious movement? *Mr. Brown.* It is, in my judgment, the greatest service that a man can render to God. *Bystander.*

[1] *The American Conflict*, by Horace Greeley, Hartford, 1864–1866, I, 294.
[2] *History of the Rise and Fall of the Slave Power in America*, by Henry Wilson, Boston, 1872–1877, II, 595.

Do you consider yourself an instrument in the hands of Providence? *Mr. Brown.* I do. *Bystander.* Upon what principle do you justify your acts? *Mr. Brown.* Upon the Golden Rule. I pity the poor in bondage that have none to help them; that is why I am here; not to gratify any personal animosity or vindictive spirit. It is my sympathy with the oppressed and the wronged, that are as good as you and as precious in the sight of God. . . . *Mr. Vallandigham.* Who are your advisers in this movement? *Mr. Brown.* I cannot answer that. I have numerous sympathizers throughout the entire North. . . . I want you to understand, Gentlemen, (to the reporter of the *Herald*) — you may report that — I want you to understand that I respect the rights of the poorest and the weakest of the colored people oppressed by the slavery system, just as much as I do those of the most wealthy and powerful. This is the idea that has moved me, and that alone. We expected no reward except the satisfaction of endeavoring to do for those in distress and greatly oppressed as we would be done by. The cry of distress of the oppressed is my reason, and the only thing that prompted me to come here. . . . I wish to say further, that you had better, all you people of the South, prepare yourselves for a settlement of this question that must come up for settlement sooner than you are prepared for it. The sooner you are prepared, the better. You may dispose of me very easily. I am nearly disposed of now; but this question is still to be settled, this negro question, I mean; the end of that is not yet." [1]

With such eloquence Brown won the heart of the North and made of himself a hero, whose trial, following within a few weeks, became in reality a trial of the antislavery North by the state courts of Virginia. Every act done, every word spoken in the drama in the Charlestown Court House was reported and read throughout the country, the prisoner's

The *Liberator*, October 28, 1859.

perfect frankness in admitting everything, his uniform courtesy to the court, his patience while lying on the bed of pain before judge and jury, with many wounds still gaping and fresh, and finally the undue haste of the whole procedure. Neither for securing sympathetic counsel for the accused nor for summoning distant witnesses was ample time allowed. All was haste.

When, on November first, after a verdict of "guilty of treason and conspiring and advising with slaves and others to rebel, and murder in the first degree" had been suddenly reached, Brown was brought into court and asked if he could give any reasons why sentence should not be passed upon him, though surprised and confused, he spoke as follows: "In the first place I deny everything but what I have all along admitted, the design on my part to free the slaves. I intended certainly to have made a clean thing of that matter, as I did last winter when I went into Missouri and there took slaves without the snapping of a gun on either side, moved them through the country, and finally left them in Canada. I designed to have done the same thing again on a larger scale. That was all I intended. I never did intend murder or treason or the destruction of property, or to incite or excite slaves to rebellion or to make insurrection. I have another objection, and that is, it is unjust that I should suffer such a penalty. Had I interfered in the manner which I admit has been fairly proved (for I admire the truthfulness and candor of the greater portion of the witnesses who have testified in this case), had I so interfered in behalf of the rich, the powerful, the intelligent, the so-called great, or in behalf of any of their friends, either father, mother, brother, sister, wife, or children, or any of that class, and suffered and sacrificed what I have in this interference, it would have been all right, and every man in this court would have deemed it an act worthy of reward rather than of punishment.

"This court acknowledges, as I suppose, the validity of

the law of God.   I see a book kissed here, which I suppose to be the Bible or at least the New Testament.   That teaches me that all things 'whatsoever I would that men should do to me, I should do even so to them.'   It teaches me further to remember those that are in bonds as bound with them. I endeavored to act upon that instruction.   I say that I am yet too young to understand that God is any respecter of persons.   I believe that to have interfered as I have done, as I have always freely admitted I have done, in behalf of His despised poor, was not wrong, but right.   Now if it be deemed necessary that I should forfeit my life for the furtherance of the ends of justice, and mingle my blood further with the blood of my children, and with the blood of millions in this slave country, whose rights are disregarded by wicked, cruel, and unjust enactments, I submit — so let it be done. . . ." [1]

For one month more, till the day of execution, Brown languished in prison, denying himself to all callers and interviewers, refusing the hundreds of requests for his autograph, devoting himself, rather, almost entirely to voluminous correspondence.   Many of his letters were published, and for loftiness of thought, appropriateness of diction and sentiment, and sweetness and tenderness of spirit, they may be ranked among the world's great letters.   Where did the untutored man learn the English language?   Where, if not in the same school as the great War President, Abraham Lincoln?   Letters of sympathy were answered, gifts acknowledged, the care of his wife and family recommended to friends, a "perfectly practical" education outlined for his children. In many letters he sought to comfort his family.   "Dear wife and children — every one," he wrote; "I will begin by saying that I have in some degree recovered from my wounds, but that I am quite weak in my back and sore about

[1] *The American Conflict*, by Horace Greeley, Hartford, 1864–1866, I, 294.

my left kidney. My appetite has been quite good for most
of the time since I was hurt. I am supplied with almost
everything I could desire to make me comfortable, and the
little I do lack (some articles of clothing which I lost) I may
perhaps get again. I am besides quite cheerful, having
(as I trust) the peace of God, which 'passeth all understanding' to 'rule in my heart,' and the testimony (in some degree)
of a good conscience that I have lived not altogether in vain.
I can trust God with both the time and the manner of my
death, believing, as I now do, that for me at this time to seal
my testimony (for God and humanity) with my blood, will
do vastly more toward advancing the cause I have earnestly
endeavored to support than all I have done in all my life
before. I beg of you all meekly and quietly to submit to
this, not feeling yourself in the least degraded on that account.
Remember, dear wife and children all, that Jesus of Naza-
reth suffered a most excruciating death on the cross as a
felon, under the most aggravating circumstances. Think,
also, of the prophets and apostles and Christians of former
days, who went through greater tribulation than you or I;
and (try to) be reconciled. May God Almighty comfort all
your hearts, and soon wipe away all tears from your eyes.
To Him be endless praise. Think, too, of the crushed
millions who have no comforter. I charge you all never
(in all your trials) to forget the griefs of 'the poor that cry
and of them that have none to comfort them.' . . . I greatly
long to hear from some one of you and to learn anything
that in any way affects your welfare. I sent you ten dollars
the other day. Did you get it? I have also endeavored to
stir up Christian friends to visit and write to you in your
deep affliction. I have no doubt that some of them, at least,
will heed the call. Write to me, care of Captain John Avis,
Charlestown, Jefferson County, Virginia. 'Finally, my
beloved,' 'be of good comfort.' May all your names be
written in the 'Lamb's Book of Life,' may you all have the

purifying and sustaining influence of the Christian religion, is the earnest prayer of your affectionate husband and father,

JOHN BROWN.

"P.S. I cannot remember a night so dark as to have hindered the coming day, nor a storm so furious and dreadful as to prevent the return of warm sunshine and a cloudless sky. But, beloved ones, do remember that this is not your rest, that in this world you have no abiding place or continuing city. To God and His infinite mercy I always commend you. J.B."

Slaveholding and slavery-supporting clergymen of the community, seeking to comfort him, he summarily repulsed. To one who sought to harmonize Christianity and slavery he replied: "My dear sir, you know nothing about Christianity; you will have to learn the A B C's in the lesson of Christianity, as I find you entirely ignorant of the meaning of the word. I, of course, respect you as a gentleman, but it is as a heathen gentleman." Here the argument closed.[1]

The day of execution was Friday, December 2. Brown stepped from the jail with "radiant countenance"; passing a little negro baby he stooped tenderly and kissed it; at a negro woman, exclaiming as he passed, "God bless you, old man! I wish I could help you, but I can't," he looked in silence with tears in his eyes. Attended by militia he rode alone in a wagon to the gray stubble field on the edge of the city, the place of execution, where thousands of soldiers were drawn up in waiting. "It has been a characteristic of me from infancy not to suffer from physical fear. I have suffered a thousand times more from bashfulness than from fear," he declared on the journey. Almost his last words

[1] *The American Conflict*, by Horace Greeley, Hartford, 1864–1866, I, 296.

were to his jailer : "I have no words to thank you for all your kindness to me." [1] Thus the felon's death was turned to triumph, and in the North the same spirit of triumph marked the many celebrations in honor of the event, mingling with the tone of sadness and transforming it.[2]

Frank Leslie's Illustrated Weekly published a . striking full-page picture of the execution. At a public meeting in Cleveland the martyr's words were hung up in banners : "John Brown, the hero of 1859," "Remember those that are in bonds as bound with them," "If I had interfered in behalf of the great, the wealthy, and the wise, no one would have blamed me," "I do not think I can better serve the cause I love so much than to die for it." In Newburyport, Massachusetts, stores were draped in mourning and bells tolled ; in West Newbury a factory draped ; in Amesbury the flags of the mills kept at half-mast, the bells tolled, many stores and offices draped, and a public meeting held in the evening ; in Haverhill, Georgetown, Danvers, and Lynn there were the same demonstrations. In Albany, New York, one hundred guns were fired. In the Massachusetts State Senate a motion to adjourn at the hour of execution was lost by only three votes. Thousands of Brown's pictures were sold, and also thousands of copies of his prison letters bound in pamphlet form. Within four weeks Redpath's life of Brown was out, and in Massachusetts alone twenty thousand copies were quickly sold. Numberless church services and public meetings were held, called by the abolition societies "for the furtherance of the antislavery cause, and renewedly to consecrate themselves to the patriotic and Christian work of effecting the abolition of that most dangerous, unnatural, cruel, and impious system of slavery, which is the fruitful source of all our sectional heartburnings and conflicts."

[1] *The American Conflict*, by Horace Greeley, Hartford, 1864–1866, I, 296.
[2] In all, seven of the conspirators were executed, some two weeks after Brown and some as late as March of the next year.

At one of these meetings in Boston William Lloyd Garrison passionately cried : "I do not rise on this occasion to define my position (*laughter*) ; that I believe Virginia and the South clearly understand, and I as clearly understand theirs. Between us there is an 'irrepressible conflict' (*applause*) ; and I am for carrying it on until it is finished in victory or in death (*renewed applause*). For thirty years I have been endeavoring to effect by peaceful, moral, and religious instrumentalities, the abolition of American slavery ; and if possible, I hate slavery thirty times more than when I began, and I am thirty times more, if possible, an abolitionist of the most uncompromising character (*loud applause*). . . . A word or two in regard to the characteristics of John Brown. He was of the old Puritan stock, a Cromwellian, who believed in God and at the same time in 'keeping his powder dry.' He believed in 'the sword of the Lord and of Gideon,' and acted accordingly. Herein I differed widely from him. But certainly he was no infidel, oh, no ! How it would have added to the fiendish malignity of the *New York Observer*, if John Brown had only been an infidel, evangelically speaking ! The man who brands him as a traitor is a calumniator (*applause*). The man who says that his object was to promote murder, or insurrection, or rebellion, is, in the language of the Apostle, 'a liar, and the truth is not in him.' John Brown meant to effect if possible a peaceful exodus from Virginia. But, it is asked, 'Did he not have stored up a large supply of Sharp's rifles and spears ? What did they mean ?' Nothing offensive, nothing aggressive. Only this : he designed getting as many slaves as he could to join him, and then putting into their hands those instruments of self-defense. But, mark you, self-defense ; not in standing their ground, but in their retreat to the mountains ; or in their flight to Canada ; not with any design to shed the blood or harm the hair of a single slaveholder in the state of Virginia, if a conflict could be avoided. . . . See the ferocious spirit

of the Virginians in their treatment of the living and the
dead. Let me give you a single specimen, as narrated by
an eyewitness. This is Southern testimony. 'The dead
lay on the streets and in the river and were subjected to every
indignity that a wild and madly excited people could heap
upon them. Curses were freely uttered against them and
kicks and blows inflicted upon them. The large mulatto
that shot Mr. Turner was lying in the gutter in front of the
arsenal, with a horrible wound in the neck, and though dead
and gory, vengeance was unsatisfied, and many, as they
ran sticks into his wound, or beat him with them, wished
that he had a thousand lives, that all of them might be
forfeited in expiation and avengement of the foul deed he
had committed. Leeman lay upon a rock in the river and
was made target for the practice of those who had captured
Sharp's rifles in the affray. Shot after shot was fired at him,
and when tired of this sport, a man waded out to where he
lay and set him up in grotesque attitude, and finally pushed
him off, and he floated down the stream.' Oh! the spirit
engendered by slavery! Is there anything like it upon
earth? . . .

"Was John Brown justified in this attempt? Yes, if
Washington was in his, if Warren and Hancock were in
theirs. If men are justified in striking a blow for freedom,
when the question is one of a threepenny tax on tea, I say
they are a thousand times more justified, when it is to save
fathers, mothers, wives, and children from the slave coffle
and the auction block and to restore to them their God-
given rights (*loud applause*). Was John Brown justified in
interfering in behalf of the slave population of Virginia, to
secure their freedom and independence? Yes, if Lafayette
was justified in interfering to help our revolutionary fathers.
If Kosciusko, if Pulaski, if Steuben, if de Kalb, if all who
joined them from abroad were justified in that act, then
John Brown was incomparably more so. . . .

"Who instigated John Brown? Let us see. It must have been Patrick Henry of Virginia, — 'Give me liberty or give me death.' Why do they not dig up his bones and give them to the consuming fire, to show their abhorrence of his memory? It must have been Thomas Jefferson, another Virginian, who said of the bondage of the Virginia slave, that 'one hour of it is fraught with more misery than ages of that which our fathers rose in rebellion to oppose,' and who as the author of the Declaration of Independence, proclaimed it to be a 'self-evident truth, that all men are created equal and endowed by their Creator with an inalienable right to liberty.' Beyond all question it must have been Virginia herself, who by her coat of arms, with its terrible motto, *Sic semper tyrannis*, asserts the right of the oppressed to trample their oppressors beneath their feet, and if necessary, to consign them to a bloody grave." [1]

Victor Hugo, in the following letter to a London newspaper, spoke the sentiment of enlightened Europe and re-echoed the American abolitionists : "Brown, stretched upon a truckle-bed, with six half-closed wounds, a gun-shot wound in the arm, one in his loins, two in the chest, two in the head, almost bereft of hearing, bleeding through the mattress, the spirits of his two dead sons attending him ; his four fellow prisoners crawling around him ; Stephens with four saber wounds ; justice in a hurry to have done with the case ; an attorney, Hunter, demanding that it be dispatched with sharp speed ; a judge, Parker, assenting ; the defense cut short ; scarcely any delay allowed ; forged or garbled accounts put in evidence ; the witnesses for the prisoner shut out ; the defense clogged ; two guns, loaded with grape, brought into the court, with an order to the jailer to shoot the prisoners in case of an attempt at rescue ; forty minutes' deliberation ; three sentences to death. I affirm on my honor, that all this took place, not in Turkey, but in America." [2]

---

[1] The *Liberator*, December 16, 1859.
[2] The *Liberator*, December 31, 1859.

The deeds of the abolitionists supplemented their words. Said George L. Stearns of Boston: "From first to last I understood John Brown to be a man opposed to slavery, and as such, that he would take every opportunity to free slaves where he could; I did not know in what way; I only knew that from the fact of his having done it in Missouri in the instance referred to; I furnished him with money because I considered him as one who would be of use in case such troubles arose as had arisen previously in Kansas; that was my object in furnishing the money; I did not ask him what he was to do with it." Samuel G. Howe, a physician of the highest professional and social standing in Boston, said: "I contributed to his aid at various times." "His aid — in what way?" "In the same way that I contributed to the aid of other antislavery men; men who give up their occupations, their industry, to write papers or 'to deliver lectures, or otherwise to propagate antislavery sentiments. I give as much money every year as I can possibly afford." [1]

These radicals cared little whether or not Brown was insane; they were ready for a hero, and swept on by the full tide of excitement they gave little or no heed to the most significant affidavits published by Brown's counsel when he was struggling for delay in the trial. Nineteen persons swore to statements going to show Brown's insanity for several years past, and proving beyond a doubt the extraordinary fact of the insanity of no fewer than thirteen of his near relatives, — a grandmother, two aunts, an uncle, a sister, five cousins, two sons, and a niece; all of which, when added to Brown's unusual language and behavior as to slavery, the character of the expedition, and the strange constitution found among his papers, which he had apparently drawn up in anticipation of a new government to be established,[2] would certainly seem to render belief in his monomania at

[1] *U. S. Senate Reports*, 36 Cong., 1 Sess., No. 278.
[2] See p. 21, note.

least plausible. But madman or no madman, thousands hailed him hero.[1]

Southern radicals were as much wrought up as those in the North, but with a passion all their own — the deed must not be allowed to happen again; there must be no more John Browns. It was no mere abstract question, but a most serious practical situation which now confronted the men and women of the South; saneness and sobriety of judgment seemed almost out of the question, and small wonder that a distorted notion of self-preservation and an angry debate with the North on slavery carried them away. "Do you read your Bible, Mrs. Childs?" hotly inquired Mrs. Mason of Virginia, the wife of a United States Senator, of a prominent Northern abolitionist. "If you do, read there: 'Woe unto you, hypocrites,' and take to yourself, with twofold damnation, that terrible sentence, for, rest assured, in the day of judgment it shall be more tolerable for those thus scathed by the awful words of the Son of God than for you. You would soothe with sisterly and motherly care the hoary-headed murderer of Harper's Ferry! A man whose aim and intention was to incite the horrors of a servile war — to condemn women of your own race, ere death closed their eyes on their sufferings from violence and outrage, to see their husbands and fathers murdered, their children butchered, the ground strewn with the brains of their babes. The antecedents of Brown's band proved them to have been the offscourings of the earth; and what would have been their fate had they found as many sympathizers in Virginia as they seem to have in Massachusetts. Now, compare yourself with those your sympathy would devote to such ruthless men, and say, on your word of honor, which has never been broken, would you stand by the bed of an old negro, dying of a hopeless disease, to alleviate his suffering as far as human aid could? Have you watched the last lingering

[1] The *Boston Daily Advertiser*, December 2, 1859.

illness of a consumptive, to soothe, as far as in you lay, the inevitable fate? Do you grieve with those near you, even though their sorrows resulted from their own misconduct? Did you ever sit up until the 'wee hours' to complete a dress for a motherless child, that she might appear on Christmas day in a new one, along with her more fortunate companions? We do these things and more for our servants, and why? Because we endeavor to do our duty in that state of life it has pleased God to place us. . . . You reverence Brown for his clemency to his prisoners! Prisoners! and how taken? Unsuspecting workmen, going to their daily tasks, unarmed gentlemen, taken from their bed at the dead hour of night by six men doubly and trebly armed. Suppose he had hurt a hair of their heads, do you suppose any of the band of desperadoes would have left the engine house alive? And did he not know that his treatment of them was his only hope of life then or of clemency afterwards?"

Without noticing the Southern woman's natural fear of a servile insurrection, Mrs. Childs replied: "I have no disposition to retort upon you the twofold damnation to which you consign me. On the contrary, I sincerely wish you well, both in this world and the next. If the anathema proved a safety valve to your boiling spirit, it did some good to you, while it fell harmless upon me. . . . You refer me to the Bible, from which you quote the favorite text of slaveholders, 'Servants, be subject to your masters with all fear; not only to the good and gentle, but also to the froward.' 1 Peter 2 : 18. Abolitionists also have their favorite texts, to some of which I would call your attention. 'Remember those that are in bonds as bound with them.' Hebrews 13 : 3. 'Thou shalt not deliver unto his master the servant which is escaped from his master unto thee. He shall dwell with thee where it liketh him best. Thou shalt not oppress him.' Deuteronomy 23 : 15, 16. . . . I would especially commend to slave owners the following portions of that volume, wherein you say God has revealed the duty of masters. 'Masters, give unto your servants that which is just and equal, knowing that you also have a Master in Heaven.' Colossians 4 : 1. 'Neither be ye called masters, for one is your master, even Christ, and all ye are brethren.' Matthew 23 : 8–10. 'Whatsoever ye would that men should do unto you, do ye even so to them.' Matthew 7 : 12. 'Woe unto him that useth his neighbor's service without wages, and giveth him not for his work.' Jeremiah 22 : 13. . . .

"If the appropriateness of these texts is not apparent, I will try to make it so, by evidence drawn entirely from Southern sources. . . . The universal rule of the slave states is that 'the child follows the condition of its mother.' This is an index to many things. Marriages between white and colored people are forbidden by law; yet a very large number of the slaves are white or yellow. When Lafayette visited this country in his old age, he said he was very much struck by the great change in the colored population in Virginia; that in the time of the Revolution nearly all the household slaves were black, but when he returned to America he found very few of them black. The advertisements in Southern newspapers often describe runaway slaves that 'pass themselves for white people.' Sometimes they are described as having 'straight black hair, blue eyes, and clear complexion.' This would not be unless their fathers, grandfathers, and great-grandfathers had been white men. But as their mothers were slaves, the law pronounces them slaves, subject to be sold on the auction block whenever the necessities or consciences of the masters or mistresses require it. The sale of one's own children, brothers or sisters, has an ugly aspect to those who are unaccustomed to it; obviously, it cannot have a good moral influence, that law and custom should render licentiousness a profitable vice.

"Throughout the slave states the testimony of no colored person, bond or free, can be received against a white man.

You have some laws which on the face of them would seem to restrain men from murdering or mutilating slaves; but they are rendered nearly null by the law I have cited. Any drunken master, overseer, or patrol may go into the negro cabins and commit what outrages he pleases with perfect impunity, if no white person is present who chooses to witness against him. North Carolina and Georgia have a large loophole of escape even if white persons are present, when murder is committed. A law to punish persons for 'maliciously killing a slave' has this remarkable qualification, 'always providing that this act shall not extend to any slave dying of moderate correction.' We at the North find it difficult to understand how moderate punishment can cause death. . . .

"By your laws all a slave's earnings belong to his master. He can neither receive donations nor transmit property. Your laws also systematically aim at keeping the minds of the colored people in the most abject state of ignorance. If white people attempt to teach them to read or write, they are punished by imprisonment and fines; if they attempt to teach others, they are punished with from twenty to thirty-nine lashes. . . .

"The reliable source of information is the advertisements in the Southern newspapers. In the *North Carolina* (Raleigh) *Standard* Mr. Micajah Ricks advertises a 'negro woman and two children. A few days before she went off, I burned her with a hot iron on the left side of the face. I tried to make the letter M.' In the *Natchez Courier* Mr. J. P. Ashford advertises a runaway negro girl 'with a good many teeth missing and the letter A branded on her cheek and forehead.' In the *Lexington* (Kentucky) *Observer* Mr. William Overstreet advertises a runaway negro 'with his left eye out, scars from a disk on his left arm, and much scarred with a whip.' I might quote from hundreds of such advertisements.

c

"Another source of information is afforded by your fugitives from justice, with many of whom I have conversed freely. . . .

"Another source of information is furnished by emancipated slave holders. . . .

"Looking at the system of slavery in the light of all this evidence, do you candidly think that we deserve 'twofold damnation' for detesting it? Can you not believe that we hate the system and yet be truly your friends? I make allowance for the excited state of your mind and for the prejudice induced by education. I do not care to change your opinion of me; but do wish that you would be persuaded to examine this subject dispassionately for the sake of the prosperity of Virginia, and the welfare of unborn generations, both white and colored. For thirty years abolitionists have been trying to reason with slaveholders through the press and in the Halls of Congress. Their efforts, though directed to the masters only, have been met with violence and abuse equal to that poured on the head of John Brown. Yet surely we, as a portion of the Union involved in the expense, degeneracy, the danger and the disgrace of this iniquitous and fatal system, have a right to speak about it and a right to be heard also. . . .

"To the personal questions you ask me, I will reply in the name of all the women of New England. It would be extremely difficult to find any woman in our villages who does not sew for the poor and watch with the sick, whenever occasion requires. We pay our domestics generous wages, with which they can purchase as many Christmas gowns as they please, a process far better for their characters as well as our own, than to receive their clothing as a charity, after being deprived of just payment for their labor. I have never known an instance where the pangs of maternity did not meet with requisite assistance; and here at the North, after we have helped the mothers we do not sell the babies. I really believe what you state concerning the kindness of many Virginia matrons; but, after all, the best that can be done in that way is a poor equivalent for the perpetual wrong done to the slave, and the terrible liabilities to which they are always subject. Kind masters and mistresses among you are merely lucky accidents. If any one chooses to be a brutal despot, your laws and customs give him complete power to do so ." [1]

Drastic action on the part of the South attended the angry discussion. Stating its attitude toward the presence in their midst of any detested Yankee from John Brown's country, the *Atlanta Confederacy* declared that they regarded every man in their midst as an enemy to the institutions of the South who did not declare boldly that he or she believed African slavery a social, moral, and political blessing; whether born at the South or at the North, any person holding other than these sentiments was unsound and should be requested to leave the country. From every one a confession of faith on slavery was sought. "Beecher said that he would preach the same doctrines in Virginia as in Massachusetts," exclaimed a Southerner in Congress, two weeks after Brown's death; "I ask you why you do not come on?" "I will answer the gentleman if he will permit me," quickly retorted a Northerner. "I will tell the gentleman why Mr. Beecher would not preach in Virginia; because liberty of speech is denied in the South, and if he were to go there he would get a coat of tar and feathers." "Yes, sir," assented the Southerner; "not only would he be denied liberty of speech but he would be denied personal liberty also and would be hung higher than Haman." On the last day of the year 1859 twelve families, including thirty-nine persons, arrived in Cincinnati, Ohio, from Berea, Madison County, Kentucky, whence they had been forcibly expelled for abolitionism. Madison County, near the center of the state, had a popu-

[1] The *Liberator*, December 31, 1859.

lation of fifteen thousand people, one third of whom were slaves; the largest town, Berea, was an antislavery center under the influence of Rev. John G. Fee, who had organized several churches in the vicinity, from membership in all of which sympathizers with slavery were excluded. There was a seminary in which antislavery was openly taught, a school, supported by public money, for children of all colors, and an abolition postmaster who regularly handled abolition mail from the North. Opposition to slavery, moral opposition and that alone, moved the community. The fatal sixteenth of October arrived, and Fee, then in New York, was reported as having said that he sympathized with Brown and that John Browns were needed in Kentucky. Then came a public meeting of outraged slaveholders, the inevitable vigilance committee, and the abolitionists of Berea had to go. The Governor of the state, to whom in their trouble they appealed, gave them no aid.

James Powers, a stonecutter at work on the new Capitol building at Columbia, South Carolina, was arrested for seditious speech in regard to Brown and slavery, taken before the mayor and committed to prison, whence he was dragged by a mob, whipped, tarred and feathered, and sent North. In all its details the story was widely heralded in such papers as the *New York Tribune*, the *New York Evening Post*, and the *New York Independent*. James Crangale, who suffered a like fate in Augusta, Georgia, finally reached New York to publish his story in the same way. Small H. Fisk, a shoe dealer in Savannah, Georgia, and a native of Massachusetts, was charged with expressing general abolition sentiments and with reading one evening to some negroes in his store. He was called out of the store at night, gagged before he could make resistance, and driven outside the city, where he was tarred and feathered. The *News* of the city added, "Not a spot of his skin was left visible, and his hair was trimmed close to his head." A peddler of fruit trees and shrubbery from Rochester, New York, driven from Asheville, North Carolina, was hauled before a great public meeting at Knoxville, Tennessee, and after inflammatory speeches by prominent men was given three days in which to get out. Two luckless men from Savannah, Georgia, with their heads shaved on one side, arrived in New York, and later to the same place came two young ladies from Richmond, Virginia, where they had lost their positions as school-teachers. A book agent was arrested in Alabama for selling Fleetwood's *Life of Christ* and was brought before the Methodist Episcopal Conference for judgment; the report of this body read as follows: "We have examined this man's case. We find no evidence to convict him with tampering with slaves, but as he is from the North and engaged in selling a book published in the North, we have a right to suspect him of being an abolitionist, and we, therefore, recommend, in order to guard ourselves against possible danger, that he be immediately conducted by the military out of this county into the next adjoining." A single issue of a local Florida paper, January, 1860, contained three editorial notices to the public to watch out for certain suspected Northerners; while in Richmond, Virginia, the Young Men's Christian Association with much bravado withdrew a previous invitation to Bayard Taylor, because of his connection with the editorial staff of the unendurable *New York Tribune*, to deliver a lecture in Richmond under its auspices.

This was the feeling in every Southern community; suspicion constantly attended a Northerner in the South, he had no freedom of speech or action, he was not wanted, neither was he safe. Thus determined were the slaveholders to guard against more John Browns.[1] It was a natural position.

[1] The *Provisional Constitution and Ordinances for the People of the United States*, found among Brown's papers, was in one sense a justification of the South in this position. This document sketched a government very similar to that of the United States, but spoke of slavery as the cause

There were those more conservative Southerners who ridiculed Governor Wise as "General Fussation" for keeping so many thousand militia at Harper's Ferry for four weeks and more at an expense to the state of $200,000; they deemed the display mere politics, designed to make the Governor President. But the critics could not stay the common hostility toward Northern people. Throughout the year 1860 hundreds of luckless people from the free states were expelled from the slave country with more or less violence, until the matter became an issue in the presidential campaign.[1]

By formal state law in Virginia, Maryland, North Carolina, Alabama, and Texas, copies of Northern newspapers, such as the *New York Tribune*, the *New York Christian Advocate*, the *Albany Evening Journal*, the *Springfield Republican*, and *Harper's Weekly*, upon being received in the local post offices were burned by the postmasters, and to this outrage the pliant administration at Washington offered no objection beyond informing the Southerners that before they destroyed the papers they must examine them copy by copy and not burn all issues because of one. Southern students, resident in the North, were affected by the prevailing excitement. The departure southward of over two hundred medical students from Philadelphia, possibly for a regular vacation, though this contingency was never mentioned, was widely heralded south of the Ohio River as a sign of the times; passing through Richmond they listened to bombastic Governor Wise in a most fiery speech, filled with praise for shaking the dust of the unfriendly North from their feet and with denunciation of John Brown's land. In Missouri, the legislature

of the constitution, spoke of the "enemy," and "confiscated property" given up to the common store, of "prisoners," of those who gave up slaves "voluntarily" and of the "neutrals." This was a menace which Brown's words in prison could not assuage. See *U. S. Senate Reports*, 36 Cong., 1 Sess., No. 278.

[1] See pp. 215–217.

refused to the antislavery Methodist Episcopal Church a charter for a university, to be located at the state capital; they favored education, but not the antislavery kind.

A favorite threat concerned commercial intercourse. As is well known, the South in this regard was dependent on the North; in the words of Governor Wise everything in the South came from the Yankees, from the churns in the dairies to the clocks in the parlor. But public meetings were now called to advocate direct trade with Europe.[1] State legislatures considered bills to encourage such trade by tax exemption, while at the same time heavier taxes were to be levied on the Northern traveling salesmen; prominent men appeared in homespun, and to cap the climax the editor of a Georgian paper published a white and black list of New York merchants, proslavery and antislavery, with the former of whom it was recommended that the South should trade and should taboo the latter. When the editor later appeared in New York to correct his lists, the vials of Horace Greeley's wrath could no longer be contained; to be kicked into the nastiest part of the gutter was the only fate suitable for the contemptible blackmailer. Yet scores of New York merchants affected to welcome the Southerner and with many favors sought a place on the white list. Perhaps the success of the movement was the secret spring of the *Tribune* editor's outburst, for the commercial element of the city was strongly pro-Southern and remained so throughout the year.

A veiled and indefinite purpose, a vague threat, perhaps, was couched in the immediate formation of local military companies in many Southern towns, where daily and weekly drills and tournaments were common.

In the Southern legislatures a determined effort was made to give political support to Virginia. Scarcely was John

[1] Southern commercial conventions had long agitated this question, but had never accomplished anything.

Brown dead when South Carolina passed the following resolutions: *"Whereas,* the state of South Carolina, by her ordinance of A.D. 1852, affirmed her right to secede from the Confederacy whenever the occasion should arise, justifying her, in her judgment, in taking that step; and in the resolution adopted by her convention declared that she forbore the immediate exercise of that right, from considerations of expediency only; and whereas, more than seven years have elapsed since that convention adjourned, and in the intervening time the assaults upon the institution of slavery and upon the rights and equality of the Southern states, have increasingly continued, with increasing violence, and in new and alarming forms, be it therefore, First, *Resolved,* That the slaveholding states should have a convention for united action. . . . Third, That delegates especially be sent to Virginia to express to the authorities of that state the cordial sympathies of the people of South Carolina with the people of Virginia, and their earnest desire to unite with them in measures of common defense."

Upon the receipt of this call, bitter contests were precipitated in the various states, which ran for a few weeks and ended in the defeat of the proposed convention; not one state followed the lead of South Carolina. The Carolinian Commissioner made long speeches both before the legislature and before the people of Virginia, breathing defiance to the North and by every art of the orator attempting to stir the Virginians to action. But he failed. The sober, second thought of the people, though greatly agitated, was not yet ready for extremes.

Proslavery political leaders, framing their views preparatory to the coming presidential campaign, also fell victims to the prevailing excitement and clothed their sentiments in language unusually radical. The following typical resolutions were framed in Georgia on the day that Brown died: "We, a portion of the citizens of McIntosh County, believing that a fearful crisis in our national existence is at hand, and that the attempt to raise an insurrection at Harper's Ferry is but a faint index of the impending evil that threatens the slaveholding states, deem it the duty of every citizen to think calmly, resolve with firmness, and act with decision, do announce to the Union and to the whole world the views we entertain, and the course we think ought to be pursued. *Resolved*, That by the laws both of God and man, the slave is the property of his master, and that by the constitution of the United States the general government is bound to protect us in the possession of this species of property, both by statute and treaty. *Resolved*, That those states that encourage or permit the abolitionists to devise plans to rob us of our slaves, have violated and are still violating the constitution of the United States. Resolved, That, although we would be glad to see our Union go on prospering and to prosper, yet recent events show that our rights are not only disregarded but are assailed, and we are threatened with all the desolation and horrors attendant upon a servile war. *Resolved*, That we call upon the non-slaveholding states to carry out in good faith the constitution of the Union, by putting down the abolitionists and their abettors, and if they persist in their hostility to our institutions we feel it a duty to ourselves and a duty to our institutions to sever our connections with them. *Resolved*, That the greatest curse that has ever befallen the South was to submit to any compromise. That in every compromise that we have made we have been defrauded out of our just rights. That in the future we intend to declare to the Northern states our rights, and these rights we intend to maintain, if it costs our heart's last drop of blood. That we recommend to our delegates to the Charleston convention to contend for the rights of the South; and if voted down by the Northern states, that the Southern delegates withdraw, and call upon the South to call a convention to nominate candidates for president and vice president, to be run by the people of the South, pledged to stand up and defend our Southern rights. *Resolved*, That the cause of Virginia is the cause of the South, and that we stand ready and willing to march to her aid or any other Southern state when assailed." [1]

The conservative classes in the North, used from long custom to taking their principles from the Southern radicals, now stuck fast to their old friends and roundly denounced John Brown and all his followers; they insisted that slavery was right and that the South should not be disturbed and goaded into secession. The editor of the *Columbus* (Ohio) *Statesman*, a prominent Democratic politician and a regular attendant at the Methodist Episcopal Church, suddenly arose and left the church and vowed that he never would return when his pastor in a public discourse spoke of Brown as "one who stepped from the gallows to the portals of Heaven"; for similar reasons six Democrats withdrew from a Massachusetts church service. Everywhere churches were distraught. In many cities "Union-saving" meetings were held, conservative gatherings called to attest anew the value of the union of the states, fraternal devotion to the Southern members of the Confederacy, a determination to do them justice, and undying hatred of John Brown. In Lowell, Massachusetts, Portsmouth, New Hampshire, New York, Albany, Rochester, etc., slavery was praised. Said Mr. Charles O'Conor, a leader of the New York bar, at a meeting in that city: "I insist that negro slavery is not only just (hisses and disorder) — I maintain, gentlemen, that negro slavery is not unjust, that it is benign in its influence on the white man and on the black man; that it is ordained by nature itself; that it carries with it duties for the black man and duties for the white, which duties cannot be performed except by the preservation, and if the gentlemen please it, the perpetuation of the system of negro slavery." [2] Said

[1] The *New York Herald*, January 1, 1860.
[2] The *Liberator*, January 20, 1860.

Caleb Cushing, whom many called the most unscrupulous of Northern politicians: "I showed you how under the influence of their malign teachings all party action North and South was running in the channel of a desperate and deplorable sectionalism, and that above all, here in Massachusetts, all the political influences dominant in the state were founded upon the single emotion of hate, aye! hate, treacherous ferocious hate of our fellow-citizens in the Southern states. Under the influence of this monomania, they have set up in this commonwealth a religion of hate, aye! a religion of hate such as belongs only to the condemned devils in hell. I say it is a religion of hate and blasphemy. Oh God! that such things are in this our day." [1]

The meeting in Rochester, New York, framed the following resolutions: "*Whereas*, recent events, occurring in different portions of our common country, have made prominent the continued union of the States composing our Confederacy; and whereas it has been thought proper for the citizens of Rochester to assemble in public meeting to declare their sentiments on this question. Therefore, *Resolved*, That we affirm and reiterate our fealty and attachment to the union of these states. . . . *Resolved*, That in our relations with the Southern states, we will, as far as in our power, cheerfully accord to them what we claim for ourselves, the free and unmolested exercise of our sovereign rights and privileges, and will manfully and faithfully aid them in their defense against unhallowed and treasonable designs of any combination of men. . . . *Resolved*, That we hold in utter disregard and contempt the cant and sneers of all those disorganizing and seditious fanatics who go about the streets of our cities and towns, claiming to be wiser than their fathers and better than their neighbors, and hold mutinous public meetings and secret conclaves, to impress upon the unsuspecting and peaceful of our fellow-citizens the dangerous

[1] The *Congressional Globe*, 36 Cong., 1 Sess., Vol. I, p. 311.

and unholy doctrine that he, who is not an abolitionist, is a thief, a robber, and a murderer; and we hold him morally guilty of such crimes, who openly or covertly endeavors to incite the slaves of the South to rapine and violence, or encourages fanatical emissaries to go forth on the errand of promoting such an end. *Resolved*, That the late insurrectionary movement of John Brown and those who conspired in person with him, in his treasonable and murderous assault upon the peaceful citizens of Virginia, has our most unqualified condemnation and severest rebuke, and we consider his punishment and that of his confederates not only just but demanded both by the offended laws of the country and by the magnitude and dangerous tendency of the offense; and should a like occasion arise, we pledge ourselves, if need be, and to the utmost of our power, in person and with our fortunes, to protect and defend the constitutional rights and privileges of the South. . . . *Resolved*, That while we revere the teachings from the pulpits of the free states, so far as they are confined to the legitimate objects of church organization, we consider all interferences from that source, with the constitutional rights of our Southern brethren touching the institution of slavery not only entirely unwarranted but calculated to incite disloyal and treasonable action, and to engender strife and disaffection. . . ." [1]

In the opinion of these ultraconservative, proslavery, Northern Democrats the true causes and incentives of the treasonable acts of Brown and other crazy adventurers were the brutal and bloody "irrepressible conflict" teachings of William H. Seward. Combating this view was the unpalatable doctrine, set forth by Ex-President Fillmore in a letter to the New York "Union-saving" meeting and for obvious reasons not read there. This eminent statesman announced it as his belief that the Harper's Ferry episode was the direct result of the Civil War in Kansas, and that the principle of

[1] The *Congressional Globe*, 36 Cong., 1 Sess., Vol. I, p. 296.

popular sovereignty, as there applied, was the true Pandora
box to which to trace the flood of evils then threatening to
overwhelm the constitution and sweep away the foundations
of the government; few laws were in his opinion so barren of
good and so fruitful of evil as the Kansas-Nebraska Act.

While some of the Southern papers praised the Union
meetings, many at the same time denounced them as too
late and as representing only the minority; what the South
wanted of the North was not public meetings, processions,
speeches, and resolutions, but votes. Mere "Union-saving"
by irresponsible public gatherings, which could easily be
assembled in large centers of population, was moreover
glaringly inconsistent with the retention on the statute books
of the formally enacted personal liberty laws.

To the Republicans of the North "Union-saving" was
even more ridiculous than to the Southerners. In the first
place, such meetings were not new. They were held after
the death of President Taylor, when that President's ap-
pointees were fighting the new President for the promised
spoils of office, after the enactment of the Fugitive Slave Law
and its enforcement, after both the Kansas-Nebraska Act
and the assault on Senator Sumner, and under Buchanan
during the struggle over the Lecompton constitution, in each
case following closely upon offensive acts of the government
and plainly under the auspices of administration men, who
pushed them for the purposes of shielding themselves and
turning public attention to other channels. It was not
difficult to gather men into a meeting in favor of a popular
idea (the nearer a truism the better), to officer it with respectable men (the more neutral the better), to get speakers and
resolution writers, and having all ready, to start the thing in
motion, then to let the resolutions be for self-evident propositions which no man disputed. There was nothing better
calculated to hide the actual situation than this "Union-
saving" device; in its declarations, the real cause of the

Brown uprising, the administration policy in Kansas, was always passed over.

The positive declarations of opinion by the Republicans concerning Brown and Harper's Ferry, although purposely guarded in order to save them from the charge of radical abolitionism, were yet well calculated to identify them with moderate antislavery. Horace Greeley, in the *New York Tribune*, wrote: "There are eras in which death is not merely heroic but beneficent and fruitful. Who shall say that this was not John Brown's time to die?... It will be easier to die in a good cause, even on the gallows, since John Brown has hallowed that mode of exit from the troubles and temptations of this mortal existence. Then, as to the 'irrepressible conflict,' who does not see that this sacrifice must inevitably intensify its progress and hasten its end?... So let us be reverently grateful for the privilege of living in a world rendered noble by the daring of heroes, the suffering of martyrs, among whom let none doubt that history will accord an honored niche to old John Brown." William Cullen Bryant, in the *New York Evening Post*, wrote: "A large part of the civilized world will, as a large part of the world does already, lay on his tomb the honors of martyrdom, and while the honors remain there, his memory will be more terrible to slaveholders than his living presence could ever have been, because it will bring recruits to his cause who would never have served under his banner while he was wielding carnal weapons." [1]

The *New York Independent* said: "No man can study the demeanor of Brown during his trial, and read his final speech to the court, without feeling that with all his errors of judgment and his fatal mistake in the mode of his attack upon slavery, this forlorn old man is exhibiting a type of heroism which the world has hardly seen since Cromwell and Sydney

[1] These two quotations are taken from the *New York Herald*, December 5, 1859.

shook tyrants with terror. . . . He stands not only as a brave man in a community of cowards, but a moral hero and prophet." [1] The *New York Times* said : "At the same time it cannot be doubted that Brown's personal bearing through-out the trial, his courage, his courtesy, his perfect self-pos-session, and his evident conviction of the rightfulness of his acts have awakened a personal sympathy for him even in the hearts of those who most detest his principles and his con-duct ; . . . it can hardly be possible that any man should read the words of the brave fanatic without a glow of half compassionate admiration." [2] The day following the execu-tion this paper declared that thousands had sympathy for Brown who were convinced that he should die.

That the same sentiments characterized the lesser Repub-lican papers was manifested in every part of the country. The *Winsted* (Connecticut) *Herald* said, "For one we con-fess that we love him, we honor him, we applaud him." The *New Haven Journal and Courier* declared that John Brown was hung "because he acted on the belief that the Declara-tion of Independence was more than a generality." The *New Haven Palladium* wrote : "John Brown had no murder, no treason, in his heart. His mission was one of freedom. . . . He was a good man and a true friend of his race, and he died a Christian death." The *Norwich Bulletin:* "John Brown died a martyr to the cause ; we have said so once, we say so again." The *Hartford Press:* "Slavery must come down peacefully, or scenes of horror shall mark its overthrow in blood." [3]

The Republicans, therefore, as well as their radical and conservative brethren in the North and the radicals of the South were strongly influenced by the John Brown affair.

[1] The *New York Independent*, November 10, 1859.

[2] The *New York Times*, November 2 and 3, 1859.

[3] The *New York Journal of Commerce*, March 3, 1860, contains these quotations from the Connecticut papers.

The country was slowly recovering from the business depression of 1857, and the Kansas question and the Lecompton constitution were rapidly becoming matters of the past; the nation was enjoying more peace than for many months and seemed destined to go into the presidential campaign without any urgent and immediate question of dispute, when suddenly the firebrand of Harper's Ferry flared forth and kindled public sentiment into new life. This was the influence of John Brown on the politics of the country. By the creation of sudden and intense excitement, which rendered deliberation and moderation well-nigh impossible, he forced the political parties of the country to assume extreme positions and declare extreme principles before they were prepared to do so; and from these positions and principles, once assumed and declared, there could be no receding. The only change possible was progress into more advanced radicalism. John Brown must, therefore, bear the immediate responsibility for the extremes of the presidential campaign of 1860.

CHAPTER II

ON December 5, three days after the execution of Brown, while the country was still under the spell of the unusual passions and excitement aroused by that dramatic event, the Thirty-sixth Congress of the United States met in its first regular session. In the House of Representatives, where the first duty was to effect organization, balloting for speaker began almost at once, one hundred and seventeen votes being necessary to a choice. In the first ballot Bocock of Virginia, the leading Democratic candidate, received eighty-six votes, Sherman of Ohio and Grow of Pennsylvania, the Republican candidates, sixty-six and forty-three votes respectively. When the result of this ballot was announced, Clark of Missouri arose for remarks, and after some confusion, incident to the fact that in the absence of a regular speaker the temporary presiding officer, the clerk, refused to decide points of order but insisted that the House should decide for itself, he introduced the following resolution: "*Whereas*, certain members of this House, now in nomination for speaker, did indorse the book hereinafter mentioned, *Resolved*, That the doctrines and sentiments of a certain book, called *The Impending Crisis in the South, How to meet It*, are insurrectionary and hostile to the peace and tranquillity of the country, and that no member of this House, who has indorsed and recommended it, is fit to be speaker of the House."

In this way an antislavery book, written by a poor white

of North Carolina, was suddenly raised into national prominence; it had first appeared in 1857 without attracting attention, had later been severely castigated in the Senate of the
United States without widespread comment, and with the
indorsement of sixty-eight Republican Congressmen, including both Sherman and Grow, and leading Republican
editors, had been used as a campaign document in the fall
campaign of 1859. The prevailing excitement now lent it
new significance. In the week of the death of Brown the
book had been resurrected and laid before the country in
large extracts in the columns of the *New York Herald.* Hope
was kindled again in the hearts of the Democrats, who had
been badly beaten in the previous fall elections, losing even
Pennsylvania, their old stronghold; combined with the
Virginia raid, the new book might arouse such a conservative
reaction as to completely rejuvenate the party. Thus
buoyed anew, the administration party girded itself for one
of the most bitter parliamentary struggles in the history of the
national House.

The book itself, whose author, Hinton Rowan Helper, was
but twenty-seven years of age, indeed proved "insurrectionary and hostile to the domestic peace and tranquillity of the
country." Its outline was simple. It opened with a comparison of the free and slave states, altogether to the advantage
of the former. When the first census was taken in 1790,
New York had a population of 340,120, Virginia twice that
number or 748,308; sixty years later New York had 3,097,-
394, Virginia 1,421,661. In 1791 the exports of New York
equaled $2,505,465 and those of Virginia $3,130,865, but
in 1852 those of New York amounted to $87,484,450 and
those of Virginia to $2,724,657; although in 1790 the im-
ports of the two states were about equal, in 1853 those of the
Northern state were $178,270,999 and of the Southern state
only $399,000. The products of mining, manufacturing,
and the mechanic arts in the one case were valued in 1850 at

$237,597,249, in the other at $29,705,387 ; in the same year the real and personal property in Virginia, excluding slaves, exceeded $390,000,000 ; in New York, where there were no slaves, $1,080,000,000. New York City was worth more than the whole state of Virginia. In 1790 North Carolina had 393,000 people, 15,000 more than Massachusetts ; in 1850 Massachusetts, with 994,000, was 125,000 ahead. The exports and imports of the New England state in 1853 were valued at $58,000,000, while those of North Carolina were so small as to be unworthy of record ; products of mining, manufacturing, and the mechanic arts in the one instance reached $150,000,000, in the other $9,000,000. Boston alone could almost buy North Carolina, while in the whole state of Massachusetts, with no slaves, real and personal property was valued at $570,000,000, and in North Carolina, with slaves, at only $266,000,000. In 1760 the one city of Charleston, South Carolina, imported $2,600,000 worth of articles, and in 1855 only $1,750,000 worth ; Philadelphia, in 1854, $21,000,000 worth. The products of mining, manufacturing, and the mechanic arts in Pennsylvania in 1850 totalled $155,000,000, in South Carolina $7,000,000 ; the cash value of Pennsylvania's farms was $422,000,000, of those in South Carolina $86,000,000 ; and the real and personal property in Pennsylvania, with no slaves, was put at $729,000,000 ; in South Carolina, with 384,000 slaves, at $288,000,000. Pennsylvania spent $1,348,000 on her schools, possessed 393 libraries other than private, and 310 newspapers and periodicals, of which 84,898,672 copies circulated ; whereas South Carolina expended on her schools $200,000, had 26 libraries, and 46 newspapers and periodicals with 7,145,930 copies in circulation. Many other details were given. Incontrovertible facts afforded ample evidence that something was wrong with the South, racially, politically, and morally ; else how had the North so far outstripped her ?

It was well known to Southerners that they were compelled

to go North for almost everything of utility and adornment, from watches, shoe pegs, and paintings to cotton mills, steamships, and statuary ; there was no foreign trade in the South, no princely Southern merchants. "And now to the point. In our opinion — an opinion which has been formed from data obtained by assiduous researches and comparisons, from laborious investigation, logical reasoning, and earnest reflection — the causes which have impeded the progress and prosperity of the South, which have dwindled our commerce and other similar pursuits into the most contemptible insignificance ; sunk a large majority of our people into galling poverty and ignorance, rendered a small minority conceited and tyrannical, and driven the rest away from their homes ; entailed upon us a humiliating dependence on the free states ; disgraced us in the recesses of our own souls, and brought us under reproach in the eyes of all enlightened and civilized nations, may be traced to one common source, and there find solution in the most hateful and horrible word that was ever incorporated into the vocabulary of human economy — slavery." It was the first and most sacred duty of every Southerner, without evasion or compromise, to declare himself an unqualified abolitionist ; the only thing to save the South from the vortex of utter ruin was complete abolition. There must be no more yielding to the domination of the inflated oligarchy.

Away with the agricultural boasts of the South. Comparing agricultural records the author found that there was a balance of $44,000,000 in favor of the North ; the one Northern crop of hay was worth more than the cotton, tobacco, rice, hay, and hemp of all the Southern states. Moreover, the North secured more profit even from Southern agriculture than did the South herself, for the cotton was carried to its destination in the ships of the Northerners, spun in their factories, woven in their looms, insured in their offices, and returned again South in their ships.

The soil under slave culture sickened and died. Said C. C. Clay of Alabama : "I can show you with sorrow in the older portions of Alabama the sad memorials of the artless and exhausting culture of cotton. Our small planters, after taking the cream off their lands, unable to restore them by rest, manures, and otherwise, are going West and South, in search of other virgin lands, which they may and will despoil in like manner. Our wealthier planters with greater means, and no more skill, are buying out their poorer neighbors, extending their plantations, and adding to their slave force. The wealthy few, who are able to live on smaller profits, and to give their blasted fields some rest, are thus pushing off the many." The author then quoted from an address by Henry A. Wise to Virginians : "Commerce has long ago spread her sails and sailed away from you. You have not as yet dug more than coal enough to warm yourselves at your own hearths ; you have set no tilt hammers to strike blows worthy of Gods in your iron foundries ; you have not yet spun more than coarse cotton enough in the way of manufactures, to clothe your own slaves. You have no commerce, no mining, no manufactures. You have relied alone on the single power of agriculture, and such agriculture! Your sedge patches outshine the sun. Your inattention to your only source of wealth has seared the very bosom of Mother Earth. Instead of having to feed cattle on a thousand hills, you have had to chase the stumped-tailed steer through the sedge patches to procure a tough beefsteak."

Definite recommendations followed as to how to get rid of slavery. First, thorough political organization and independent political action on the part of the nonslaveholding whites of the South ; second, ineligibility of slaveholders to membership in the organization — never another vote to any one who advocated the retention and perpetuation of human slavery ; third, no coöperation with proslavery politicians, no fellowship with them in religion, no affiliation with them in society; fourth, no patronage to proslavery merchants, no guestship in slave-waiting hotels, no fees to proslavery lawyers, no employment of proslavery physicians, no audience to proslavery parsons; fifth, no more hiring of slaves by nonslaveholders; sixth, abrupt discontinuance of subscription to proslavery newspapers; seventh, the greatest possible encouragement to free white labor; eighth, immediate death to slavery, or if no immediate, then unqualified proscription of its advocates during the period of its existence; ninth, a tax of sixty dollars on every slaveholder for each and every negro in his possession at the present time or at any time between now and July 4, 1863; tenth, an additional tax of forty dollars per annum to be levied annually on every slaveholder for each and every negro found in his possession after July 4, 1863.

"This, then, is the outline of our scheme for the abolition of slavery in the Southern states. Let it be acted upon with due promptitude and as certain as truth is mightier than error, fifteen years will not elapse before every foot of territory, from the mouth of the Delaware to the emboguing of the Rio Grande, will glitter with jewels of freedom. . . . But, sirs, slaveholders, chevaliers, and lords of the lash, we are unwilling to allow you to cheat the negroes out of all the rights and claims to which, as human beings, they are most sacredly entitled. Not alone for ourselves as individuals, but for others also, particularly for five or six million of nonslaveholding whites, whom your iniquitous statism has debarred from almost all the mental and material comforts of life, do we speak, when we say, you must sooner or later emancipate your slaves, and pay each and every one of them at least sixty dollars cash in hand. By doing this you will be restoring to them their natural rights and remunerating them at the rate of less than twenty-six cents per annum for the long and cheerless period of their servitude, from the 20th of August, 1620, when on the James River in Virginia, they became the unhappy slaves of unhappy tyrants. Moreover, by doing this you will be performing but a simple act of justice to the nonslaveholding whites, upon whom the system of slavery has weighed scarcely less heavily than upon the negroes themselves. You will also be applying a saving balm to your own outraged hearts and consciences, and your children, yourself in fact, freed from the accursed stain of slavery, will become respectable, useful, and honorable members of society." Finally the author taunted and defied the slaveholders as follows: "And now, sirs, we have thus laid down our ultimatum. What are you going to do about it? Something dreadful, of course! Perhaps you will dissolve the Union again. Do it, if you dare! Our motto, and we would have you to understand it, is 'the abolition of slavery and the perpetuation of the American Union.' If by any means you do succeed in your treasonable attempts to take the South out of the Union to-day, we will bring her back to-morrow; if she goes away with you, she will return without you. Do not mistake the meaning of the last clause of the last sentence. We could elucidate it so thoroughly that no intelligent person could fail to comprehend it; but for reasons, which may hereafter appear, we forego the task. Henceforth there are other interests to be consulted in the South, aside from the interests of negroes and slaveholders. A profound sense of duty incites us to make the greatest possible efforts for the abolition of slavery; an equally profound sense of duty calls for a continuation of those efforts until the very last foe to freedom shall have been utterly vanquished. . . . Thus, terror engenderers of the South, have we fully and frankly defined our position; we have no modifications to propose, no compromises to offer, nothing to retract. Frown, sirs, fret, foam, prepare your weapons, threat, strike, shoot, stab, bring on civil war, dissolve the Union, nay, annihilate the solar system if you will, do all this, more, less, better less, anything — do what you will, sirs, you can neither foil or intimidate us; our purpose is as firmly fixed as the eternal pillars of heaven; we have determined to abolish slavery, and so help us God, abolish it we will!"

The author then gave an elaborate set of quotations to prove that the Southern statesmen quite generally in the early days of the republic, Northern statesmen of all times, and leaders of all civilized nations from antiquity to modern times, were arrayed against slavery; the testimony of the churches and of the Bible was likewise against it. Washington wrote, "I never mean, unless some particular set of circumstances should compel me to it, to possess another slave by purchase, it being among my first wishes to see some plan adopted by which slavery in this country may be abolished by law." Jefferson proposed a plan of emancipation, and added: "Indeed, I tremble for my country when I reflect that God is just; that his justice cannot sleep forever; that considering numbers, nature, and natural means only, a revolution of the wheel of fortune, an exchange of situation, is among possible events; that it may become probable by supernatural influence! The Almighty has no attributes that can take sides with us in such a contest." Madison and Monroe were opposed to slavery. Patrick Henry wrote, "It would rejoice my very soul that every one of my fellow-beings were emancipated." Henry Clay said, "So long as God allows the vital current to flow through my veins, I will never, never, never, by word or thought, by mind or will, aid in admitting one rod of free territory to the everlasting curse of human bondage." [1]

---

[1] The book closes with further facts and figures in comparison of the two sections. The North, with 780,576 hands, turned out $842,586,058 worth of manufactured product; the South, with 161,733 hands, $165,413,027 worth. The one group of states had 3682 miles of canals, 17,855 miles of railroads, a bank capital of $230,100,340, and a militia force of 1,381,843, while the other had 1116 miles of canals, 6859 miles of railroads, $102,078,940 bank capital, and a militia force of 792,876. The

In the eyes of slaveholders such a book, containing such advice, was rebellion, and the men who gave it their indorsement, understanding the scope and purpose of their act, deserved a nameless fate. Republicans in the House, forced by Clark's motion to take the defensive, although they mildly admitted their circulation of the despised book as party literature, indulged but little in direct attacks on the South, whereas, on the other hand, the Southerners were aggressive in the extreme. A part of almost every day the House devoted to a fruitless ballot or two for speaker, the remainder of the time to the speeches of the mob. For it was a great unruly mob over which by circumstances the clerk was forced to preside. Members were seated on wooden benches, arranged in a semicircle around the speaker's desk; a wide central aisle, with the Republican benches on the one side and the Democratic on the other, like an arena, seemed to invite the hostile camps to combat. Despite numberless challenges to come forth and state and defend his opinion of Helperism, Sherman, who was the leading Republican candidate after the first ballot, as often refused so long as the Democrats refused to withdraw the offensive resolution. Points of order were discussed, questions of procedure propounded; the whole range of Republican and Democratic policy was now run over, now the possibilities of the coming presidential campaign weighed in the balance. The facts and figures of the *Crisis* the Southerners could not dispute, and they wisely never attempted to do so, but they raged and threatened. Said Pryor of Virginia, "We have

one section had 62,433 public schools, 72,621 teachers, and 2,169,901 school children, the other 18,507 schools, 19,307 teachers, and 581,861 school children; there were in the one section 14,911 libraries other than private, with 3,888,234 volumes, in the other 695 libraries with 649,577 volumes; in the North 1790 newspapers and periodicals with 334,146,281 copies circulated, and in the South 704 newspapers and periodicals with 81,038,693 copies circulated; Northerners in the one year took out 1929 patents, Southerners 268.

threatened and resolved, and resolved and threatened, and backed out from our threats, until, so help me God! I will never utter another threat or another resolution; but as the stroke follows the lightning's flash, so, with me, acts shall be coincident and commensurate with words." Curry of Alabama, "I am not ashamed or afraid publicly to avow that the election of William H. Seward or Salmon P. Chase, or any other representative of the Republican party, upon a sectional platform, ought to be resisted to the disruption of every tie that binds this confederation together." Crawford of Georgia: "Now, in regard to the election of a Black Republican President, I have this to say, and I speak the sentiment of every Democrat on this floor from the state of Georgia, we will never submit to the inauguration of a Black Republican President. (*Applause from the Democratic benches and hisses from the Republicans.*) I repeat it, sir; and I have authority to say so; no Democratic representative from Georgia on this floor will ever submit to the inauguration of a Black Republican President. (*Renewed hisses and applause.*)" Singleton of Mississippi, "If you desire to know my counsel to the people of Mississippi, it is, that they take measures immediately in conjunction with the other Southern states, to separate from you." Gartrell of Georgia, "I shall announce the solemn fact, disagreeable though it may be to you as well as to me, to my people as well as to yours, that if this course of aggression shall be continued, the people of the South, of the slaveholding states, will be compelled by every principle of justice, honor, and self-preservation, to disrupt every tie that binds them to the Union, peacefully if they can, forcibly if they must." [1]

On some occasions passion went beyond the bounds of parliamentary order. In a rough-and-tumble fight one day,

[1] The *Congressional Globe*, 36 Cong., 1 Sess., Vol. I, pp. 840–841, gives these and other threats. See *the same*, Vol. IV, App., p. 53, for an angry encounter between Kilgore of the North and Singleton of the South.

amid intense excitement, a pistol fell from the pocket of a member from New York. Early in the session Branch of North Carolina challenged Grow of Pennsylvania to a duel, which the latter promptly refused. At another time Logan of Illinois drew a pistol on a colleague. "By God, if I can't talk, I can do something else," he exclaimed. Yet mutual good will was not lacking; inflammatory speeches and angry encounters on the floor were usually over in a few minutes, and gave place to good feeling, to chatting, smoking, and drinking in mutual good-fellowship. Even Sherman, arch-traitor, denounced as unfit to live and as unfit to die, after all was over might be seen walking off, arm in arm, with his castigators.

The responsibility for the failure to elect the speaker was justly laid to the door of the two small parties or factions, the Anti-Lecompton Democrats and the Americans, who steadfastly refused to vote for Sherman or to allow the adoption of the plurality rule for the election. The substitution of a rule of this kind in place of a majority vote had been the only means of ending the struggle of 1849 in the House with the election of Howell Cobb of Georgia on the sixty-second ballot, and that of 1856 with the election of Banks of Massachusetts on the one hundred and thirty-third ballot; and in the minds of the Republicans, who easily commanded the highest vote, such a rule was now desirable.

Finally patronage, "the cohesive power of public plunder," accomplished the work. After the contest had dragged itself out for two months, continuing uninterruptedly through the Christmas holidays,[1] the Republicans gave up the radical Sherman and threw their votes to Pennington, a member of the People's Party of New Jersey, who had uniformly voted for Sherman, but had not signed the offensive indorsement of the Helper book because he was not a member of the House when that indorsement had appeared; the Anti-

---

[1] Christmas and New Year's came on Sunday this year.

Lecompton Democrats and the Americans gave the new candidate the three or four votes that Sherman had always lacked and thus an election was accomplished. An Anti-Lecomptonite was made clerk, an American sergeant at arms, and together the two small parties divided several important committee assignments.[1]

The new speaker, sixty-three years of age and of a distinguished New Jersey family, was a graduate of Princeton College and by profession a lawyer; for seven years he had served his state with distinction as governor, in which position he had achieved a national reputation as an anti-slavery man. He had refused the governorship of the territory of Minnesota proffered him by President Taylor, and later an appointment as judge to settle claims with Mexico. Elected to Congress by the People's Party, or as it was sometimes called, the Opposition, his new honor, conferred by Republican votes, was calculated to facilitate the merging of his party into the larger opposition or Republican party both in New Jersey and in the neighboring state of Pennsylvania. Along with Muhlenburg, the first speaker, and Henry Clay, Pennington enjoyed the distinction of elevation to the speakership at the beginning of his first term as mem-

---

[1] In the long interval covering December and January the members of the House could receive no salary from the government as they had not been sworn in and there was also no speaker to sign the salary warrants. In the contingency the former sergeant at arms, active candidate for re-election, privately borrowed money and advanced it regularly to the members in easy loans, in the hope that thus he could win the post again; but he had his pains for nothing, as the office went to another. It was suggested at the time, that inasmuch as there was no speaker to swear the members in, an ordinary justice be secured to perform the task; the speaker was not necessary to this function. Pennington announced his committees almost at once; Sherman had had these made up for a long time, and the successful candidate adopted these assignments as his own. Probably he had to promise to do this in order to secure the Republican vote. Here, then, was an instance in which the speaker practically did not select his own committees but allowed a party to dictate the choices to him.

ber of the House; as a new man he had no record and was not yet definitely a member of any faction, and thus his name was a good one to win support from various groups.[1] Tall and stately, courteous and affable, he was yet without practical legislative experience, and proved a poor speaker, entirely dependent upon accommodating members and intelligent pages.[2]

The effect on the country of this long contest was intense. Every phase of the two months' battle, every excoriation of Helperism, every bit of Southern bluster, every Northern argument and expostulation, every physical clash, was eagerly read about the next morning by hundreds of thousands. Numerous Northern cities greeted the election of Pennington with the firing of one hundred guns, while the Richmond papers draped themselves in mourning. Northern bookstores and news stands sold one hundred and fifty thousand copies of the incendiary *Crisis*, the popularity of which recalled *Uncle Tom's Cabin*. In the South the dreaded book was suppressed and supporters of it persecuted after the fashion of John Brown's sympathizers. So intent were Southerners on keeping the incendiary sentiments from the common people and from the negroes that they made practically no mention of Helper and his book in their local press. An exclusive boat club in Washington, D.C., requested the withdrawal of a member who indorsed Helper.

---

[1] This principle was to receive application later in the selection of Lincoln as the party's candidate for the presidency. See p. 127.

[2] He was defeated for reëlection to the House, November, 1860. In a campaign speech in the fall, Pennington declared that he knew several weeks before his election to the speakership that sufficient votes to elect him could be obtained at any time; the Republicans, however, coveted the moral influence of the victory and clung to Sherman as long as possible. The *New York Tribune*, February 18, 1860, gives an account of the courteous reception by Pennington, while he was governor of New Jersey, of a communication from a world antislavery convention in London, praying for the abolition of slavery in America. The Southern governors spurned the circular.

In a bill regulating the Police Commissioners of Baltimore, Maryland, the state legislature inserted the following clause, "Provided that no Black Republican or indorser or supporter of the Helper book shall be appointed to office under the said Board"; that is, no Helperite could be a policeman. In the charter of a street railway for the same city there was this clause, "That no Black Republican or indorser or supporter of the Helper book shall receive any of the benefits or privileges of this act or be employed in any capacity by the said railroad company"; that is, no Helperite could ride in the street cars. This was the same legislature that censured the American, Henry Winter Davis, member of Congress from Baltimore, for throwing his vote to Pennington. In the town square at High Point, North Carolina, ten copies of the *Crisis* were publicly burned. A farmer of Alexandria County, Virginia, was arrested for buying four copies of the book, and thrust into jail under bonds of $2000. Rev. Daniel Worth, a missionary of the American Missionary Association, was arrested at Greensboro, North Carolina, for selling the hated book and in default of $15,000 bail was allowed to languish some three months in jail. At the trial four copies of Helper were produced, which it was proved that Worth had sold. One buyer, learning of Worth's arrest, buried his copy; another hid his in a hollow log; another testified that Worth on selling a copy to him, told him to be careful whom he allowed to see it. A sentence of one year in prison followed. Tried again on the same charge, Worth was convicted but immediately released on bail, and finally escaped to New York, where both he and Helper addressed large popular audiences in the interests of their cause. The story of Worth's persecution was a favorite one in the Northern papers.

CHAPTER III

AFTER the final organization of the House the record of Congress was much less that of a legislative body than of a great factory for the manufacture of public opinion ; speeches were made and things were done for home consumption, to influence voters. Probably more than at present the people were influenced by Congress, just as the frequent congressional clashes were themselves in turn but a reflection of the known attitude of the home communities. There was formal discussion of the tariff, polygamy, the Pacific Railroad, the Homestead Act, and a few other acts of general public policy, but the one unfailing topic, to which all others inevitably led, was the sectional question of slavery.

In the House perhaps the most famous speech on either side of this question, and certainly the most famous Republican utterance there on the subject, was that of Owen Lovejoy of Illinois. The speech should be read in its entirety, for no adequate idea of it can be gained from mere description or quotation. The subject was the extermination, so far as the federal government had power, of the "twin relics of barbarism," polygamy and slavery, to which policy the Republican party pledged itself in its platform of 1856. The deathblow had already been dealt the former, so that the speaker would consider slavery alone. After some technical objections to his speaking, he proceeded as follows : "We are told that where slavery will pay, slaveholders will go. Precisely upon the same principle we might say that where

47

robbery will pay, robbery will go; where piracy will pay, piracy will go; and where adipose human flesh is cheaper than that of beeves, cannibalism will go, because it will pay. Sir, than robbery, than piracy, than polygamy, slaveholding is worse, more criminal, more injurious to man, and consequently more offensive to God. Slaveholding has been justly designated as the sum of all villainy. Put every crime perpetrated among men into a moral crucible, and dissolve and combine them all, and the resultant amalgam is slaveholding. It has the violence of robbery. *A Member.* You are joking. *Mr Lovejoy.* No, sir, I am speaking in dead earnest. It has the violence of robbery, the blood and cruelty of piracy; it has the offensive and brutal lusts of polygamy, all combined and concentrated in itself, with aggravations that neither one of these crimes ever knew or dreamed of."

The justification of slavery, so far as he knew, rested on three grounds, the infirmity of the enslaved race, the civilizing and christianizing influences of slavery, and the guarantees of the federal constitution. As to the first point: "We may concede it as a matter of fact that it (the negro race) is infirm; but does it follow, therefore, that it is right to enslave a man because he is infirm? This, to me, is a most abhorrent doctrine. It would place the weak everywhere at the mercy of the strong; it would place the poor at the mercy of the rich; it would place those that are deficient in intellect at the mercy of those who are gifted in mental endowment. The principle of enslaving human beings because they are inferior is this: if a man is a cripple, trip him; if he is old and weak and bowed with the weight of years, strike him, for he cannot strike back; if idotic, take advantage of him; and if a child, deceive him. This, sir, this is the doctrine of Democrats, and the doctrine of devils as well, and there is no place in the universe outside the five points of hell and the Democratic party where the practice and the prevalence of such doctrines would not be a disgrace. (*Laughter*) If the strong of the earth are to enslave the weak here, it would justify angels in enslaving men, because they are superior; and archangels in turn would be justified in subjugating those who are inferior in intellect and position, and ultimately it would transform Jehovah into an infinite Juggernaut rolling the huge wheels of His omnipotence (here Mr. Lovejoy advanced from his seat on the Republican benches out into the long aisle in front of the Democratic benches). *Mr. Pryor* (advancing from the Democratic side to meet him): The gentleman from Illinois shall not approach this side of the House, shaking his fists and talking in the way he has talked. It is bad enough to be compelled to sit here and hear him utter his treasonable and insulting language, but he shall not, sir, come upon this side of the House, shaking his fists in our faces." Great confusion followed, and Mr. Pryor spoke up: "Let the gentleman speak from his seat, and say all under the rules he is entitled to say. . . . He shall not come here gesticulating in a menacing and ruffianly manner." Here some one tried to pour oil on the waters by saying that Lovejoy should speak from his seat; all knew him to be a man of courage and that he could not be intimidated. "*Mr. Pryor.* No one wants to intimidate him. *Mr. Lovejoy.* Nobody can intimidate him." Thirty or forty members were now gathered about the two principals in the long aisle; finally it was moved that the committee rise, whereupon the speaker took the chair and asked for order. "*Mr. Barksdale.* Order that black-hearted scoundrel and niggerstealing thief to take his seat and this side of the House will do it. *Mr. McQueen.* We will allow nobody to come over from that side of the House and bully us on this side." Finally order was restored, and Mr. Lovejoy went on to finish his sentence: "axle-deep, amid the enslaved and mangled and bleeding bodies of human beings (*laughter on*

E

the Democratic side) on the ground that he was infinitely
superior, and that they were an inferior race.   *Mr. Gartrell.*
The man is crazy."

As to the civilizing of the negroes : "It is a strange mode
of Christianizing a race to turn them over into brutism without legal marriage.   Among the four millions of slaves in
this country there is not a single husband or wife.   There is
not legally a single father or mother.   There is not a single
home or hearthstone among these four millions. . . .   Christianizing them, sir, Christianizing them by a new process.
The slave states have a right to an exclusive patent on it.
Taking them out in sight of the church, as one was taken out
not long ago in the state of Tennessee by a Presbyterian
elder, and laid down on his face on the ground, his hands and
his feet extended to their utmost tension and tied to pickets,
and the Gospel whipped into him with the broadside of a
handsaw, discolored whelks of sanctification being raised
between the teeth every time this Gospel agency fell upon
the naked and quivering flesh of the tortured convert.
(*Laughter*)   Christianized as a young girl was Christianized
in this city since this session of Congress, by being whipped
and sent to the garret and found dead in the morning, with
the blood oozing from nose and ears."   The orator pictured
the funeral, the fine black coffin and the decorating ribbons,
and ridiculed the Southern boast of Christian funerals for
slaves.   "See, Mr. Lovejoy, there is a slave funeral.   Is
that treating them like brutes ?   Look into the coffin !   Look
into the carriage !"

On the third point the speaker denied the constitutionality
of slavery ; slavery was not in the constitution, and when
he took the oath of office as Congressman he did not swear
to uphold slavery.   He knew that Congress could not touch
slavery in the states, and yet he justified himself in discussing it because he hoped to hold it up to the scorn of all the
world and ultimately to secure its removal.

He approved of Helper's book and of John Brown. "I tell you, Mr. Chairman, and I tell you all, that if I were a slave and I had the power, and were it necessary to achieve my freedom, I would not hesitate to fill up and bridge the chasm that yawns between the hell of slavery and the heaven of freedom with the carcasses of the slain." [1]

As a result of this ferocious speech and the violence attending it, Pryor of Virginia, Lovejoy's leading antagonist, though a very young man, challenged Potter of Wisconsin to a duel, undoubtedly counting on the latter's refusal and the discomfiture thereby of the North. The doughty Westerner, however, turned the tables by accepting the challenge and naming bowie knives as the weapons. This the Southerner felt called upon to refuse, and the proud F.F.V. name of Pryor temporarily became a byword and a joke in the Northern papers. During the Republican national convention a month later in Chicago Potter was presented with a bowie knife seven feet long, appropriately inscribed.

Not once but a number of times the lie was passed in the House, and on one occasion the Vice President of the United States was called upon to intervene in a fist fight between two members of the House on the steps of the Capitol. In these various ways the violence that attended the speakership contest was prolonged to the very end of the session.

The other House of Congress, the Senate of the United States, immediately upon assembling in December, was plunged into a discussion of the slavery question just as was the House of Representatives, but while the one body considered Helper's book, the other debated John Brown. As promptly as the celebrated Clark motion in the House came the motion of Senator Mason of Virginia in the Senate for a special committee to inquire into the facts of the Harper's Ferry raid, to determine whether there was any opposition to the troops of the United States, whether any Vir-

[1] The *Congressional Globe*, 36 Cong., 1 Sess., Vol. IV, App., p. 202.

ginia citizens or troops were murdered, whether there was "any organization intended to subvert the government of any of the states of the Union," "what was the character of such organization," "whether any citizens of the United States, not present, were implicated therein, or accessory thereto, by contributions of money, ammunitions, or otherwise," "whether any and what legislation may, in their opinion, be necessary on the part of the United States for the future preservation of the peace of the country"; said committee also should "have power to send for persons and papers."

Fortunately this motion to a large extent served to throw the consideration of the matter into the committee away from the open Senate, so that the latter body, debating John Brown, was saved a repetition of the excitement of the pitched battle in the House over Helper; but few Senators in open session made provoking speeches on Brown. Though the sittings of the committee were open to the public, the testimony there was but meagerly reported in the newspapers and general interest in the hearings was small. Indeed, as Brown's race was run, and his principles amply vindicated, the inquiry was almost academic, nay, political, as some believed, designed, in general, to throw discredit upon the Republican party and in particular to make Senator Mason President.

Strangely enough, a fine point of constitutional law, not directly connected with Brown himself, but arising out of the proceedings of the committee, was followed by the public with more eagerness than was any of the testimony; this was the right of a legislative body to imprison a contumacious witness for contempt to one of its committees. A popular liberty right was at stake.

Four witnesses, summoned before the committee, failed to come and were ordered to be arrested by the sergeant at arms, John Brown, Jr., of Ohio, James Redpath of Massachusetts, Frank B. Sanborn of Massachusetts, and Thaddeus

Hyatt of New York. Brown evaded arrest and Redpath could not be found. Sanborn was taken in an outrageous manner at Concord, Massachusetts, by the sergeant at arms, who called him out of his home at night and forcibly carried him off without showing his warrant or giving any reason for the arrest. The next morning the prisoner secured his own release by a writ of habeas corpus, issued by a judge of the state court, and later on a fictitious charge had himself arrested by state officials, in order that he might remain in the jurisdiction of the state of Massachusetts. He was then safe, for the Senate did not choose to enter into a controversy with the state for the possession of the prisoner.

Hyatt, at first fleeing from arrest, finally gave himself up and voluntarily went to Washington with his lawyers to argue the case. Standing before the bar of the Senate and not before the committee, he gave his answer in the form of a long constitutional argument of over two hours' duration, read to empty benches by two clerks in succession, who frequently turned two or three pages at a time. The prisoner was willing to appear before the committee and answer all questions if he were allowed to do so of his own free will, but he said that he would not if constrained by the threat of arrest; the act of 1857 which sought to compel witnesses at Congressional investigations to testify to their own disgrace he regarded as contrary to common law and unconstitutional. By the Constitution of the United States the Senate had no power to constitute itself accuser, judge, jury, and executive official, without recourse to regular indictment and without witnesses.[1] In favor of the Senate was

[1] Senator Sumner thought that the Senate had the power to compel answers from witnesses, in determining elections, returns and qualifications of members, in punishing misbehavior of members, in inquiring into the conduct of Senate officials, and in cases where a man abused the privileges of the Senate. But the case in hand constituted a new point, and both the Constitution and reason and precedent were against the proposed new exercise of the right. See the *Congressional Globe*, 36 Cong., 1 Sess., Vol. II, p. 1100.

the contention that a committee hearing without such power would be rendered useless; looking in the same direction were many English and American colonial cases, and two American cases since 1789, the last as late as 1857.[1]

Party lines were broken, prominent Democrats being for the accused and prominent Republicans against him, and by a vote of forty-four to ten the self-surrendered prisoner was remanded to the Washington jail in care of the sergeant at arms, to remain until such time as he should see fit to obey the power of the Senate and answer the questions of the committee. Proving obdurate, he languished in his prison for thirteen and one-half weeks and was only released when the committee completed its labors and made its report. Thus Hyatt suffered, a victim in the opinion of many to the galling slavocracy of the United States Senate, and a hero in the eyes of the Northern radicals; the list of the antislavery martyrs was growing fast, Brown, Helper, Worth, Hyatt, and there were others to be added. That some of the opponents of slavery, however, did not admire Hyatt's conduct is clearly shown by the curt questions of the *New York Tribune;* was not Hyatt impractical? Why, instead of tamely giving up, did he not follow the example of Sanborn and release himself by habeas corpus? Greeley did not think that Hyatt's martyrdom had done the cause any good.

When confronted by the business of actual legislation during the first two months of its session, the Senate found itself balked by the nonorganization of the House of Representatives, and the interesting question arose whether one house could perform its part in legislation before the other

---

[1] Wilckelhausen *vs.* Willet in New York. The plaintiff sued the sheriff for allowing a debtor to escape out of his hands into the control of the sergeant at arms of the House of Representatives, at the warrant of the speaker of the House. The judge decided that the warrant had the force of a habeas corpus and was binding on the sheriff.

house was able to proceed. Reason seemed to point to an affirmative answer, courtesy, form, and precedent in the opposite direction. The decision seemed to depend on whether or not there was any Congress, and this latter question further to depend on the solution of the question whether or not there was any House of Representatives. There was surely a Senate. The constitutional mandate that the House of Representatives should choose its speaker and other officers seemed clearly to indicate that the House existed before the choice of these officers; furthermore, failure to take the oath of office did not, as some maintained, constitute proof of the nonexistence of the House, as the taking of the oath three days after the organization of the first House proved. The date of the taking of the oath was a mere matter of law and not of the Constitution. All this was admitted. But it seemed courteous for the upper house, before proceeding to legislate, to wait until officially informed of the organization of the lower house; precedent also dictated the same course. In 1839 the Senate waited three weeks for the House, in 1849 three weeks and one day, and in 1856 two months. This it was finally determined to do in 1860, and for two months the Senate refrained from legislation and gave itself up entirely to executive business.[1]

When legislation became possible the Senate considered the same questions as did the House. Politics held sway much more than in the popular branch, owing undoubtedly to the presence in the Senate's membership of many avowed candidates for the presidency, especially of Douglas, the popular sovereignty champion. Frequently the Republi-

[1] Credentials were examined, resolutions submitted, memorials presented and referred, petitions and papers received, and many speeches delivered. See the *Congressional Globe*, 36 Cong., 1 Sess., Vol. I, pp. 494–517. The delay in 1839 was occasioned by a contested election case, in 1849 and in 1856 by a contest over the speakership.

cans poured their wrathful vituperation on the institution of slavery, but succeeded in calling forth only a few positive statements in its behalf, while at least one great and notable attack went entirely unanswered. This was Senator Sumner's speech on the admission of Kansas into the Union, entitled "The Barbarism of Slavery." After long and patient travel in two continents in search of recovery from the murderous blows dealt him by Brooks in the Senate Chamber four years previously, the Massachusetts statesman now returned for his "revenge," and in June, two months after Lovejoy's effort, he delivered a four hours' speech on slavery, which for stubborn logic, bitter invective, and stinging, exasperating frankness, has seldom, if ever, been equalled. The style had all the speaker's well-known literary and oratorical traits. Pedantic references to classical and medieval history abounded; vigorous use of language, sharp epithets, and grace and charm of style characterized the whole, but through it all ran a pervading egotism and painful elaboration, with nothing of the abandon, the spontaneity, and utter sinking of self, that characterized the great speech in the House. The practical usefulness of the attack, too, was seriously questioned; the spirit displayed was too vigorous to do good.[1]

"Slavery is the sum of all villainies," said the speaker in opening, quoting John Wesley; it was always the scab, the canker, the barebones and the shame of the country. "Founded in violence, sustained only by violence, such a law must, by a sure law of compensation, blast the master as well as the slave; blast the community of which they are a part; blast the government which does not forbid the outrage; and the longer it exists and the more completely it prevails, must its blasting influences penetrate the whole social system. Barbarous in origin, barbarous in its law,

---

[1] It was said at the time that Senator Sumner committed his speeches to memory.

barbarous in all its pretensions, barbarous in the instruments it employs, barbarous in consequences, barbarous in spirit, barbarous wherever it shows itself, slavery must breed barbarism, while it develops everywhere, alike in the individual and in the society to which he belongs, the essential elements of barbarism." In regard to the law of slavery he continued : "The slave is held simply for the use of his master, to whose behests his life, liberty, and happiness are devoted, and by whom he may be bartered, leased, mortgaged, bequeathed, invoiced, shipped as cargo, stored as goods, sold on execution, knocked off at public auction, and even staked at the gaming table on the hazard of a card or a die, — all according to law, . . . He may be marked like a hog, branded like a mule, yoked like an ox, hobbled like a horse, driven like an ass, sheared like a sheep, maimed like a cur, and constantly beaten like a brute, — all according to law." There were five objectionable elements in the law of slavery, — property in man, abrogation of marriage, absence of the parental relation, the closing of the gates of knowledge, and the appropriation of all toil, — at the end of the consideration of each of which points the orator would exclaim : "Sir, is not slavery barbarous?" Consideration of the practical results of slavery led to a valuable and exhaustive comparison of the North and the South, similar to Helper's comparison, and like the latter overwhelmingly in favor of the North. The character of the slaveholder was shown up by the usual quotations from statesmen and authors, and by a painstaking citation of facts drawn from the whole range of history.

When the speaker closed, Senator Chestnut of South Carolina rose for a brief reply. Although he was sorry that the orator of the day was back at his post, he would not attack him and make a hero of him, one "who had been crawling through the back doors to whine at the feet of the British aristocracy, craving pity, and reaping a rich harvest of contempt, the slanderer of states and of men." Thereupon

Sumner, who had been claiming that slavery made the slave-holder barbarous, rose and made one of the finest retorts in the records of the Senate. "This is a better illustration than any I have cited. I ask the Senate that I may use it in my speech as an appendix." [1]

[1] The *Congressional Globe*, 36 Cong., 1 Sess., Vol. III, p. 2590 ff.

CHAPTER IV

JOHN Brown's raid heightened the discussion of slavery among the people at large as well as in Congress. Editorials on the subject became more informing and more full of argument, news items more inclusive of the happenings in the slavery world; in the large dailies and religious weeklies, at church, at home, in the store and in the street, slavery was brought home to men and women in every conceivable form. By the very progress of events countless new currents and eddies in public opinion were forming, which the politicians of the time found it necessary to take into account before daring to formulate their platforms, and which the present generation must understand if it would appreciate the politics of the period.

The cruel, the unusual sides of slavery, as the institution existed in the South, were continually held up to view. On the point, did the Southern masters ever burn their slaves at the stake? angry colloquies were waged both in Congress and before the people; the Northerner, answering the question in the affirmative, was a "liar and a scoundrel," his statements were "utterly false," they were "foul and false slanders." There was no retraction on either side. Horace Greeley set to work and in widely quoted articles on the editorial page of the *New York Tribune* produced what seemed irrefutable evidence. In a careful historical survey covering the previous thirty years twelve occurrences of the crime were brought to light. The *St. Louis Evening News* now republished, and the *Tribune* copied, the accounts which had appeared originally in the St. Louis papers, of a lynching of three negroes the previous year in that state by a crowd of one thousand people. The details of the crime, the stripping of the negro to the waist, his desperation, the fire licking up the body and its quick effects seen in the writhing of the victim and his shrieks and appeals for mercy, his clutching at the hot chains and dropping them, his pitiable death, all were described in the most harrowing fashion, obviously with the conscious effort to inflame the passions and sensibilities of the readers. Thousands and tens of thousands of people read Greeley's presentation of the matter, written in his most vigorous style.[1] Numerous instances of the crime in 1860, taken from Southern papers themselves, were brought to light in further proof of the Northern charges. Two negroes were burned in Arkansas and a subscription was taken up to indemnify the owners for their loss. The *Vicksburg Sun* reported the burning of a negro in Mississippi, "whose fate was decreed by a council of highly respectable gentlemen." The *Augusta* (Georgia) *Chronicle* told of a case in that state, the *Columbus* (Georgia) *Chronicle* of another in the same state. In each instance the victim was guilty of some fiendish crime, murder, arson, or rape, which richly deserved severe punishment. The frequent lynching of white murderers and horse thieves on the wild frontiers of the country, in Iowa, Nebraska, and Arkansas, passed almost unnoticed; only let the unfortunate wrongdoer be a black slave and his murderers Southern slaveholders, and the Republican papers teemed with glaring accounts.

The oft-repeated descriptions of the slave auction scarcely need mention. As may be expected, the disgusting points

[1] The *New York Tribune*, March 12 and 20, 1860; for a very excited speech on the subject, see the *Congressional Globe*, 36 Cong., 1 Sess., Vol. II, p. 1032.

were those most dwelt upon, the examination of the physical characteristics of the slave, his teeth, legs and arms, and the coarse, indelicate questions often addressed by the bidders to the young female slaves. Few could read the story without pity and anger. Charges, already quoted in this book,[1] and scores of others of a similar nature, concerned the denial to the slave of legal marriage, education, and wages, the cruel punishments, and the brandings with the hot irons. The masters' advertisements of runaways were instanced, with their heartless descriptions of the tell-tale physical marks and wounds on the bodies of the culprits, and the equally cruel advertisements of the slave-catchers' well-trained packs of dogs, guaranteed in every case to secure the recapture of fugitives.

To set forth the lengthy notices of all these details, repeated over and over again, is beyond the compass of this book; their importance, however, can hardly be overestimated, for they show the spirit of a large part of the Northern press, the kind of reading that was daily laid before multitudes. The accounts were exaggerated, one-sided, and told for a purpose; from them all, critical scholars could not construct an accurate account of the institution in question. Nevertheless, they inflamed and influenced men's minds, and constituted an important chapter in the history of the times.

Defenses of slavery, although seldom indulged in at any length in Congress, from time to time appeared in the public prints. Said Edward A. Pollard, in *Black Diamonds Gathered in the Darkey Houses of the South:* "Surely God proceeds mysteriously to us in his works of Love and Redemption. . . . The translation of African savages from their country as slaves—a great, improving, and progressive work of civilization — we also discover to be one of the largest works of Christianity, endowing a people with a knowledge

[1] See pp. 56–58.

of the Christian God, and they, in turn, enlightening us as to
his Grace, and the solemn and precious mystery of the conversion of the soul to Christ. . . . I think the remarkable
characteristic of our 'peculiar institution,' in improving the
African race humanly, socially, and religiously, is alone sufficient to justify it. . . . He has been plucked from the
wilds of Africa and saved to Christ." [1] The *New York
Herald* regarded slavery "as a great blessing in the tropical
climates, and in the Southern states of our Republic, a blessing to the slave, to the master, and to the whole of this
Union, one of the great sources of our national prosperity." [2]
President Lord of Dartmouth College praised slavery and
believed that "without a miracle" the Yankees themselves
would yet call for slaves in New England. [3]

According to Congressman Reagan of Texas, to free the
slaves would be a crime against reason and humanity; the
four million negro slaves were better fed, clothed, and protected from violence and wrong, more intelligent and possessed of more religious advantages, than any other four
millions of the human race anywhere. Another Southerner
believed that to free the blacks would amount virtually to
an annexation of the Southern states to Hayti and the Congo,
for it would establish here the same state of things that
existed there, free polygamy, free laziness, free stealing from
the nearest sheepfold or henroost, and seizure as slaves of
the most docile by the most savage. Slavery was simply a
means of repressing the liberty of idleness. The masters
did not permit their slaves to live as savages or as vagabonds,
but set them to work in fields with competent guides. To
force a negro to work enough to pay for his housing and keep
from infancy to old age was no easy matter, and inasmuch as

---

[1] *Black Diamonds Gathered in the Darkey Houses of the South*, by Edward
A. Pollard, New York, 1859, p. 82. f.

[2] The *New York Herald*, June 2, 1860.

[3] The *Liberator*, March 23, 1860.

no white man could be expected to do this for nothing, permanent property in the black and ownership of his industrial product was guaranteed to the white as inducement to undertake the task. Where negroes were numerous, there was no alternative between discipline and freedom. "The industrial education of a negro multitude cannot be managed without fixed and responsible masters, endowed with all necessary authority by law, and stimulated by some surer reward than the chance wages to be derived from negro consciousness and negro gratitude. No man would house and clothe and feed a family of negroes from birth to maturity for such amount of work as they might please to give him after they were grown up." [1]

Touching those phases of slavery that came nearer home, Northern people formed more intelligent ideas than concerning conditions in the South. Slaves were everywhere appearing out of the South, now peacefully seeking aid and comfort, now fugitive on the way to Canada, now in the company of their masters ; and each made his own appeal, silent or otherwise, to the freedom-loving people about him.

Mused Horace Greeley in the *New York Independent:* "A poor woman, born of an unfortunate race and of the least desirable color, calls at your fireside or at your place of business, and interrupts your labors or your meditations with a request that you read her soiled and sweat-stained papers. Their purport, which you have already guessed, is this ; she lives in Maryland or eastern Virginia and has a daughter, fourteen to sixteen years of age, who is about to be sent to New Orleans and there to be sold to the highest bidder, unless she can ransom her from slavery by the payment of several hundred dollars, towards which she solicits a subscription from you. . . . In your perplexity your wandering eye rests on some representation of the Man of Sorrows, who had not where to lay his head, and your mind recalls the burden

[1] The *Liberator*, September 28, 1860.

of his benign utterance : 'Inasmuch as ye have done it to one of the least of these my brethren, ye have done it unto me !' What is the natural result of this timely recollection? " [1]

One Sunday morning a little slave girl appeared in the Sunday School of Henry Ward Beecher's church in Brooklyn, New York; her mother was a slave in Washington and her father a slave-dealer. Five of her brothers and sisters had already been sold South, and in the late Christmas holidays came the word that she, the sixth and last, was to be sold for breeding purposes for eight hundred dollars. After some difficulty the victim was brought North and now sought alms. This was the story told to the fashionable gathering of four hundred white boys and girls, none of them whiter than the little slave. The special collection of two hundred dollars only inadequately represented the sympathy aroused. The great preacher himself, at the end of the morning sermon, brought the slave to the platform and in simple but eloquent language presented her cause to the large congregation. The shameful fate was prevented. Added Greeley the next morning in the *Tribune:* "How noble is chivalry ! To beget white daughters and then have them sold as breeders !" [2]

Such an occurrence was not uncommon in the Northern churches. Cards in the newspapers often called for the charity; on several occasions the Republican members of the national House of Representatives at Washington generously gave their aid for the same cause.

Again mused the *Tribune* editor : "A hunted and weary fugitive crosses your doorstep, imploring protection and sustenance. He has traveled through many long and tedious nights, avoiding cities and thronged highways, keeping as far to the woods and traveling by night only, through dew-drenched weeds and briers which have torn most of his

---

[1] The *New York Independent*, October 4, 1860.
[2] The *New York Tribune*, February 6, 1860.

coarse and flimsy garments from his limbs, guided only by the often shrouded light of the North Star. Perplexed by what seems a divided duty, you naturally ask, 'What would my Saviour desire me to do in the premises?' " [1]

Owen Lovejoy's answer to the question was.: "I have no more hesitation in helping a fugitive slave than I have in snatching a lamb from the jaws of a wolf, or disengaging an infant from the talons of an eagle. Not a bit. Long enough has the nation crouched and cowered in the presence of this stupendous wrong." Thousands felt the same and acted on their feelings.

Forcible rescues of fugitives out of the hands of the United States officials, who had arrested them under the national fugitive slave law, constantly occurred. The famous Ottawa rescue was fresh in the public mind throughout the year. In that small town in Illinois, while the first news of John Brown's raid was spreading over the country, a large mob, amid intense excitement, forcibly rescued a negro out of the hands of the officers of the law and secured his escape. John Hossack and two associates, leaders in the affray, were promptly arrested, conveyed to Chicago for safe keeping, and after long delay finally brought to trial. Conviction, fines, and short terms of imprisonment followed, but through the inability of the prisoners to pay the fines and costs the imprisonment seemed destined to be very long. The presidential campaign was now far advanced; but the mayor of Chicago, a strong antislavery man and editor of the leading Republican paper of the Northwest, had the strength of his convictions and opened his office for public subscriptions. In a few days' time, from all over the Northwestern states, seventeen hundred dollars poured in, and in a very exciting public meeting, with the election but four weeks off, the prisoners were released. Antislavery had produced a new hero at the very moment the people were called upon to

[1] The *New York Independent*, October 4, 1860.

deliver their judgment at the polls. Hossack took his position alongside of Brown, Helper, Worth, and Hyatt.

Late in April there was a notable rescue at Troy, New York. A crowd of one thousand people, including many free negroes, gathered about the office of the United States Commissioner, where that official, on testimony of witnesses from Virginia, had just remanded to his old master a negro who had long lived quietly in the community as a hard-working mechanic; the prisoner was about to be taken from the building when the deputy sheriff arrived with a writ of habeas corpus, and while this was being served, the crowd, with tremendous cheering and enthusiasm, rushed the officers off their feet. In the tumult the prisoner escaped to the river, was carried across to the opposite shore in a skiff, was there again arrested, but again promptly rescued, this time never to be recaptured. Similar cases were reported in the local newspapers throughout the spring and early summer in various sections. Fugitive slaves, going North, were reported at Auburn, New York; New York City; Boston, Greenfield, Massachusetts, Rochester, Cincinnati, etc.; at New York and Philadelphia, without any excitement, captured fugitives were rendered back to their masters.

Over against the law of Congress under which these rescues were declared a crime and punished by the national government, were the so-called personal liberty laws of the Northern states. These statutes, which sought to frustrate the national law, were under another name the most practical nullification laws ever set in motion by states against a law of the United States. Soon after the enactment of the objectionable fugitive slave law of 1850 Vermont led the way in resistance by declaring that state officials, under pain of fine and imprisonment, should not help execute the national law; the use of the jails in the state was forbidden to the Southern masters, the Attorney-General of the state was required to defend the slaves, and to the latter trial by jury was guaranteed; to take a fugitive unlawfully from the state was forbidden under pain of fine and imprisonment; slaves brought into the state were declared free, and persons attempting to hold such as slaves might be punished by a sentence of from one to fifteen years in the penitentiary and by a fine of not over two thousand dollars. The Michigan legislature followed in like tenor; then came Wisconsin with the most extreme of all such laws. In this Western state, in addition to the impediments created in Vermont, there was habeas corpus for the black on the mere statement of the Attorney-General; all the expenses of the action were to be paid by the state, and to take a negro out of the state was most severely prohibited. Almost every Northern state had laws on the subject with varying restrictions and provisions, enacted during the decade, 1850–1860, and in active operation in 1860. States that prohibited officers and citizens from aiding in execution of the national law were Maine, New Hampshire, Vermont, Massachusetts, Rhode Island, Connecticut, New York, Pennsylvania, New Jersey, Michigan and Wisconsin; states that denied the use of all public buildings to the master were Maine, Vermont, Rhode Island and Michigan; states that provided defense for the fugitives were Maine, Vermont, Massachusetts, New York, Pennsylvania, Michigan, and Wisconsin; states that declared all fugitives within the state free were Maine, New Hampshire, and Vermont; New Hampshire declared free any black within her borders.[1]

The two sets of laws, so antagonistic in their provisions and purposes, the one national and the other state, led to many a conflict in the courts, one of the most famous of which now

[1] See a valuable report on the subject by the joint committee of the two houses of the Virginia Legislature on Harper's Ferry, in the *New York Herald*, January 30, 1860; copies of all the laws are in the appendix to this report. The *New York Tribune*, February 15, 1860, gives a report of a committee of the New York legislature on the subject. In 1860 there were some attempts to make these state laws more stringent.

came to a head. Sherman M. Booth, the editor of an abolition paper in Milwaukee, Wisconsin, was arrested in 1854
for aiding in the rescue of the fugitive Joshua Glover from
the Milwaukee County jail. Freed by the habeas corpus of
the state Supreme Court, then twice rearrested and twice
again freed by the same means, Booth for a time was lost
sight of in a contest between the Supreme Court of the
United States, which insisted on asserting its power to review
a habeas corpus writ of a state court, and the state Supreme
Court, which insisted on declaring that habeas corpus was
original in the states and not subject to review by the Supreme Court of the United States. Due to complications
in the composition of the state tribunal, this body by a vote
of one to one refused to obey the order of the court at Washington to remand Booth to prison, and for several years the
latter was free. Finally the membership in the state court
changed, and in March, 1860, came another order from
Washington for the culprit's arrest, and again a one to one
vote in the state court, but this time against a habeas corpus
writ for the prisoner, who was now kept closely guarded in
the Milwaukee Custom House. There he remained for five
or six months, in prison for his opinions, another antislavery
hero, a fit companion for Brown, Helper, Worth, Hyatt, and
Hossack. Presently he was rescued by a mob; twice, amid
intense excitement and uproar, his rearrest was attempted
but frustrated, on one occasion by an armed guard of sixty-
two citizens; at last, however, he was taken while off his
guard, on his way home from a Republican campaign meeting. The presidential election was now less than four weeks
off, so that at that crisis Booth, like Hossack, loomed large
in the public mind, especially in the antislavery Northwest.
The list of antislavery heroes in all parts of the country was
large. For almost the entire year Booth's case helped to estrange section from section, the aggrieved South from the outraged North. To the one section, which charged that the other

was guilty of rank nullification of United States law and resistance to the United States courts, the constant reply was
that Wisconsin was but standing out for right and freedom.
Other cases of judicial conflict served to fan the sectional
fires. On technicalities the Governors of Ohio and of Iowa
refused to give up to Virginia certain members of the John
Brown band who had fled to their states; Virginia affected
to feel highly insulted, and the Governor and the legislature
in official documents, which were more or less widely published in the newspapers, made the most of the situation for
the Southern cause. On the ground that in Ohio it was no
crime to steal slaves the Governor of the state refused to
extradite to Tennessee a man accused of this crime in that
state, and not until the formal charges were altered did the
Ohio Executive yield; for the same reason he would not
give up to Kentucky a man accused there of aiding slaves to
escape. Similarly, the Governor of Illinois displeased the
Governor of Kentucky. All these cases achieved prominence.

When not fugitive, but traveling in the North with their
masters, Southern slaves were liable to capture and liberation by the radical abolitionists and free negroes, either
acting forcibly or by the ever-present habeas corpus. The
Savannah Blues, a famous military organization, set upon
in this way in New York, saved their servants only by stout
physical resistance. A master, taking his slaves from Virginia to Missouri by boat and coming ashore at Cincinnati,
saved his property by the favor of a judge, who refused a
habeas corpus for the slaves on the ground that slaveholders
must be accorded some rights on the dividing river between
slavery and freedom. Terrifying threats were held over a
pleasure party near Detroit. This case arose out of the
defiance of a law then recently enacted by the Michigan
legislature, inflicting fine and imprisonment on all who
brought slaves into the state. Although cordially invited

by Northern railroads, including the Michigan Central, the coming into the state of the party of excursionists, between two and three hundred in number, was greeted at the small town of Marshall, Michigan, with the following handbill : "Republicans to the rescue ! Two hundred Southern slaveholders with their slaves will pass through our city this afternoon and will dine at the depot. This is a flagrant violation of the laws of the state. . . . Republicans to arms ! Strike for the memory of John Brown !"

The Lemmon case in the courts of the state of New York brought the judicial side of this question of the freedom of the personal servants of Southern masters in the free states prominently before the public. In 1850 Jonathan Lemmon, his wife, and eight slaves, on their way from Virginia to Texas, came to New York, where a writ of habeas corpus led to the liberation of the blacks, who forthwith fled to Canada. Although the property was gone beyond recovery, Lemmon carried the case to the Supreme Court of the state, where after some years the original action against Lemmon was affirmed. The Court of Appeals was next reached, and there in the spring of 1860, while politics and the "irrepressible conflict" were already agitating the people as never before, the case was argued by Charles O'Conor on the side of slavery against William M. Evarts on the side of freedom. The decision affirmed the position of the lower courts, and so far as the state tribunals were concerned declared that no black could be held a slave in the state. Because of the intense popular interest the arguments of the rival lawyers were widely published, and when the result was known it was deemed on all sides that a strong blow had been struck for freedom. Yet although in line with a long series of precedents, the decision was plainly a denial of the principles of the more famous Dred Scott case in the United States Supreme Court, and according to common expectation would soon be carried on appeal by the state of Virginia to that highest national tribunal. There, beyond a doubt, a decision definitcly nationalizing slavery would be given, and the Lemmon case would take its place in the judicial annals of the country, infamous or famous according to the point of view. From this the nation was saved by the outbreak of war.[1]

Occasionally Northern John Browns raided the border line of slavery. Near Hannibal, Missouri, according to the *Daily Missouri Republican* of St. Louis, the thieving operations of abolitionists contrived to carry four Missouri negroes across the river to freedom in Illinois; an exciting chase followed and the blacks were recovered, although the robbers escaped. Excitement in the vicinity was at fever heat. In La Grange County, in the same state, two white men were caught by the regulators running off a negro; after confession the culprits were hung, then cut down, whipped and ordered from the state.

To retaliate for these various and sundry attacks on their property, abundant opportunity was afforded to the Southerners along the border line by the presence in the free states of the free negroes. These unfortunates differed in no way from slaves in color and habits and could frequently be kidnapped and hurried into the slave states and converted into money. Their very presence near slavery invited manstealing. Many were the exciting kidnapping tales going the rounds of the papers. The *Lawrence Sentinel* of Lawrence, Kansas, complained that hardly a paper in that territory failed day after day to contain notices of such a case. In some places there were organized gangs to carry on the traffic. The crime was reported from Iowa City, Iowa, Lancaster, Pennsylvania, Watertown, New York, Sandusky and Cincinnati, Ohio, Galena and Grafton, Illinois.

---

[1] O'Conor's argument, in abstract, was published in the *New York Times*, January 25, 1860; that of Evarts in full appeared in the *New York Independent* in tho month of April of the same year.

The following story of the last-named case appeared originally in the *Chicago Tribune* and was copied in many an Eastern paper. Scores of equally harrowing tales could be collected. Five colored men were decoyed into a grocery store in Clifton, Illinois, and there suddenly confronted by seven or eight heavily armed whites; after a tussle in which two of the blacks escaped, the three remaining ones were handcuffed, thrown into a wagon, driven off to the Illinois Central Railroad, and with the connivance of Irish section hands and of a compliant railroad conductor were placed on the train and taken to St. Louis. Disposal of the booty was not so easy. In answer to the query: "Who is your master?" one of the prisoners averred that he was then and always had been free, and the second refused to answer: whipping and hunger failing to change the story the two were sold South. While this was going on, one Aimé Pernard, a farmer living near the city, whom the third victim, called Jim, claimed as his former master, was visited by one of the kidnappers with offers to buy the chances of capture of his slave after five years' absence; one hundred dollars was offered; the offer was trebled and quadrupled, and at last multiplied by ten, but all to no purpose; Pernard would not sell. But his suspicions were aroused. With some search he located his property, paid the customary fees allowed by the laws of the state to the captors of fugitive slaves, together with the jailor's fees, and took his slave home. Free papers followed, a railroad ticket was purchased, and Jim was sent back home to his wife and family, a free man. The story was dressed out in the most extravagant language. "'Niggers have no feeling. It don't hurt them to have their domestic life made the plaything of white men's cupidity and lust,' say the man-sellers. That strong woman's joy as she clasped her husband in her arms, her devout thanksgiving to God that her life was not left dark; her breaking down under the flood of emotion which the glad event aroused, her sobs and plaints interrupted only by the united prayers to the Father of whites and blacks alike; the deep feeling that Jim displayed; the delicious joy, ennobled by the new consciousness of freedom and security in the possession of a wife and home, — these, leaving not a dry eye in the little crowd of onlookers, disprove the charge." [1]

As unfailing as were these stories and episodes in regard to the domestic phases of slavery, they were probably equalled in prominence and general interest as news items by the notices of the continued progress of the foreign slave trade. Hardly a single issue of any prominent newspaper failed to contain something on the abominable traffic. Native Africans, as for two hundred and fifty years past, were still being kidnapped and brought into servitude, either clandestinely in the United States or openly in the Spanish province of Cuba.

At the very end of 1859 the yacht *Wanderer*, amid much rejoicing on the part of the Southern people, landed several hundred Africans on the shores of Georgia. The *Wildfire*, sailing from New York, December, 1859, in the vicinity of the Congo River in Africa secured a cargo of six hundred and three negroes, of whom five hundred and twenty remained when the vessel was captured off Cuba; the *William*, leaving the Congo nine days before the *Wildfire*, with seven hundred and ninety blacks, arrived in Cuban waters to be taken with five hundred and thirteen of her victims still on board. On Christmas Eve, 1859, the *Orion* was seized off the coast of Africa and conveyed to the Island of St. Helena, having eight hundred and seventy-four negroes on board, six hundred and seventy-four males and two hundred females; one hundred and forty-six died on the short voyage. It would be tedious to relate the details of every capture. The *New*

---

[1] The *Albany Evening Journal*, August 17, 1860. The ladies of Clifton thanked Pernard for his generosity and invited him to Clifton; Pernard declined the invitation. This correspondence was published.

York Evening Post published a list of eight-five American vessels apprehended as slave traders in the previous eighteen months, while the *New York Herald* at the same time placed the number as at least one hundred. Almost every day, and certainly every week, the metropolitan dailies reported captures and escapes. One slaver in four, it was estimated, was taken.

The traffic, which had gradually declined during the decade of the forties and perhaps even to a later date, was now greater than for a number of years and was rapidly increasing. According to the statistics of the British Foreign Office, approximately one hundred and thirty-five thousand natives were exported from Africa as slaves in 1835; in 1859 from thirty-five to forty thousand arrived in Cuba, principally Havana, which was the world's greatest slave market. The charges that a large number of fresh Africans reached the Southern shores of the United States were not proved.[1]

Profits, which were the motive of the nefarious commerce, were enormous. Secured in Africa for a mere song, ten to fifteen dollars each, every negro safely landed in Cuba yielded from three to four hundred dollars net gain, or three hundred thousand dollars on a cargo of one thousand; one cargo of four hundred and fifty was sold in Trinidad for six hundred and fifty dollars each, and in the United States, where prices of blacks had increased almost one hundred per cent in the past decade and were then ranging from two thousand to twenty-five hundred dollars for able-bodied "American negroes," much more than six hundred and fifty dollars must have been realized for fresh, able-bodied Africans. It was commonly stated that if three out of four of the slave ships suffered capture and one got through in safety, the owner would feel repaid; if the cargo was landed, the loss of the vessel was but little.

---

[1] Beyond the several hundred brought in by the *Wanderer*, no definite data was furnished, although various local papers in the Gulf States chronicled the arrival of small parties.

In Cuba the strongest stay of the market was the prosperity of the sugar industry, in the United States the prosperity of the sugar and cotton industries.

Descriptions abounded of the passage of a slaver over to American waters; the following is typical. "The scene between the decks was shocking. Stowed in a sitting posture, with their knees drawn up close to their breast, were over five hundred human beings, whose skin was black, mostly children and young persons, and some women. So close were they packed that they could not move, and could hardly breathe. In this suffocating position they were struggling for life. The strong were killing the weak to make room for themselves, and that a little more of God's air might be had. Disease was among them in many forms, and especially opthalmia. Seasick, homesick, starving, crying for air and water, these poor wretches crowded their floating charnel house. But the slavers were merciful, for they helped the slave to die. When one was sick nigh unto death, they would kindly assist him or her overboard, before the soul had left the body. The quality of their mercy was not strained either, for they sometimes would substitute another death for drowning — the negro was knocked on the head with an axe. Disease breaking out, it was supposed to be contagious, and the sufferers were made away with without any scruples of the troublesome thing called conscience. An idea of the mortality on board of the *Tavernier* may be formed when I state that after her capture by the *Viper*, upon her passage over to St. Helena, whither she was sent in charge of a prize crew, nearly one hundred of her negroes died. This was during a run of only about ten days duration."

Although probably but few of the unfortunates reached the United States, the proslavery administration in four important respects was yet charged with responsibility for the existence of the trade beyond her borders; at New York

and the other cities on the sea board, where the ships were
fitted out, the revenue laws were but poorly enforced; the
naval squadrons in Cuban and African waters, charged with
the duty of suppressing the trade, were hampered by inadequate laws, regulations, and instructions; the proslavery
United States Senate refused to make these laws more stringent; and the United States courts were far from strict in
punishing infractions of the law.

New York was the chief commercial depot for the fitting
out of the slavers, just as Havana was the chief market for
the sale of slaves, and few ships, destined for the illegal trade,
experienced any difficulty in securing from the New York
Custom House legal clearance papers. With a bribe to the
proper officials of from five hundred to four thousand dollars
the intended slaver could easily get away, although proper
inspection would readily disclose its unlawful purpose and
render it liable to seizure. A lawful voyage was scarcely
compatible with the following telltale cargo: lumber, which
could not be used in Africa but was intended for the purpose
of building slave decks; many buckets and sponges to wash
down the slaves; disinfectants for use on the decks; stills
for cooking purposes; casks, ostensibly to be used in the palm
oil trade on the African coast but in reality for the carrying
of fresh water on board the slavers; and finally various trin-
kets, looking-glasses, handkerchiefs, calico prints, denims,
beads, etc., of practical value only among the simple-minded
Africans. Such a list was evidence enough that the ship was
bound for the Congo coast for slave-trading purposes, — evidence enough to the public if not to the officials.

The nation's responsibility was a joint one, shared by
Great Britain. Under the Webster-Ashburton treaty the
two powers were coöperating with each other, though not
very harmoniously and successfully, for the suppression of
the traffic. Each was maintaining a squadron of naval
vessels in both Cuban and African waters, and each was

guaranteeing to the crews of its vessels the payment of prize money for captures; but where the English, with their swift steam vessels and the certain assurance of twenty-five dollars for every negro taken, made six captures, the Americans with sailing vessels or worn-out steamships and the same prospect of reward, took but one. The instructions of the Washington government to its representatives were clearly inadequate and were justly criticized by Lord John Russell of the British Foreign Office and by the world in general. When the American officials made a mistake in carrying out their instructions, they were personally liable to damages; this rendered them too careful. They could take no vessel which was palpably equipped for receiving slaves but had not yet received its cargo; no American could capture a vessel with a foreign flag, and vessels without a flag and without papers also went unmolested, and thus, when the time of danger arrived, many a ship from New York escaped merely by hoisting a foreign flag or by throwing overboard both flag and papers. On the other hand, if a New York slaver fell in with a British man-of-war, she could save herself by her United States flag, for the Southern statesmen who had long directed American diplomacy, insisted that to allow Englishmen to board an American vessel under such circumstances amounted in reality to submitting to the accursed right of search, and slave trade or no slave trade, this could never be allowed.[1] Sometimes the American trader, flying the American flag, could be induced by the British to throw overboard its flag and papers and become a British prize, by the offer of immunity to the officers and crew and the threat that, if they did not give up, they would be turned over to the Americans and sent home for trial.

[1] In 1858 numerous captures by the English in the Gulf of Mexico of slave traders flying the American flag almost led to war, and were only stopped by President Buchanan by a vigorous assertion of the Southern principle.

These principles, complained the British, simply granted practical immunity, made the slave trade easy, and led to the hoisting of the American flag by all slavers, whatever their nationality.

Over all attempts to improve these defects of national policy by means of legislation the Democratic United States Senate held an efficient veto; two stringent bills on the subject, drawn from the Republican point of view, one introduced by Senator Seward of New York and the other by Senator Wilson of Massachusetts, were defeated by decisive votes.

Finally the courts were blamed. In spite of the Congressional prohibition of the traffic and in spite of the threat of the death penalty for participation in the same, the traffic was flourishing with impunity, and in the whole history of the country not one man had been executed for breaking the law. United States District Attorney Roosevelt of New York, who was bound to President Buchanan by social ties and who therefore may fairly be assumed to have spoken the mind of the President, even went so far as to state publicly that the latter would "probably pardon" any one convicted under the law; he thought that public opinion had ceased to regard the slave trade as piracy and would not uphold the infliction of the death penalty. Judge Magrath of the United States District Court at Charleston, South Carolina, in the case of Captain Currie of the yacht *Wanderer*, ruled that under the law of 1820 to buy blacks in Africa and bring them to the United States was not piracy; in order to secure a conviction under this decision it must be proved that the prisoner had actually helped steal and enslave the blacks on the African shores before embarkation. In Alabama in the same court Judge Jones declared that under the United States law it was not piracy to buy and hold in slavery lately imported blacks after they had once gotten into the country. How short the step from these decisions to a declaration by the United States Supreme Court affirming them! and this was precisely what was feared by many, that the administration was getting ready for the opening of the slave trade through the Supreme Court of the United States. In the face of actual facts, the pious sentences of the President's annual message were not taken seriously.[1]

In the North practically all parties united in condemning the inhuman traffic, Republicans, Democrats, and Abolitionists; but while the Democrats generally refrained from attacking the administration policy openly, the Republicans and Abolitionists subjected it to bitter criticism. The slave-breeding Border states for economic reasons stood with the Republicans in favor of the strict enforcement of the law. Although proslavery, they desired to restrict the supply of slaves in order to keep up prices; additional Africans would increase the supply and cheapen prices. The extreme South, and especially the growing Southwest, on economic grounds, took the opposite position; there were mineral deposits to open, virgin fields yet to bring under cultivation, broad acres, then under foreign flags, perhaps soon to be annexed and claimed to slavery. To develop these resources the labor supply should be increased, not diminished; the foreign slave trade should be legalized, not prohibited. This was the almost unanimous position of the Southern Commercial Convention, held in Vicksburg, Mississippi, in 1859, and of thirty or more Mississippi newspapers. By reopening the

[1] It should be added that in October, 1860, the part owner of the ship *Orion* was convicted in Boston of engaging in the slave trade and sentenced to two years in jail and to pay a fine of $2000; the first mate got two years in jail and the second mate twenty-one months. This was the work of a Northern jury; no Southern jury ever convicted. One ruse employed by an American trader was to carry two crews and two sets of officers, American and foreign, generally Spanish or Portuguese; then, if captured by an American ship, it would be claimed that the crew and officers were foreign and the boat foreign also, the Americans being merely passengers; if captured by the English, the opposite claim would be made.

trade the large class of poor whites, too poor to own slaves, might be drawn over to the side of slavery; their farms were small and were gradually growing smaller under the encroachments of the large landholders. Cheapen the price of slaves, and these thousands of small holders, thus enabled to own blacks, would be enlisted in the defense of the institution. Slavery was now proving a blessing; why not, therefore, erase from the statute books a law enacted when the South still believed slavery to be a curse? "I tell you, fellow Democrats," said a prominent Georgian in the national Democratic convention at Charleston, South Carolina, "that the African slave trader is the true Union man. I tell you that the slave trade of Virginia is more immoral, more unchristian, in every possible point of view, than the African slave trade, which goes to Africa and brings a heathen and worthless man here and makes him a useful man, Christianizes him, and sends him and his posterity down the stream of time to join in the blessings of civilization." It was certainly right to go to Africa and get a slave for a few dollars, if it was right to go to Virginia and get one for two thousand dollars.

An unexpected event served to bring the discussion to a head. Three slavers, seized with their cargoes in Cuban waters, were taken by their American captors, contrary to their custom, not to Liberia, for that was at the moment impracticable in the wretched condition of the slaves, but to hastily constructed barracks at Key West, Florida. What should the nation do with its new charges? An earnest debate followed. Bring the fifteen hundred Africans to the North, said some, and let them find homes and work there as free men; put them to work as slaves on the Southern railroads, said others; still others would have them let out as apprentices. By a state law no free negro could be brought into the state of Florida; why not, then, pass a Northern "Personal Liberty" law in the state legislature, queried a local Florida paper, annul the national slave trade law, make it a crime to carry out this national law, and imprison all who attempted to carry the Key West Africans out of the state? If a slave becomes a free man by going North, why not let the South act on the opposite principle that a negro, coming into the South, becomes a slave?

In the conflict of opinions, the President determined for himself. He felt bound by the law of 1819, authorizing him to provide for the safe keeping, support, and removal of such negroes from the United States, and to appoint an agent to receive them in Africa and aid them; President Monroe had so interpreted the law, and so it had been interpreted by President Buchanan himself two years earlier. Therefore, Congress, at the President's request, passed an act appropriating two hundred and twenty-five thousand dollars for the purpose, and after special agreement between the President and the American Colonization Society the negroes were carried away to Africa under the auspices of the latter organization. There they were to be assisted for one year, with the privileges of citizenship, means of education, and chances to make their own living freely given them under Christian influences. Probably out of the fifteen hundred who were landed at Key West few over one thousand reached Liberia; three hundred died in Florida and some on the voyage to Africa.[1]

In striking contrast to this prominence of the foreign slave trade in the mind of the North, was the actual dearth of news as to the domestic slave trade. The abolitionists continued to pass their usual resolutions against the interstate traffic, but the news items on the subject in their own

---

[1] It was rumored that many of the three hundred who "died" at Key West were in reality stolen; but this could not be proved. It was the custom of the British to set the captured Africans and crew at liberty, to destroy the vessel, and to send the liberated Africans to the British West Indies to serve as apprentices.

G

papers, and indeed in the press in general, scarcely mentioned details, and in the public presentation of slavery in the North the interstate trade held a relatively unimportant position. Fugitive and obscure notices in the St. Louis papers mentioned the trade at that point, where "scarcely a day passes but gangs of these unfortunate creatures are seen, trailing in couples, with drivers in the front and in the rear, down the principal streets leading to the river. Missouri is undoubtedly being depleted of her young and vigorous slaves." A certain trader was authority for the statement that from Virginia, North Carolina, and Tennessee, one hundred thousand slaves were taken annually into the Southwest. If the trade was thus vigorous, while the notices of it in the papers were meager, the inference is that it was carried on under fairly favorable conditions.[1]

The problem of the free negro was ever present. Scarcely above the slaves in social position, and in many respects more feared and despised, this neglected class, like their enslaved brothers, suffered the vengeance of the Southern reaction roused by John Brown. They were a lazy, worthless, vagabond set, always ready to be tampered with by the Northern John Browns, and always themselves ready to tamper with slaves and aid in their escape. At the beginning of the year, while the story of the white exiles from Berea, Kentucky, was filling the public mind, forty blacks arrived in Cincinnati from Arkansas with an even more piteous appeal; on pain of being made slaves if they remained in their homes after January 1, 1860, they had been driven away as exiles. Where could they go?

Laws against free negroes were of long standing, and while at every reënactment they were made more severe, the severity now seemed redoubled. The Missouri legislature,

---

[1] For the statements in this paragraph the authorities are the Northern newspapers, together with the large collection of local Southern papers in the Library of Congress at Washington.

copying the Arkansas act, passed a bill declaring first, that there could be no emancipation of slaves in that state unless the master gave bond of two thousand dollars that the freed negroes would leave the state; second, that every free negro or mulatto over eighteen should leave the state before the next September or be sold at public auction as a slave for life; third, that all free negroes under eighteen should be bound as apprentices till they were twenty-one, when they must leave; and fourth, that every free negro coming into the state after the next September should be reduced to slavery if he remained over twenty-four hours. On constitutional grounds the Governor of the state vetoed this bill, thus establishing a precedent that was in a short time followed by the Governor of Florida in vetoing a similar bill passed by the legislature of that state. Maryland enacted the same measure and submitted it to the people for their approval or disapproval at the coming presidential election; the same was attempted and passed through a single house of the Legislature in Kentucky, Tennessee, and Mississippi, but failed of final enactment in each case. Not only humanity and progressive civilization stood in the way, but also the plain provisions of the Constitution of the United States, which guaranteed a speedy and public trial, by an impartial jury, for all crimes except in cases of impeachment, and declared that no person should be deprived of life, liberty, or property without due process of law; the same provisions were in the majority of the state constitutions. Yet the fact stands out that in spite of these great legal principles six Southern states attempted arbitrarily to make slaves of free men. Certainly the excitement and the provocation must have been great.

South Carolina accomplished the same end by different means. After August every free black in the state was required to have a guardian or trustee, who would enter him in the tax assessments as his property; a copper badge, with a number attached, was to be the outward sign of the new relationship. Without a trustee, a negro would be sold; without a badge, he would be fined and imprisoned. If the trustee proved avaricious and sold his charge or disposed of the property, there could be no redress. With this fate impending, nearly a thousand negroes left Charleston alone for New York and Philadelphia within three months' time. In Philadelphia one copper plate which read, "Charleston 1860 — servant 1243," aroused much interest. In several states free negroes were allowed voluntarily to enslave themselves, and, strange as it may seem, the papers chronicled instances of servitude under these laws by the victim's own free will.

Older laws on the subject of the free negroes of the South were brought to the attention of the Northern public, such as those in Virginia requiring sale at public auction for nonpayment of taxes and for conviction for crime, or those in Texas requiring the same for all free negroes entering the state. This last provision against the incoming of free negroes from one state into another was general in the South.

At least three Northern states, Indiana, Illinois, and Oregon, by law prohibited free negroes from entering their borders, and all other Northern states were at least chary in their welcome. Here was inconsistency. Negroes were loved, but at a distance. By almost universal custom militia service and jury duty were forbidden them; they were not wanted in the passenger coaches, sleeping cars, steamboats, and street cars, and when they ventured across these portals they were usually ejected; there were separate schools for their children, and when by law they were allowed to send their children to school along with the white children, the latter most strenuously objected to sitting in the school-room near them. Outside of Connecticut, they could vote under certain restrictions in all New England and in New

York, but in Connecticut and several Western states the ballot was refused them.

For the free negroes, then, of whom there were over a half million in the nation, what should be done? The old sentiment in favor of colonization seemed to regain some of its former strength, without accomplishing anything more definite, however, than had been accomplished in the past. Pointing to the pitiful wretches, the North reviled the South, the South reviled the North. Neither side practised as much justice as it saw fit to require of the other.

The discord in the Christian churches of the land over the prevailing question may well be imagined. Should these organizations denounce slavery and exclude slaveholders from their fellowship, or should they not? The Methodist Episcopal Church in particular, with its closely knit organization and large annual gatherings North and South, was brought face to face with the inevitable question. Swept along by a tide of prosperity during the first part of the century, it had closed its eyes to its antislavery beginnings and remained peaceful, with slaveholders and nonslaveholders in its ranks, until the abolition upheavals of 1830–1840; then several annual conferences, after hot debate, disciplined members for militant antislavery; in 1840 an antislavery wing, the Wesleyan Methodist Church, split off from the mother church, and finally in 1844, in the year of the exciting presidential election just preceding the Mexican war, came the memorable schism which resulted in the Methodist Church North and the Methodist Church South, two separate organizations. In this first great rupture the dividing issue was not an antislavery test for membership, but the broader question as to whether or not a presiding Bishop should be allowed to hold slaves. While the proslavery wing in its narrow field at once enjoyed peace and prosperity, the same was not true of its Northern sister, for the proslavery "Border Conferences" in Delaware, Maryland, the District of Columbia, Virginia, Kentucky, Missouri, and Arkansas still remained in the old church, and peace was short-lived. In the exciting presidential year of 1856 the church a second time faced the issue, the North in general opposing slavery and the Border states favoring it. Nothing was decided, and again, a third time, in the presidential year of 1860, the denomination came together in general conference to discuss the ever-recurring question. The picture may easily be drawn. Individual churches, in the preaching services, in the Sunday Schools, and in the prayer meetings debated *pro and con* the instructions to be given to the quarterly conferences, these in turn were forced to frame instructions to the annual conferences, and these to the general conference; the religious weeklies of the denomination took sides; and from one end to the other the largest church of the North sat in judgment on the most fundamental social institution of sister states. That the picture is not overdrawn is evidenced by the many references in the daily press.

For four weeks the great conference at Buffalo wrestled with the petitions of the contending factions and at last adopted a rule in the *General Rules of the Societies* to forbid "the buying, selling, or holding of men, women, and children with an intention to enslave them"; heretofore only the "buying and selling" had been prohibited; now the word "holding" was added.[1] Similarly a chapter in the *Book of Discipline* was amended to read: "*Question.* What shall be done for the extirpation of the evil of slavery? *Answer.* We declare that we are as much as ever convinced of the great evil of slavery. We believe that the buying, selling, or holding of human beings as chattels is inconsistent

---

[1] The committee received memorials against a change from 32 annual conferences, signed by 3999 memorialists and 39 quarterly conferences; for a change and extirpation of slavery there were petitions from 33 annual conferences, signed by 45,857 people and 49 quarterly conferences. There was some bitter debate in the quarterly and annual conferences.

with the Golden Rule, and with that rule in our discipline which requires all that desire to continue among us 'to do no harm and to avoid evil of every kind.' We, therefore, affectionately admonish all our preachers and people to keep themselves from this great evil, and to seek its extirpation by all lawful Christian means." The new rule was to be only advisory, not statutory. Thus, although antislavery won the day, the triumph was far from complete, for the slaveholders were not yet positively prohibited from membership in the church.

Factions of the Baptist Church and of the Presbyterian Church were also at variance one with another on the never-dying question, although the issue was not now so acute in these denominations as among the Methodists. The Protestant Episcopal Church seemed strongly proslavery, as was shown by the action of a large diocesan convention of the Church in New York City, in refusing to condemn even the slave trade. Some smaller denominations were already positively excluding slaveholders from membership, notably the United Presbyterians with fifty thousand members, the Freewill Baptists with sixty thousand members, the United Brethren in Christ with eighty thousand, and the Wesleyan Methodists with twenty thousand; hundreds of individual Congregational churches also were on the same side.

The large interdenominational benevolent organizations fell victims of the same spirit of strife. Neither the American Sunday School Union nor the American Tract Society nor the American Board of Commissioners for Foreign Missions could be deemed truly Christian brotherhoods if acceptance or tolerance of slavery was unchristian. In the face of most bitter comment and possibly to the detriment of its work in foreign lands, the last-named body refused to commit itself on slavery one way or the other, and continued to retain slaveholders in membership until its friends and supporters began visibly to fall off; not till late in the year 1860 did it bring itself to denounce the slave trade. Such a leading individual organization as Plymouth Church, Brooklyn, rejected the determined stand of its distinguished pastor, Henry Ward Beecher, and in a most bitter and exciting annual meeting, thrice adjourned, departed from its long custom by withholding a part of its missionary collections from the same society. The American Tract Society of New York, the proslavery branch of the original society,[1] suffered almost perpetual persecution and ridicule, at the hands of Horace Greeley in the *New York Tribune* and of Henry Ward Beecher in the *New York Independent*, for its mutilation of tracts in favor of the South. One example follows. Gurney's *Habitual Exercise of Love toward God* contains these words: "If this love had always prevailed, where would have been the sword of the crusader? where the odious system which permits to man property in his fellow-man, and converts rational beings into marketable chattels?" These last two clauses were printed by the society to read: "Where the tortures of the Inquisition? where every system of oppression and wrong by which he who has the power revels in luxury at the expense of his fellow-man?"

Among the important religious papers the *New York Observer* supported slavery and the South and roundly denounced antislavery. Nothing of the great moral ferment and revolution, nothing on human rights and liberty, touched its pages; not even an outline description of American religious life could be culled from its pages. A fair inference from it would be that it represented the Christian world, not of the United States of America, but of far-distant missionary lands. The paper was dead so far as the morals of America were concerned. This explains the contemptuous reference to the *Observer* by William Lloyd Garrison in his

[1] The American Tract Society of Boston was the antislavery branch.

speech in Boston on the night of the execution of John Brown; it explains the perfect volleys of hot satire and jibe poked at it by the *New York Independent* and the *New York Evangelist*. The former laid eight questions before its thousands of readers for every answer to which, by the *Observer*, by a simple "yes" or "no," it would contribute twenty-five dollars to missions. The questions themselves reveal the passionate nature of the controversy. "First, Is it wrong to sell human beings, guiltless of crime? Second, Is it wrong to hold human beings as property, subject to be bought and sold? Third, Is it wrong to separate by force or law husbands and wives, parents and children, when neither crime nor vice, nor insanity in either of the parties, calls for such separation? Fourth, Have slaves an equal right with other persons to marry according to their own choice, and should such marriage, when contracted, be held sacred and inviolable? Fifth, Has the slave woman an absolute right to her chastity, and is the master who violates that chastity guilty of a crime? Sixth, Have slaves a right to read the Bible, and is it a crime to forbid them to be taught to read? Seventh, Is the system of slavery as it exists in the Southern states a blessing to the country, which should be cherished and perpetuated by national legislation? Eighth, Is the system of slavery, as by law established in the Southern states, morally right?" The answers never came, and the *New York Observer* was brought into contempt.[1]

Pausing now at this stage of our narrative to survey the popular conditions that succeeded John Brown's raid before passing on to the politics of the year. it will be agreed that

---

[1] The editor of the *Observer*, be it said, lost his position later in the year, and he wrote a long pamphlet in defense of the position on slavery which the paper had taken under his guidance. It cannot be said, however, that the tone of the paper at the end of the year differed from the tone exhibited during the first of the year under the deposed editor.

the Union of the States was truly "a house divided against itself" and that an "irrepressible conflict" was agitating every part. The one side with an overflow of zeal that too readily responded to the negro's Macedonian cry, "Come over into Macedonia and help us," sent John Browns to prey upon slavery and hailed them as heroes for their acts; denounced slavery in every form and welcomed attacks upon it; and held up to scorn the moral character of the slaveholders. By formal state law Northerners nullified the Congressional Fugitive Slave Law, the nation's pledge of fair dealing with the South, and with alacrity aided the fugitives to flee from their masters; servants of Southern travelers in the North were not safe. Too frequently Northerners obstinately refused to return to the South its criminal fugitives from justice. In the national Congress, in state legislatures, in courts, in public meetings, in religious services, in the general religious and charitable societies, in the secular and in the religious press, in books and in countless ways the one section persisted in dishonoring that which the other section held in honor. The South, with the natural instinct of self-defense, repelled the John Browns with great fury, burned the Northern newspapers in their midst, and infringed constantly on the freedom of the press and of speech. Through the courts the Southerners were threatening to force their system on the free Northern states and to bring to naught the laws against the foreign slave trade; they persistently kidnapped the free negroes of the North when the opportunity offered, and they seemed to forget all modern civilization in the treatment they extended to their own free negroes.

This inevitable march of daily events was fast reaching a crisis that would settle the fate of the Union or at least greatly affect its future; every day the end drew nearer. It was a situation that political conventions and platforms might recognize but could not control. The people were in command, and they themselves were being hurried along by unseen and irresistible forces, now by this seemingly small event and now by that.   Every act, every expression of sentiment, every edition of a daily paper, though a small thing, was a contribution to the swelling tide of the "irrepressible conflict" in the "house divided against itself." Through knowledge of this kind it is now proposed to study the political crisis.

CHAPTER V

THE DEMOCRATIC CONVENTIONS

ALTHOUGH it has been found necessary to separate into more or less distinct parts the popular presentation of slavery and its discussion by politicians, in reality the two were inseparably connected. Politicians, bent on framing their views for the coming campaign, observed the same daily events that the people observed, discussed the same things that the people discussed, and like them, were swept blindly along, helpless victims of the "irrepressible conflict." Their utterances, no matter how abstractly expressed, reflected the tense excitement that surrounded them.

As a result of the policy of territorial expansion, which had added to the country's domain millions of acres at the close of the Mexican War and for the most part had guided the councils of the nation since that time, problems of territorial government were now foremost, and a definite decision was called for as to the extension of slavery to the new domains. On this point the Democratic party was split into two hostile factions, between the followers of Stephen Arnold Douglas, United States Senator from Illinois, who favored popular sovereignty on the subject of slavery in the territories, and those who believed in the principles of John C. Calhoun, William L. Yancey, and Chief Justice Taney, enunciated in the Dred Scott decision, that slavery spread over the territories with the Constitution. Historically each position was good Democratic doctrine, for during the preceding twelve or thirteen years now the one view and now

the other was in the ascendency. As early as 1847, immediately after the attempt in Congress to pass the Wilmot
Proviso in favor of Congressional restriction of slavery in
the territory to be acquired from Mexico, factions appeared ;
Northern Democrats almost to a man, and a few Southerners
expressed themselves as preferring Wilmot's principle of
Congressional restriction, the majority of Southerners came
out in opposition to any form of national restriction and in
favor of territorial control, while a minority of Southerners
in South Carolina, Georgia, and Alabama, under the political
leadership of William L. Yancey of Alabama, stood definitely
for the principle that the constitution of its own force carried
slavery into the territories.   The great Southwest in Mississippi, Louisiana, and Texas, full of the sturdy reliance of the
frontier, opposed Yancey and favored territorial control or
popular sovereignty.   Differences   seemed   irreconcilable.
In the crisis, Lewis Cass of Michigan, a prominent candidate
for the Democratic nomination for the Presidency, deserted
his freedom-loving associates of the North and in his so-called
Nicholson letter, with a conscious purpose to please as many
factions as possible, brought forward a new statement of
popular sovereignty as a compromise platform upon which
all factions might unite.   On this platform he won the
nomination.   He declared that the principle of national
interference in the territories should be limited to the creation of proper territorial governments, "leaving in the meantime, to the people inhabiting them, to regulate their internal
concerns in their own way.   They are just as able to do so
as the people of the states." [1]

After Cass's stinging defeat at the polls, the Yanceyites,
who had bolted the national convention that had nominated

[1] This letter was written December 24, 1847, to A. O. P. Nicholson.
Douglas pointed out that before the letter was published, it was handed
about for approval to many prominent politicians both in the North
and in the South. Others had expressed the idea many times before Cass.

him as the compromise candidate and had adopted the straddle platform, became more irreconcilable than ever; two years later, in 1850, they opposed the celebrated compromise measures of that year, in which it was sought to sink all differences, and in the presidential campaign of 1852, when Whigs as well as Democrats proclaimed the finality of these compromises, they still stood apart and ran a ticket of their own. They were irreconcilable, unconquered and unconquerable; the schism seemed irremediable.

Another reconciliation, however, was attempted, this time under the guiding hand of Douglas in 1854. In his Kansas-Nebraska act, by repealing the Missouri restriction of 1820 Douglas now restored to the South its lost chance to secure a foothold for slavery in the Northwest; he wrote into the law of the land that it was the "true intent and meaning of this act, not to legislate slavery into any state or territory, nor to exclude it therefrom, but to leave the people thereof perfectly free to form and regulate their domestic institutions in their own way"; and in order to confirm the still wavering Southerners, he added to the preceding the clause, "subject only to the Constitution of the United States." This last phrase, the great statesman declared, was intended to bring the whole question before the Supreme Court of the United States, where, if the Southerners were receding too much from the growing doctrines of Yancey, they might find ample redress. The declaration was accepted and never was a law more popular in the South than this one of Douglas. Reconciliation of factions seemed complete. Throughout the country, North and South, the Southerners joined the Illinoisian and his adherents in praising popular sovereignty. The Supreme Court decision, be it remembered, had not yet been announced; it was yet to come, and there was nothing to check the flow of Southern oratory in favor of the new statesmanship.

Candidate Buchanan, in his letter of acceptance of the

Presidential nomination in 1856, used the following language : "This legislation (the Kansas-Nebraska act) is founded upon principles as ancient as free government itself, and in accordance with them has simply declared that the people of a territory, like those of a state, shall decide for themselves whether slavery shall or shall not exist within their limits, . . . This principle will surely not be controverted by any individual of the party professing devotion to popular government." Cobb of Georgia, later President Buchanan's secretary of the treasury, in a campaign speech declared that the will of the majority of the people of Kansas should decide the question; he would not "plant slavery upon the soil of any portion of God's earth against the will of the people." The Democratic vice-presidential candidate, Breckenridge, praised the act because "it acknowledged the right of the people of a territory to settle the question for themselves." Douglas himself in 1860, referring back to a political speech which he had made in 1852 in Breckenridge's home in Lexington, Kentucky, described the Vice President's position at that early date in the following picturesque language : "I stood in the rain addressing those people for three mortal hours, and drenched in rain, during which I described the principles of nonintervention and popularity as I have explained them to you to-night. Breckenridge stood by my side and patted me on the back. At any important part of the speech he called for three cheers for the 'little giant.' " Going on, he referred in the following words to a great meeting at Tippecanoe, Indiana, in 1856 : "We made speeches from the same stand. He (Breckenridge), having priority of me as a candidate, spoke first, and when he came to expound this doctrine of nonintervention, this right of the people to govern themselves in the territories, I was so delighted with his arguments that I got right up behind him and told him to 'go it.' . . . (Then when Douglas himself was speaking) On all the telling points, when I was giving the abolitionists particular 'Jessie' and bringing the Democrats up to the point, Breckenridge would stand at my back, clap me on the back, and indorse my sentiments. I assure you that at that time I did not doubt that Breckenridge was sound on the dogma." [1]

This reconciliation, now apparently so complete under the happy inspiration of Douglas, was destined to be but short-lived. Within a few months came Chief Justice Taney's revolutionary declarations in the Dred Scott decision to the effect that slaves were property, were protected by all the constitutional guarantees of property, and went where the Constitution went; neither a territorial legislature nor Congress nor any power could exclude slavery from a territory because they could not exclude the Constitution therefrom. Straightway the slave states were in an uproar. They had given Douglas a trial. Their hearts had been set on California and later on Kansas, and in a contest with the North under popular sovereignty, they had lost them both; they loved their party, but were now forced to behold the spectacle of a new and aggressive antislavery organization growing up in the North under the very ægis of practical Democratic administration. Disaster after disaster seemed to be piling up, and the belief was beginning to spread that it was of no use for the South to continue further the struggle with the North for the territories under the conditions laid down by Douglas, for in any contest between slavery and freedom the free states were bound to win. It was a bitter confession. Then, like magic, under the spell of the Chief Justice, the pendulum swung back, the slaveholders renounced compromise and turned to the extreme Southern doctrine, now given dignity and importance by persons in high station. Instead of settlement of the slavery question by the inhabitants themselves of the territories, Southerners

---

[1] For a Bell-Everett treatment of the popular sovereignty record of the Breckenridgeites, see pp. 332–335.

would now have it settled beforehand and in favor of the
South before even the first pioneers set out. They always
bowed to the decisions of the Supreme Court, they piously
but erroneously contended, but they believed in bowing a
little lower when these decisions were in their favor. The
Dred Scott decision was but the judicial determination of
the long dispute, promised by Douglas in the words, "subject only to the Constitution of the United States," and as
such he was now called upon to accept it.

Douglas determined otherwise. The Dred Scott decision
from his point of view was in no sense a settlement of the point
at issue; that case fixed only the principle that a negro, as
a noncitizen, could not bring suit in the courts of the United
States. For the Chief Justice to deliver learned and weighty
utterances in favor of the extreme Southern political principles of Calhoun and Yancey was only to dabble in politics
— not judicial determination at all. Douglas showed that
no territorial legislature was mentioned in the record of the
case and that no territorial enactment was before the court;
no one fact in the case even so much as alluded to a territorial legislature — the counsel in the case did not think
that it was there and did not argue the point.

Upholders of each side of the broken compromise now
took hostile and irreconcilable positions; but the Illinois
Senator went one step further and angered the South still
more. Not only was the Dred Scott case obnoxious; any
decision that the court might render in the future would be
powerless to weaken local control of slavery by territorial
legislatures. "It matters not what way the Supreme Court
may hereafter decide as to the abstract question, whether
slavery may or may not go into a territory under the Constitution, the people have the lawful means to introduce it
or exclude it as they please, for the reason that slavery cannot
exist a day or an hour anywhere unless it is supported by
local police regulations. These police regulations can only

H

be established by the local legislature; and if the people are opposed to slavery, they will elect representatives to that body, who will, by unfriendly legislation, effectually prevent the introduction of it into their midst. If, on the contrary, they are for it, their legislature will favor its extension. Hence, no matter what the decision of the Supreme Court may be on that abstract question, still the right of the people to make a slave territory or a free territory is perfect and complete under the Nebraska bill. I hope Mr. Lincoln deems my answer satisfactory on that point." The same had been held by Douglas and others for years, but has come down to the present generation under the name of the "Freeport doctrine," because at that small town in Illinois in a joint meeting with his opponent, Abraham Lincoln, during the Senatorial campaign of 1858, Douglas was forced to assume the position prominently through the adroitness of his adversary.[1]

The Southerners, therefore, in turning away from Douglas and his ideas, were justifying themselves on a Supreme Court decision, when in his opinion there was no such decision, one, moreover, which, even if it did exist, could not impair popular sovereignty. They were in error. They should come back to accepted Democratic dogma, regular through more than a score of years. Douglas conceded that they had the right to change their position from year to year if they saw fit; let them not, however, deny that his principle was good Democratic doctrine and that they themselves in 1856 had most ardently defended it. Yet the Southerners did make this denial; they had praised Douglas's position in 1856 — this they could not deny; but they contended that they had never understood it as Douglas now said that he did.

In a large sense both sides of the dispute were in the right, for popular sovereignty in 1856 and popular sovereignty

[1] For Douglas's tricky explanation of this in the South, see pp. 289–290.

in 1860, that is, before and after the Dred Scott decision, were not one and the same thing. In the earlier campaign the element of time was not considered important; people praised the principle indiscriminately, whether they believed that the right began as soon as the first settlers arrived in the territory or only after the grant of statehood. Consequently in 1860, after the time element had been emphasized by the Chief Justice through the declaration that popular control of slavery in the territories began only at the time when statehood began, Southerners might well say that they had had this distinction in mind in 1856, just as for six or eight years previously, but that they had not expressed it because they were assured that the point was unimportant. In the Southern mind their own principle was as time-honored as that of Douglas.[1]

The last clash between the factions before the primaries, conventions, and discussions attending the national convention of 1860 to nominate a presidential standard-bearer was the struggle over the admission of Kansas into the Union under the Lecompton constitution. Now in a brutally concrete way the inevitable consequences of the two opposing sets of principles were worked out before the public. All the power, patronage, and strategy of the administration, all the manipulation that political shrewdness could invent, were brought to bear to induce Kansas, contrary

[1] Douglas insisted on a sharp distinction between popular sovereignty and squatter sovereignty; the latter name, though popularly applied to his principle, in reality was a thing by itself. When Americans first organized a government in Oregon without any sanction of law, Calhoun and others spoke of them as squatters, and of their government as squatter sovereignty. In the same way, settlers set up a provisional government in Nevada, Dakota, and in Colorado; in the last-named place squatter sovereignty was in operation in 1860, in defiance of the laws of the United States and of the laws of the territory of Kansas. Quite a different thing was popular sovereignty; this was the right of the people, after the territory was organized by a law of Congress, to govern themselves till statehood.

to her own desires, to adopt a constitution that would fasten slavery upon her, while all the fighting powers of the aroused "Little Giant" were brought to bear to allow Kansas to stand by her own choice. The contest was the more desperate in view of the close approach of the next presidential election. A new slave state that for months had seemed impossible before the onrushes of Northern freedom-loving immigrants, could now be grasped at for the last time; now, if ever, could the Southern partisans prove the popularity and vote-getting power of their position. On the other hand, Douglas saw or thought he saw, in the presence of the swelling tide of Northern antislavery, the utter political worthlessness of the Southern idea. To make himself president he must not offer new offense to the growing Northern sentiment; he must not lay himself open to the charge of inconsistency and truckling to the South; he must stick to his position and oppose the Lecompton constitution on the ground that it was a denial of popular sovereignty. Expediency was keeping him true to his record, but he seemed a hero. By his stand his followers in Congress, throughout the Northern states and in Kansas were so invigorated that the Lecompton project was defeated and Kansas lost to slavery.

Proof was now irrefragable that Douglas was the enemy of the South, and that section turned from him forever. His mighty attempt in the Kansas-Nebraska act to propitiate the Moloch of slavery, temporarily successful, in the end proved his undoing. Seward, Greeley, — no Black Republican could do more damage to Southern interests.

Growing out of this battle royal over Kansas rose the persistent charge that while Douglas was hard pressed in his late Senatorial campaign in Illinois by the proslavery administration interests, he had gone too far into the camp of the enemy to gain supporters and had considered joining the Republican party. Evidence piled up. In the parlor of his Washington home the great Democrat frequently had consulted with the Republicans, including Greeley, to whom he had said again and again, "We could do this, we could do that." Letters and other testimony were produced showing that Greeley, Burlingame, and Wilson of Massachusetts and other Eastern leaders had written to the Illinois Republicans requesting that they oppose no candidate to the reëlection of Douglas to the Senate; the latter was free soil enough for him, Greeley was reported to have said. Another declared that Douglas had said to him that he "had checked all his baggage and taken a through ticket into the Republican ranks." Lincoln's testimony was cited; although as the candidate opposed to Douglas, Lincoln was defeated he was still glad that his fellow Republicans of Illinois did not take the Eastern advice, but had preserved their own organization with their own candidate. To the political efficacy of these charges against Douglas the hostile Southern press of the time bears ample evidence.[1]

This long historical survey, with its platforms, laws, speeches, arguments and counter arguments, after the organization of Congress, largely occupied the time of the leaders of the Democratic party in the nation at large and particularly that of the Democratic leaders in the United States Senate. President Buchanan in his annual message at the opening of Congress was first in the lists. "I cordially congratulate you upon the final settlement by the Supreme Court of the United States of the question of slavery in the territories, which had presented an aspect so truly formidable at the commencement of my administration. The right has been established of every citizen to take his property of every

---

[1] For a strong speech on this subject, see the *Congressional Globe*, 36 Cong., 1 Sess., Vol. IV, App., pp. 159–163; also the *Springfield Republican*, March 16, 1860; the *New York Evening Post*, March 3, 1860; *The American Conflict*, by Horace Greeley, Hartford, 1864–1866, I, 301; *Abraham Lincoln; Complete Works*, ed. by Nicolay and Hay, New York, 1894, I, 592.

kind, including slaves, into the common territories belonging equally to all the states of the Confederacy, and to have it protected there under the Federal constitution. Neither Congress nor a territorial legislature nor any human power has any authority to annul or repair this vested right. The supreme judicial tribunal of the country, which is a coördinate branch of the government, has sanctioned and affirmed these principles of constitutional law, so manifestly just in themselves and so well calculated to promote peace and harmony among the states." In the same vein speech after speech was hurled at the popular sovereignty champion by the most eloquent Senators. Sometimes the argument followed the logic, fallacious and contrariwise, of the opposing sets of principles, and here Jefferson Davis of Mississippi was Douglas's foremost opponent. In famous resolutions which the Mississippi Senator introduced in the Senate early in February, he embodied the Calhoun-Yancey-Taney principles, and provoked debate and strife for over three months. An advanced position was quickly developed; not only did slavery go with the Constitution beyond the power of either territory or Congress to eradicate it, but it was the bounden duty of Congress to enact a national slave code, which should do for slavery in the territories that which Douglas in his "Freeport doctrine" declared that the people could or could not do for themselves by territorial law. This was the extreme demand of the proslavery interests regarding territorial law.[1]

At other times the argument touched on personalities, with Benjamin of Louisiana playing the chief rôle. In and out of Congress Democrats and Republicans alike dissected Douglas's character, and with surprising unanimity laid him bare as a self-seeking, inconsistent, double-faced man, who could be trusted by neither friend nor enemy. To go back no

[1] For the speech of Davis, see the *Congressional Globe*, 36 Cong., 1 Sess., Vol. III, p. 1937.

further than 1854 : for his own profit in that year he betrayed
the antislavery Democrats of the North and by a fair promise deceived the proslavery Southerners. This promise,
when political necessity demanded it, he threw overboard in
his Freeport attack on the Dred Scott decision, and for a
short while even pretended to draw near to his Republican
enemies; some charged that he was the author of the Lecompton constitution, in opposing which he made such a
public show of virtue. It was everything for Douglas and
nothing for principle.[1] "We accuse him for this, to wit :
that having bargained with us on a point on which we were
at issue, that it should be considered a judicial point; that
he would act under the decision and consider it a doctrine
of the party; that having said that to us here in the Senate,
he went home, and under the stress of a local election, his
knees gave way; his whole person trembled. His adversary
stood upon principle and was beaten; and, lo! he is the
candidate of a mighty party for the presidency of the United
States. The Senator from Illinois faltered. He got the
prize for which he faltered; but, lo! the prize of his ambition slips from his grasp because of the faltering, which he
paid as the price for the ignoble prize, ignoble under the circumstances under which he obtained it." [2]

Once again, however, in spite of everything, once again
Douglas turned his face southward for propitiation and
reconciliation. Surrounded by angry, ridiculing, sarcastic
Southern senators he rose in his place in the Senate to speak
on his bill to prevent recurrences of the John Brown raid.
Under the Congressional power to repel invasions, to protect

---

[1] Later, in his convention platform, Douglas in turn renounced the
Freeport principles by promising to abide by a future decision of the
Supreme Court on the question. For his evasive explanation before a
Southern audience of his Freeport doctrine, see pp. 289–290.

[2] This is from the greatest speech against Douglas by Senator Benjamin
of Louisiana; see the *Congressional Globe*, 36 Cong., 1 Sess., Vol. III,
p. 2233.

each state from domestic violence, and to guarantee them a Republican form of government he pleaded for a law to enable the President to prevent such invasions by the use of the troops of the United States and to punish the conspirators in the courts of the United States. "Mr. President, the method of preserving peace is plain. The system of sectional warfare must cease. The constitution has given the power and all we ask of Congress is to give the means, and we, by indictments and convictions in the Federal courts of our several states, will make such examples of the leaders of these conspiracies as will strike terror into the hearts of others, and there will be an end of this crusade." He would "open the prison doors to allow conspirators against the peace of the Republic and the domestic tranquillity of our states to select their cells wherein to drag out a miserable life as punishment for their crimes against the peace of society." [1]

Southerners laughed. They knew the man and would have none of him. The bill was never heard of again. Recalling the sedition act of 1798, many believed that the proposed measure of Douglas, if enacted into law, would inaugurate a reign of political persecution like that of the days of the old Federalists. Hearing of Douglas's speech, his former anti-Lecompton associate, Hickman of Pennsylvania, exclaimed: "Upon thy belly shalt thou go, and dirt shalt thou eat all the days of thy life!"

Never was a public man subjected to such merciless criticism from within the ranks of his own party, and never did a public man under fire make a more valiant defense. Day after day the Senate Chamber at Washington was virtually the political arena of the Democratic Party, wherein one candidate openly defended his claims upon the nomination of his party for the presidency of the United States, and eight or ten rivals, mostly Southerners, sought to badger and destroy him. Contemporary judgment inclined to the view

[1] The *Congressional Globe*, 36 Cong., 1 Sess., Vol. I, p. 552.

that Douglas was the superior of them all in the power of argument. Yet he availed nothing.

The die was cast. No longer would the South parley with a Northern man with Southern principles, no longer compromise or fall short of insistence upon their extreme position. To compromise was a losing policy. In 1848, while Yancey and others urged the extreme claims, the majority accepted a Northern straddle and were defeated; the compromise measures of 1850, the issue of the election of 1852, profited nothing, for California was lost and the fugitive slave law accomplished little; the bargain with the Northern leader in 1854 on popular sovereignty and the Supreme Court proved a delusion and a snare, for Kansas was not won and the Dred Scott decision was flaunted, the "Freeport doctrine" enunciated, and the Lecompton constitution defeated. "No more straddles, no more compromises, and down with Douglas" was the new battle cry. The only way to retrieve their failing fortunes before the successes of Black Republicanism was to make a final stand on their extreme position and to maintain themselves there at any cost. This, indeed, was the only thing possible; all other policies had failed.

Northern Democrats stood aghast at the inevitableness of the situation. But if they could not please the Southerners, who could? Could Black Republicans? The result of the dilemma was apparent to all. Their hero, though, now perhaps in their eyes more popular than ever because of his firm stand against the persecutions of the proslavery administration party, could not be deserted. "The sacred right of self-government," always Douglas's leading argument to independent and self-reliant Americans, and all the other favorite arguments, shone with undiminished splendor. Why should an American citizen lose his ability to govern himself when he crossed an imaginary boundary line between a state and a territory? Why should not the people who are to suffer the effects of legislation, themselves legislate? For the South to estrange their Northern friends was politically unwise; if the slaveholders were really bent on a quarrel, why not direct it against their inveterate antislavery enemies for real substantial grievances, such as John Brown's raid, the personal liberty laws, and the popular judgment in the North against slavery?

Stirred by this inevitable and irrepressible conflict, the Democratic party assembled itself in national convention. The story of the convention may be briefly told. In the convention hall at Charleston, South Carolina, which held three thousand people, on the twenty-first of April six hundred and six delegates came together with the power of casting three hundred and three votes; seats were provided for the national committee, for distinguished guests, and for over two thousand spectators. Caleb Cushing of Massachusetts, a strong proslavery man, was permanent chairman. After a week's earnest debate, which in a remarkable manner arrested the attention of the whole nation already greatly roused by the undying popular discussion of slavery, the committee on resolutions reported three resolutions: one, the majority report, adopted in committee by a vote of seventeen to sixteen (California and Oregon voting with the South against the North), provided for a reassertion of the Cincinnati platform of 1856 with the addition of the principles of the Dred Scott decision; another, the minority report, provided for reassertion of the Cincinnati platform, with the addition of a promise to abide by any future decision of the Supreme Court as regarded slavery in the territories; and a third, signed only by Benjamin F. Butler of Massachusetts, reasserted the Cincinnati platform, without any additions or alterations. Earnest debate in open convention followed, and by a full vote of one hundred and sixty-five to one hundred and thirty-eight the majority report was rejected and that of the minority substituted in its place. Popular sovereignty was triumphant; again it was the true party doctrine, but the victory was so hollow that Douglas never reaped any fruits from it.

As soon as the vote was announced the Alabama delegation arose and left the hall, followed by ten of the Louisiana delegates, all those from Mississippi, Texas, and Florida, and a majority of those from South Carolina, Georgia, and Arkansas; and the departure of each delegation was preceded by a solemn speech of justification and farewell. This secession accomplished, the remaining delegates proceeded to a fruitless balloting for President through fifty-seven wearisome ballots, in which Douglas was always far in the lead of the other candidates, including, among others, James Guthrie of Kentucky, R. M. T. Hunter of Virginia, and Andrew Johnson of Tennessee, without ever attaining the requisite number of votes to give him the nomination. Then the convention passed a resolution requesting the seceding states to fill up their vacant delegations, and adjourned for six weeks, to meet again in Baltimore on the eighteenth of June. The Charleston sessions had lasted two weeks.

In the meantime the seceders, increased by the addition of a few delegates from the border states of Missouri, Kentucky, Delaware, and North Carolina, immediately after their withdrawal gathered themselves into convention in the same city of Charleston, listened to a few speeches, placed themselves on record as opposed to the adoption of a new party name and to the issuing of a separate platform of principles, and then adjourned to meet in Richmond, Virginia, the eleventh of June, one week before the reassembling of the regular convention in Baltimore.

In all its history the Democratic party had never been so torn by debate as in these weeks of waiting in May and June; on the one hand, the devoted Douglasites of the North boiled with rage and anger at the insurrectionists and bolters of the South, and passionately committed themselves against admitting them back again into the second convention;

while, on the other hand, the radicals of the South, with their every step fiercely assailed by a few still devoted Douglas followers, firmly approved of the rebels, reappointed them and sent them as delegates, with few exceptions, both to Baltimore and to Richmond. Several contesting delegations were also appointed. The country at large, awestruck by the disruption of the great historic party, echoed the ominous words of Georgia's leading statesman, Howell Cobb : "It cannot be disguised that both the safety of the South and the integrity of the Union are seriously threatened. It is my honest conviction that the issue depends upon the action of the Southern people at this important juncture." "The overthrow of the national Democratic party would be a gigantic stride toward dissolution," wrote Ex-Governor Herschel V. Johnson of Georgia.

Seldom has the attention of the country been so fixed on a national convention as on that at Baltimore. The expected happened, an irreconcilable quarrel over the contesting Southern delegations. On this important question, by the very act of secession of the Southerners themselves at Charleston, the entire decision lay with the Douglas men. South Carolina and Florida sent their delegates now only to Richmond ; from Mississippi and Texas the original seceding delegates, commissioned to both Richmond and Baltimore, after a sharp contest were accepted at Baltimore but refused the proffered seats ; the original delegates from Arkansas and Georgia, sent to both adjourned conventions, were accepted at Baltimore and took their seats ; from Alabama and Louisiana alone, the bolters, commissioned to both June conventions, were rejected at Baltimore and their seats given to the rival Douglas delegates. Of the eight dissatisfied states, two were represented at Baltimore and six were without representation, four of the latter by their own choice or that of their delegates and two by the action of the convention itself. But this rejection was crucial, for it precipitated an immediate second secession, shared in by delegates from twenty states. The regulars then nominated Senator Douglas for President and Senator Fitzpatrick of Alabama for Vice President, while the seceders in an immediate convention in the same city, without waiting to go to Richmond, named Vice President Breckenridge of Kentucky for President and Senator Lane of Oregon for Vice President. The Richmond convention, attended from day to day by the South Carolina delegates and daily adjourned while waiting for the results at Baltimore, ratified the nominations of Breckenridge and Lane.[1]

Discussion of the mooted questions arising out of these conventions continued down to the very day of election, if indeed it may be considered as terminating at that time. They were questions of party procedure and convention practice, questions primarily for the student of political science, and they are best appreciated when considered in this light. The whole convention system was at stake.

At the outset the Southerners boldly challenged the principle of convention representation in their declaration that when the platform committee at Charleston, in which the states were equal because the committee was made up of one delegate from each state, had adopted the platform, this action should not have been rejected by the open convention, where the states were not equal. The action of the convention was controlled by states which were morally certain to cast no Democratic electoral votes; states which were sure for the ticket should not be overborne by states

---

[1] A valuable history of these conventions from the Douglas point of view is contained in the address to the country by the national committee of the Douglas party; see the *New York Herald*, July 19, 1860. The Breckenridge side of the dispute may be found in the address to the country of their national committee; this may be found in the *Boston Post*, in the month of August, 1860, and also in Vol. XVII of the political pamphlets in Yale University Library. *Caucuses of 1860*, by Murat Halsted, Columbus, 1860, is also valuable.

which were sure to the enemy. Especially in a time of strained relations was this unfair. The reply was equally forcible. A convention should always control its committee, its servant. To assume at the very beginning of the campaign that certain states were to be lost was both impolitic and unwise as well as discouraging. Theoretically the existing system had been devised to do the very thing that was now attacked. In the flourishing time of Democracy from Jefferson to Jackson, it finally appealed to people as unjust that only the Democratic members of Congress should participate in the right to nominate the presidential candidate; if a certain district was not represented in Congress by a Democrat, the Democrats in that district secured no representation in their party's choice. Accordingly, at the suggestion of the New Hampshire legislature in 1832, the Democratic party adopted the plan of a convention, wherein the Democrats of all districts, whether in a majority or in a minority, might be represented.[1] To prevent the control of the convention from going into the hands of delegates from states controlled by the opposition, it was decided that a two-thirds vote be required for nomination, and thereafter this had been the practice in the national conventions.[2]

The manner of application of this two-thirds rule, whether two-thirds of the whole number of delegates should be required or only two-thirds of the number voting, occasioned further dispute. At Charleston, before proceeding to nominate, it was decided that a two-thirds vote of the whole convention be required of the successful candidate, although in every Democratic convention in which the rule had been enforced after 1832 it had been "two-thirds of the vote

[1] There were other reasons of weight for the decline of the Congressional caucus.

[2] In the convention of 1840 there was no ballot; a committee of one from each state reported the nomination of Van Buren, and the report was unanimously accepted.

given" that had been stipulated.[1] In the convention of 1848, when on the fourth ballot Cass received two-thirds of the two hundred and fifty-four votes cast, although two hundred and ninety delegates were present, including the thirty-six from New York who would not vote, that candidate was declared nominated. It had never been held that a full convention was necessary to nominate; in fact, before 1860, in only two conventions, those of 1848 and 1856, had every state been represented.[2] In extenuation of the change of party practice at Charleston it was pleaded that the step was a practical necessity if further secessions of the Southern delegates were to be prevented, and for this reason, the New York delegation, friendly to Douglas, voted for it.[3]

Through almost three score of ballots the nomination was thus withheld from Douglas, whose highest vote was one hundred and fifty-one and one-half, fifty and one-half votes less than the necessary two hundred and two. At Baltimore, with two hundred and twelve electoral votes present, though not all voting, after the same candidate had received only one hundred and eighty-one and one-half votes, twenty and one-half votes less than the two hundred and two, a unanimous vote for him was carried without any objection, it was claimed, from any of the two hundred and twelve votes present. It may well be doubted if in the excitement and tumult of the moment the chairman correctly reported this *viva voce* vote; probably more than twenty delegates, con-

[1] Jackson would not allow himself to be nominated by a convention in 1832; only the vice presidential candidate was then named by the convention.

[2] For a valuable historical article on this subject, see the *Daily Missouri Republican*, St. Louis, August 9, 1860; in 1832 Missouri, in 1835 South Carolina, Alabama, and Illinois, in 1840 Connecticut, Delaware, Virginia, South Carolina, and Illinois, in 1844 South Carolina, and in 1852 South Carolina sent no delegates to the national convention of the party.

[3] It was threatened that if this vote was not passed, the whole South would secede; such a vote seemed to the South a guarantee that Douglas would not and could not be named.

trolling ten votes, shouted "no" only to have their voices drowned out and not counted. It is to be recalled that the objectionable application of the two-thirds rule at Charleston was made after the departure of the secessionists, that is, by a convention controlled by Douglas, and the same body had ample power to change its own rule. This was now done, and Douglas was declared nominated by the following resolution: "Resolved, unanimously, That Stephen A. Douglas of the state of Illinois, having now received two-thirds of all the votes given in this convention, is hereby declared nominated, in accordance with the rules governing this body, and in accordance with the uniform customs and rules of former Democratic conventions, the regular nominee of the Democratic party of the United States for the office of President of the United States."

Breckenridge was declared nominated by only one hundred and five votes in a convention of fragments, in which, while some twenty states were represented, only five had full delegations.[1] According to a strict construction of the Charleston rule, and in justice and equity to the delegates who must have been overborne by the Douglas chairman at Baltimore, both nominations were irregular; according to the Democratic practice before 1860 both nominations were regular, if the Breckenridge gathering may be called a convention. The disputes on the point were very bitter.

It was charged that the well-established unit rule, by which a state delegation might be forced to vote as a unit, was manipulated to the advantage of the North. The full Charleston convention adopted as a rule that "in any state which had not provided or directed, by its state convention, how its vote may be given, the convention will recognize the right of each delegate to cast his individual vote." This

---

[1] To put it at one hundred and five is to concede to Breckenridge every dispute as to the delegates and votes; the Douglasites put Breckenridge's vote at a far lower figure.

break from former custom released twenty-four and one-half Douglas votes, mostly in Pennsylvania, New Jersey, and Massachusetts, which by the regular operation of the unit rule would have been smothered by anti-Douglas state majorities, while at the same time by the enforcement of the unit rule where the state conventions had directed it, fifty-one anti-Douglas votes were locked up, fifteen in New York, six in Ohio, five in Indiana, etc. The rule worked both ways, however, for after the secession at Charleston individual Southern delegates remaining behind could cast no vote. President Buchanan expressed the opinion that it was this want of uniformity in the mode of voting that led to the break up.[1] If all the states had voted as units or if all the states had voted by individual delegates, in either case the majority platform would have been sustained and "the Democratic party would have been saved."

To bolt a convention was a recognized means of party warfare. In 1848 the Yanceyites seceded from the Baltimore convention and took practically the same position in 1852 when they nominated their own ticket of Troup and Quitman; in 1856 the Alabama delegation was distinctly instructed by the state convention to withdraw from the national convention unless suited as to the platform, and in 1860 five Southern states, backed by many local conventions and widespread public opinion, issued the same instructions to their delegates to the national convention. The secession at Charleston, therefore, was not a sudden innovation.

An interesting point hinged about the vice presidential nomination on the Douglas ticket. Senator Fitzgerald declined to serve, and the vacancy was filled by the national committee and not by the convention. Although to many this step was so irregular as to constitute no nomination at all, it was yet completely in accordance with party practice.

[1] *Mr. Buchanan's Administration*, by James Buchanan. New York. 1866, p. 69.

I

In a number of cases vacancies in the lists of presidential electors on the tickets of both parties, caused by resignation, were filled by the state committee, and in at least two states the nomination to the lieutenant governorship was made in the same way. The inference was plain that the power existed for all offices, although it was unique when applied to such a high office as the vice presidency. Certainly the practice would be followed at the present time.[1]

There were objections to the large number of spectators both at Charleston and Baltimore, complaint of their interference with the regular proceedings of the conventions, and suggestions that the number of delegates be cut down. Common adhesion to the importance and the rights of the states still prevented the predominance and the abuse of power by the national committee, now prevalent; but in almost every other respect the abuses of the convention system resembled those of the present day. Few modern bosses have equalled the tricks and the wiles practiced in these Democratic conventions of 1860. But neither Douglasites nor Breckenridgeites are to be greatly blamed; they were simply playing the game according to the rules as these existed at the time. The stake was high. The only valid unfavorable criticism of the whole episode concerns rather the time and the circumstances of the practices in question. Defensible in the abstract, they were certainly less defensible when their influence was liable to inflame public opinion and fan further the kindling embers of secession and civil war.

A pertinent question now suggests itself. Why did the Southern states after the Charleston secession seek to send their delegates back to the adjourned convention? In view of the firm control of the Douglasites in the convention and the implacable hatreds that had been aroused on both sides,

---

[1] It may be noticed that while Edward Everett was considering declining his nomination to the vice presidency on the Constitutional Union ticket, he suggested that the national committee might fill the vacancy.

it cannot have been expected by Yancey that his followers would be received back to the extent of surrendering to them the control, nor yet indeed can it be said that the imperious Yancey wished to repudiate his own acts. Moreover, had all been taken back, they would have but occupied the position that they occupied before the secession. Douglasites themselves, also, could not be expected to change their position and principles. Perhaps a desire to appear anxious for harmony and peace may have actuated them. But there must have been something beneath even this. It would seem that the Southerners did not expect to regain the control but that they returned for the sake of committing more mischief; they would break up the body further by inducing the border states to join them. The strategic importance of the support of these states was great. To them, as to a prize at stake, both conventions, regular and seceding, betook themselves; their delegations furnished the largest number of the new recruits to the secessionists in the second withdrawal, and from them the seceders took their candidate. If the ethics of party politics sanctioned the one secession, they certainly would sanction the return in order to make this secession larger.

What ultimate purpose actuated both secessions? Was it a desire to destroy Douglas and his principles, or the Democratic party, or the Union of the States? It is certain that the destruction of candidate Douglas was not the sole object sought, for even after the loss of the platform this end could have been secured, under the operation of the two-thirds rule, merely by remaining in the Charleston body and voting against him to the end.[1] Coupled with the desire for personal vengeance was devotion to Southern principles, and these two things together dictated the slaveholders' course.

---

[1] Possibly the Southerners were afraid to take this chance for fear that in the convention they might not be able to hold all their votes together; a break in their ranks, a stampede to Douglas perhaps, might come.

Historical perspective through the previous decade discloses the existence of these Southern principles years back, their too frequent sacrifice to the party exigency of carrying the Northern states, and the gradual formation of a purpose to yield no more. Hence the necessity of destroying Douglas and all that he stood for. Southern interests, and those alone, uncontaminated by any compromise or evasion, must be made supreme.

The death of the party was not sought; the Southerners were too good party men for that. It cannot be denied that Yancey and many of his associates ardently looked forward to a secession of the South from the Union and the formation of a Southern Confederacy; and the opinion was expressed that this goal was now consciously in the foreground, and that the destruction of the Democratic Party was sought as a step in this direction. This is to attribute to the leaders of party politics more prevision than they usually possess; they are best looked upon as the creatures of events, as opportunists. The daily happenings in the wide world of national politics brought about secession, the realization of the vague hopes of many, with an inevitableness that no men or set of men could foresee or direct; even the most ardent secessionists must have been surprised at the rapidity with which events proceeded. Not the death of the Democratic party, then, nor yet the dissolution of the Union of the states was the compelling force back of the Charleston and Baltimore secessions; the true motive was a desire to vindicate Southern principles, by securing the abasement of Stephen A. Douglas and his principles.

It was a question of how best to serve slavery. The logic of daily events proved that the institution was in great and immediate danger. The Northern Democrats would give aid in one way, the slaveholders sought it in another.

CHAPTER VI

A BOUT William H. Seward, United States Senator from New York, Republican politics centered in the opening months of 1860, just as Democratic politics centered about Stephen A. Douglas. Each was his party's intellectual genius, its boldest and most aggressive leader, greatest orator, and popular idol; each had written his name large in the legislative annals of the country in the past ten years; and each now seemed destined at last to receive that greatest of all rewards to which any American may aspire, his party's nomination for the presidency of the United States. The leaders' struggles after this prize, their rivals' desperate efforts to thwart them, make up almost the whole story of the two conventions.

The Republican party was more united than the Democratic party. Still new, with only one presidential campaign to its credit, there had not yet been time for jealousies greatly to disturb its national councils nor had two mutually exclusive sets of principles arisen to rend it in twain. Arguments on the presidential nomination, instead of going back ten years or more in search of historical proof, hinged rather on the question of availability. Why, then, did the new party, which so loved and honored its leader, fail to award him the coveted honor?

Seward fondly believed that the nomination would be his. From the time when he arrived home from a European trip late in December, 1859, fêted and honored by the city government of the metropolis of the country, and greeted everywhere along the line of the railroad by admiring crowds as a great national figure, to the time when, just before the party convention, he left the Senate Chamber in Washington for his New York home, he lived in this expectation. To his fellow-senators, and to his visitors and guests, whom he entertained lavishly throughout the winter, he predicted that he would be named. Enemies as well as friends seemed to encourage him. On the one hand was the almost unanimous love of his own party, on the other almost universal Southern hatred; scarcely a Southern orator, newspaper, or convention failed to denounce him by name as the arch fiend of political antislavery and to point to him as the next standard bearer of his party.

Seward's leadership rested primarily on the idea of the "irrepressible conflict" which he had proclaimed in a speech in Rochester, New York, in 1858, in words that forever associated his name with progressive and radical tendencies. "Shall I tell you what this collision means? They who think that it is accidental, unnecessary, the work of interested or fanatical agitators, and therefore ephemeral, mistake the case altogether. It is an irrepressible conflict between opposing and enduring forces; it means that the United States must and will, sooner or later, become entirely a slaveholding nation, or entirely a free labor nation." [1] This thought,

---

[1] The idea was not new with Seward. Probably thousands of less important people before him had thought and expressed the same. The *Richmond Enquirer*, May 6, 1856, said: "Social forces so widely differing as those of domestic slavery and attempted universal liberty, cannot long co-exist in the great Republic of Christendom. They cannot be equally adapted to the wants and interests of society. . . . The war between the two systems rages everywhere, and will continue to rage till the one conquers and the other is exterminated." In 1853 Henry Ward Beecher said: "Two great powers that will not live together are in our midst and tugging at each other's throats. They will search each other out, though you separate them a hundred times. And if by an insane blindness you shall contrive to put off the issue and send this unsettled dispute down to your children, it will go down, gathering volume and strength at every step, to waste and desolate their heritage. Clear the place. Bring in the champions."

long in the hearts and the minds of men and frequently expressed previously, when taken up and uttered by the prominent politician at once placed the speaker at the front of the radicals, and as it was passed about from person to person in countless speeches, sermons, and editorials, it made converts unceasingly. By one happy phrase that would not down, Seward became sponsor for political antislavery. He was popular with the radicals as few great leaders have ever been.

Soon he fell, ten years after Webster's seventh of March speech almost to a day. "His knees gave way, his whole person trembled"; like his great rival in the Democratic party, he faltered before "the great prize of his ambition," the presidency.

Under the guise of a plea for the admission of Kansas as a state into the Union, he made an elaborate speech in the Senate in the course of which he announced his presidential platform. Like most contemporary utterances on the subject of slavery, this speech first rehearsed the history of the contest. All was conciliation and conservatism. Not a sentence showed that the speaker ever so much as thought of the "irrepressible conflict"; under the fire of the fierce charge the world over that his radicalism was responsible for the Harper's Ferry raid, he refused either to defend the magic phrase or even to name it. He tried to show that there was no such conflict and need be none, and that the North and the South might live with one another without jealous hatred. Instead of "slave" and "free" states, which Greeley said told the story very well, he coined the phrases "capital" and "labor" states. Glowing panegyrics of the Union fell from his lips almost without number and saintlike appeals to toleration and fraternity, and theatrical horror of Brown's treason. The latter and his men were a "band of exceptional men," "inspired by enthusiasm peculiar to themselves," who "committed an act

of sedition and treason" for which they were "justly hung."
Their death was "pitiable." Slavery itself was not attacked,
no sympathy for the slaves was expressed. It was a pas-
sionless speech, utterly ignoring moral issues, as brutal and
as cold and as hard as steel, more like Stephen A. Douglas
than William H. Seward.

A great cry went up that Seward had turned conservative,
and his radical friends began to leave him as they had left
Webster ten years earlier. At this day it is plain that the
orator was under the spell of a fear of conservative reaction
that set in after the Harper's Ferry raid, when radicals began
to be afraid of themselves and became like incendiaries who
would help extinguish the flames which they themselves had
kindled. But the fear was ill-founded, as was shown
shortly in New Hampshire, Connecticut, and Rhode Island
where the spring state elections returned safe Republican
majorities. The "irrepressible conflict" had not abated
one jot, and Seward should have been acute enough to
realize it; if he did realize it, and still ignored it, he was un-
true to himself.[1]

A second class whom Seward failed to conciliate, but for
whom largely the renunciation of the "irrepressible conflict"
was made, were the ultra-conservatives in the Southern
counties of New Jersey, Pennsylvania, Ohio, Indiana, and
Illinois, where there were many people of Southern blood
and sympathies. These regions had gone Democratic in
1856 and might do so again in 1860. Their people hated
the "irrepressible conflict" and distrusted Seward for his
contention that negroes should be allowed to vote; negro

[1] In the spring election in Rhode Island the Democrats put up no ticket
of their own, but joined with a faction of the Republicans. This faction
won and the victory was hailed by some as a Democratic victory, but it
was this in no sense of the word. After the time of temptation was over,
that is, after the convention, during the progress of the presidential campaign, Seward returned to the "irrepressible conflict" with his old time
vigor. See p. 213.

equality, which the opposition with some plausibility might argue that Seward upheld, they utterly rejected. The leader had turned conservative to please them, but the conversion was too late.

Thirdly, it was essential for the new party, still unorganized in Pennsylvania and New Jersey, but destined soon to seek organization there, to draw within its ranks the remnants of the Know Nothing party in those states. This desirable end Seward's nomination could effect but poorly, since he had been one of the earliest and most persistent opponents of Know Nothingism.

Fourthly, the rich merchant class of the Northeast became conspicuously lukewarm for the New Yorker, after the hue and cry aroused by John Brown began to threaten the loss of Southern trade. They placed their own pecuniary interests ahead of the nomination of any particular candidate, on matter how eloquent, cultured, and intellectual he might be and how devoted his following.

The corruption of the New York legislature, controlled by Seward's party and bossed by Seward's boss, Thurlow Weed, was also a heavy load for the seeking candidate. In Congress Seward was known always to have voted for the most lavish expenditures and his administration at Washington, dominated by Albany standards, might be expected to be extravagant and corrupt. How could such a candidate avail against the rottenness of the Buchanan régime? The *New York Tribune* called the legislature of New York "not merely corrupt but shameless"; the *New York Evening Post* said: "Money is more powerful with our representatives at Albany than any consideration of law or justice." In the West, where the opposite reputation of "Honest Old Abe" was growing fast, this attack on Seward had much effect.

Finally, though of no little significance, Seward's political fortunes had to stem the tide of the opposition of Horace Greeley and the *New York Tribune*, as was made evident in the post-convention lamentations and disputes of New Yorkers.

This displeasure of the extreme antislavery radicals, of the more extreme conservatives of the party, of the remnants of the Know Nothing party and of the commercial classes of the Northeast, the corruption of the New York legislature, and the opposition of the influential editor together slowly combined to create the impression that Seward, even if nominated, could not be elected. He had too many enemies; the very power and prominence of his leadership was proving his undoing.

A host of minor candidates were in the field, United States Senator William Pitt Fessenden of Maine, United States Senator John P. Hale of New Hampshire, United States Senator Henry Wilson of Massachusetts, ex-Governor Banks of Massachusetts, Speaker Pennington of New Jersey, Simon Cameron of Pennsylvania, Governor Salmon P. Chase, United States Supreme Court Justice John McLean, and United States Senator Benjamin F. Wade of Ohio, Cassius M. Clay of Kentucky, Caleb Smith of Indiana, Abraham Lincoln of Illinois, and Edward Bates of Missouri. If Seward could be defeated for the nomination, which of these was the one to do it? What one could best weld together the divergent factions? Upon whom could the Seward opposition unite? It was Seward against the field.

With the party weighing such considerations, the candidate and not the platform being the chief issue, the time for the convention drew near.

Seward's birthday, the 16th of May, was the day of meeting.[1] The convention hall in Chicago, especially constructed

---

[1] This date was fixed by the national committee. The call for the convention was issued the previous December, and unlike calls of the present day, it contained an enumeration of issues on which voters were invited to enter the party. This declaration was later superseded by the regular party platform adopted by the convention.

for the purpose, held ten thousand people. Twenty-four states, four more than at the Breckenridge convention at Baltimore, were represented by four hundred and sixty-six delegates; of the slave states, North Carolina, Tennessee, Arkansas, Mississippi, Louisiana, Alabama, Georgia, Florida, and South Carolina sent no delegates, although several were present from Maryland, Delaware, Virginia, Kentucky, and Missouri, and, as alleged, from Texas. So great was the Republican anxiety to disprove the charge that the party did not exist in the South and was, therefore, wholly sectional, that a delegation of six, later shown to have been composed of one Canadian and five men from the neighboring state of Michigan, was admitted to sit for the last named state. But the palpable fraud deceived no one, for all knew that not one Republican vote had been cast in Texas in 1856 and that in all the six slave states recorded as present less than fourteen hundred votes had been mustered for the party. Delegates were admitted from the two territories, Kansas and Nebraska,[1] and from the District of Columbia.

After the initial contest over the Southern delegates was settled, a second was at once precipitated by the report of the committee on the order of business, controlled by the anti-Seward men, to the effect that the presidential nominee be required to secure a majority, not of the votes cast, but of the votes which would be cast if all the states were present. This, if adopted in the absence of so many states, would amount to a practical acceptance of the two-thirds rule of the Democrats and would be a blow so openly aimed at Seward that its defeat by a vote of three hundred and fifty-eight to ninety-four sent the latter's stock up very high. There was, finally, a slight contest over the insertion into the platform of the Declaration of Independence. Apart from these three contests and in marked contrast to the proceedings of the Democratic conventions, everything was harmony.

[1] The Democrats did not thus admit the territorial delegates.

This was commented upon. In the minds of all who recalled the split of the Democrats it was significant that the rejection of the two-thirds rule at Chicago was passed quietly. The platform was conservative. At the party's first national gathering four years earlier, when it was deemed necessary to be passionate and revolutionary in order to arouse men, slavery and polygamy were denounced as "twin relics of barbarism," and the prohibition of territorial slavery by Congressional action was strongly demanded. On this territorial issue alone the earlier campaign had been waged. Now, with the antislavery Republicans in control of practically every Northern state, the revolutionary work was over ; the times seemed no longer to demand sectional denunciation and insults to slaveholders. Less than one-third of the new platform concerned slavery, whereas five-sixths of the earlier document touched upon the subject. In the interests of conservatism the offensive phrase, "twin relics of barbarism" was now omitted, as likewise the right and duty of Congress to prohibit slavery in the territories by positive legislative enactment, though this latter power was not definitely disowned ; there was the colorless statement, to wit : "We deny the authority of Congress, of a territorial legislature, or of any individuals, to give legal existence to slavery in any territory of the United States." The intention of this clause was not defined except by inference and weak statement ; it was confessedly an attempt at evasion and came dangerously near offering the country a weak solution of popular sovereignty. Voters could see that the right of the people of the territories to control slavery within their own limits was not opposed, and that the opposite power of Congress to exclude slavery from the territories was not affirmed.[1]

[1] Perhaps the Republicans took this backward step in order to give no aid and comfort to the Breckenridgeites, who demanded a Congressional slave code for the territories ; for Congress to adopt this code would be by

The principles of 1856 had contained no guarantee of the inviolability of slavery in the states, but now a clause was inserted declaring that "the right of each state to order and control its domestic institutions is essential." John Brown was aspersed in the words: "We denounce the lawless invasion by armed force of the soil of any state or territory, no matter under what pretext, as among the gravest of crimes." The logical conclusion of the Dred Scott Decision, the extension of slavery into the free states, was not met. All this truckling (or conservatism, as it was called by staunch Republicans) was beheld with dismay by the abolitionists, who also searched in vain for denunciations of the fugitive slave law and of the existence of slavery in the District of Columbia under the sufferance of the national Congress. The slave trade was denounced. New doctrines, not mentioned at Philadelphia, were included in the demands for a protective tariff "to encourage the development of the industrial interests of the whole country," for a homestead act, for internal improvements of rivers and harbors by the national government, and for a continuation of the existing naturalization laws; a Pacific Railroad was again demanded, and the corruption of the Buchanan administration was attacked. These questions of national development, aside from the transcontinental railroad and the naturalization laws, were peculiar to the party. While the opposition was concentrating on territorial slavery, the Republicans, in the interests of conservatism, were seeking to widen the field of attention of voters to other issues.

Between the adoption of the platform on the second day and the ensuing nominations, night intervened, during which caucusing by the different state delegations went on in lively fashion; those doubtful were addressed and importuned by

inference to legislate for the territories, that is, to exercise control over them. The Republicans may therefore have thought it was not wise to go too far in the direction of Congressional control.

various orators, including the chairman of the Pennsylvania state committee, William M. Evarts of New York, and Horace Greeley. It was reported that the Republican gubernatorial candidates in the three critical states of Pennsylvania, Indiana, and Illinois, where the Seward opposition was strongest, threatened to resign in case the latter was chosen, while the Pennsylvania and Indiana candidates, Curtin and Lane, in person delivered earnest threats and entreaties against Seward to caucus after caucus. Thus, in the night hours immediately before the delegates reassembled to nominate, the anti-Sewardites delivered their last blows. Had the convention, after agreeing upon the platform, proceeded at once to the nominations, instead of putting off this part of its work to the next day, many believed that the Seward successes of the day over the two-thirds rule and the platform, for the platform well represented Seward, would have landed the coveted prize. As it was, adjournment lost it.[1]

On the first ballot twelve names appeared, on the second, eight, and on the third and last only four. So quickly was achieved one of the saddest and most fortunate steps in American politics. For the sake of success the party's representative man, the one whose services doubtless deserved its highest honors, was cast aside for one of less prominence and fewer enemies.

Lincoln's debates with Douglas in 1858 had given him some national prominence, and a few speeches in states outside of Illinois had increased his growing reputation away from home, as for example, in Ohio, New York, and Connecticut; furthermore having beaten Douglas on the popular vote in Illinois for the United States senatorship, he could

---

[1] Adjournment was probably secured by a trick. When the time for nominations came, in the regular order of business, the secretaries reported that they had not prepared paper on which to enter the results of balloting, and this announcement secured adjournment.

probably be relied upon to do it again as presidential candidate in all the Northwest. His greatest asset was obscurity. On the national stage he had not offended influential factions in doubtful and critical states; mutually jealous and antagonistic leaders he could easily unite because nothing that he had ever said or done, so far as they knew, could be an object of offense to any man. The argument of availability never received a better illustration.

Lincoln's reputation, so far as it went, was consistent. He had never hedged. It was now recalled that he had expressed the "irrepressible conflict" idea some months before Seward, and in words just as classic as those of the latter. At the outset of his senatorial campaign in 1858 he declared to the convention which nominated him: " 'A house divided against itself cannot stand.' I believe this government cannot endure permanently half slave and half free. I do not expect the Union to be dissolved — I do not expect the house to fall — but I do expect it will cease to be divided. It will become all one thing or all the other. Either the opponents of slavery will arrest the further spread of it, and place it where the public mind shall rest in the belief that it is in the course of ultimate extinction; or its advocates shall push it forward till it shall become alike lawful in all the states, old as well as new, North as well as South." Throughout the ensuing debates with Douglas, planting himself on the position that slavery was wrong, he persistently endeavored to arouse moral sentiment against the system, and this position he never ceased to put forward. In the early spring of 1860, while Seward in the Senate at Washington, in great fright, was doing his utmost to consign the "irrepressible conflict" to oblivion, Lincoln was travelling in New York and New England, hammering away at the same old thought of the moral wrong of slavery.

At Cooper Union in New York he expressed the belief that "if slavery is right, all words acts, laws, constitutions against it are themselves wrong, and should be silenced and swept away. If it is right, we cannot justly object to its nationality, its universality; if it is wrong, they cannot justly insist on its extension, its enlargement. All they ask we could readily grant, if we thought slavery right; all we ask they could as readily grant, if they thought it wrong. Their thinking it right and our thinking it wrong is the precise fact on which depends the whole controversy. Thinking it right, as they do, they are not to blame for desiring its full recognition as being right; but thinking it wrong, as we do, can we yield to them? Can we cast our votes with their view, and against our own? In view of our moral, social, and political responsibilities, can we do this?"

At New Haven, in what was in many ways the greatest of this series of speeches, Lincoln said: "If I saw a venomous snake crawling in the road, any man would say I might seize the nearest stick and kill it; but if I found that snake in bed with my children, that would be another question. I might hurt the children more than the snake, and it might bite them. Much more, if I found it in bed with my neighbor's children, and I had bound myself by a solemn compact not to meddle with his children under any circumstances, it would become me to let that particular mode of getting rid of the gentleman alone. But if there was a bed newly made up, to which the children were to be taken, and it was proposed to take a batch of young snakes and put them there with them, I take it no man would say there was any question how I ought to act. That is just the case. The new territories are the newly made bed to which our children are to go, and it lies with the nation to say whether they shall have snakes mixed up with them or not. It does not seem that there could be much hesitation what our policy should be. Now, I have spoken of a policy based on the idea that slavery is wrong, and a policy based on the idea that it is right. But an effort has been made for a policy that shall treat it as neither right nor wrong. It is based upon utter indifference. Its leading advocate has said: 'I don't care whether it is voted up or down.' . . . Its central idea is indifference. It holds that it makes no more difference to us whether the territories become free or slave states than whether my neighbor stocks his farm with horned cattle or puts it into tobacco. All recognize this policy, the plausible sugar-coated name of which is popular sovereignty. This policy chiefly stands in the way of a permanent settlement of the question. I believe there is no danger of its becoming the permanent policy of the country, for it is based on public indifference. There is nobody that 'don't care.' All the people do care, one way or the other." [1]

Lincoln ran from nothing, he sugar-coated nothing, to propitiate enemies; neither did he try to fool the public by hair-splitting distinctions nor to coax and wheedle the Southerners by soft words. He "stood upon principle," and "lo!" he was now "the candidate of a mighty party for the presidency of the United States."

The more the candidate was disclosed, the more the radicals liked him, while the conservatives, with the example before them of the divisions of the Democrats and the everlasting possibility of secession, were not estranged. The Know Nothings, opposed to slavery, freely accepted Lincoln, who had never opposed them; Whigs accepted him, because he had been one of them. He was not entangled with corrupt allies, nor antagonized by commercial interests. [2]

The Seward men, although greatly chagrined and grieved

---

[1] *Abraham Lincoln; Complete Works.* Ed. by John G. Nicolay and John Hay, New York, 1894, I, 616. The same gives the New York speech, I, 599.

[2] Hamlin's nomination to the vice presidency followed without incident on the second ballot; and was intended in some degree to comfort the New Yorkers for the defeat of their idol, since it was felt that they inclined to Hamlin for the second honors in preference to any other candidate.

K

at the defeat of their beloved leader, accepted the result with
as much grace as could be expected, and Seward himself,
without a word of complaint, pledged his loyalty to the
ticket, although he was still quietly nursing a calm, exasperating superiority to Lincoln, which lasted not only
throughout the campaign, but during the ensuing administration, and which must always be to his admirers a cause
for regret.[1]

To the student of political science the Republican convention is not as interesting as that of the Democrats. Republicans then, as now, had no unit rule or two-thirds rule
to manipulate and quarrel over, and no occasion arose to
attack the theory of convention representation. Equally
in the two conventions the influence of the National Chairman and of the National Committee was insignificant. But
at Charleston and at Baltimore the crowd of spectators was
so small that it was always within the power of the presiding
officer to clear the galleries to maintain order, while at Chicago this was impossible. With less than five hundred
delegates set down in the midst of a vast crowd of ten thousand spectators, there was one continual blast of shouting
and cheering from the opening to the close of the convention.
For the first time in American political history artificially
manufactured noise from thousands of throats intimidated,

---

[1] The Seward party in New York was very bitter against Horace
Greeley for the latter's opposition at Chicago. It had been known that
subordinate editors of the *Tribune*, Dana and Pike, were opposed to
Seward, but Greeley's opposition had not been common knowledge. The
latter was accused of treachery and badgered in many ways, until in self-
defense he published in his paper, a letter which he had written to Seward
in 1854, in which he showed how his antagonism to Seward had been of
long standing and for sufficient reasons. Thus was Greeley's attitude at
Chicago explained. It was current report that at Chicago, after the nomination of Lincoln, Greeley had been heard to exclaim: "Now I have gotten
even with Governor Seward," but this was denied. Greeley had dissolved the political partnership with Seward because the latter refused to
favor the nomination of Greeley to a state office in 1854.

and to some extent governed the deliberations of a national political convention.[1]   In the dispute over the Declaration of Independence the crowd's wild support of Giddings, Curtis, and Blair, who spoke in favor of incorporating that document into the platform, was most effective; against the thousands the advocates of the so-called two-thirds rule could make no headway; their influence for Lincoln is well known.[2]

[1] The *New York Independent*, May, 31, 1860.

[2] The convention of the Constitutional Union party, which nominated John Bell of Tennessee for President and Edward Everett of Massachusetts for Vice President, was held at Baltimore a few days before the Republican convention, but the convention itself was unimportant.   The principles of this party will be considered later in connection with the general political campaign of all the parties.

CHAPTER VII

THE Democratic conventions and the adjournment of
Congress late in June had scarcely passed when the
actual campaign set in, remarkable for its length and the
unusual division of public sentiment. There were radicals
in the North and in the South, the Republicans and the
Breckenridge Democrats, and conservatives in both sections,
the Douglas Democrats and the Bell-Everetts, and each was
bitterly arrayed against the others.

The Republicans made capital of the charge of corruption
brought against the Buchanan administration. Abundant
evidence was at hand, although extorted by means that were
perhaps unfair. Early in March the Covode Committee was
appointed in the House of Representatives by a partisan vote
and with no debate "for the purpose of investigating whether
the President of the United States or any other officer of the
government, has by money, patronage, or other improper
means sought to influence the action of Congress or of any
committee thereof, for or against the passage of any law
appertaining to the right of any state or territory; and also
to inquire into and investigate whether any officer or officers
of the government have by combination or otherwise prevented and defeated, or attempted to prevent and defeat,
the execution of any law or laws now on the statute book, or
whether the President has failed to compel the execution of
any law thereof. The said committee shall investigate and
inquire into the abuses at the Chicago and other post offices,
and at the Philadelphia and other navy yards, and as to any
abuses in connection with the public buildings and other

public works of the United States. Resolved, further that as the President in his letter to the Pittsburg Centenary celebration of the 25th of November, 1858, speaks of the 'employment of money to carry elections,' said committee shall inquire into and ascertain the amount so used in Pennsylvania or any other state or states; in what district it was expended and by whose authority it was done, and from what sources the money was derived, and report the names of the parties implicated."

These sweeping powers included in their scope almost every branch of the internal administration of the country, and together with the work of other committees in both the House and the Senate, which gave themselves to similar tasks, they show the low estate to which the power and dignity of the presidential office was reduced.

Before the committee proceeded to its task, the President, whose personal and public honor seemed to be impugned, sent in to the House an immediate message of protest, based on the constitutional argument that the President, as an independent and coördinate branch of the government, was responsible only to the people, and that over him the House of Representatives had no power except that of impeachment; and the proposed action could not possibly be construed to be an impeachment, inasmuch as the right of the accused, as a public official, to defend himself, always granted in impeachment cases, was now denied. Moreover, it was unjust that Covode, the accuser, should be constituted the President's judge, as a member of the committee. "Since the days of the Star Chamber and general warrants there has been no such proceeding in England," declared the Executive.

Precedent as well as common sense were on the side of the committee. President John Quincy Adams and President Andrew Jackson had both been subjected to a Senatorial investigation as to their use of the patronage, and President

James K. Polk during the twenty-ninth Congress wrote: "If the House of Representatives, as the grand inquest of the nation should at any time have reason to believe that there had been malversation in office by an improper use or application of the public money by a public official, and should think proper to institute an inquiry into the matter, all the archives and papers of the Executive department, public and private, would be subject to an inspection and control of a committee of their body." The action now proposed in 1860 in no sense constituted the accusation involved in impeachment proceedings, which the President gravely assumed, but was rather a preliminary step on which later impeachment proceedings might be based.[1]

Damaging facts were unearthed. In the preceding six years Congress had ordered three and one-half million dollars' worth of printing, binding, and engraving, all of which, in the opinion of Cornelius Wendell, who had done the work, could have been done for fifty per cent less than the actual cost; well over a million dollars had been wasted. Profits had gone for campaign purposes and for the support of administration papers, namely the *Constitution* in Washington, and the *Argus* and the *Pennsylvanian* in Philadelphia. Quarrels between the editors of these papers and Wendell over the booty led up to the disclosures. It was brought to light that eleven thousand dollars of this money had been paid to the editor of the *Pennsylvanian* and five thousand dollars to the editor of the *Argus*. A part of Wendell's examination follows: "Do you say, sir, to the *Argus*, by the direction of the Executive? *Answer.* Yes, sir. *Question.* I thought I understood you to say the other day that there was no compulsion exercised upon you to pay; but that you considered you were, to a certain extent, bound to give to the *Argus*. *Answer.* Under the arrangement with ——. Allow me to say that —— obtained the contract and then ——

[1] *U. S. House Reports*, 36 Cong., 1 Sess., Nos. 394 and 648.

and his friend claimed a part, and I was directed to reduce the amount to —— and to pay an amount to ——. *Question*. Who directed you? *Answer*. The Executive. *Question*. Whom do you mean by the Executive? *Answer*. James Buchanan."

The editor of the *Pennsylvanian*, asked by what authority the Postmaster General distributed certain money, to which his paper laid claim, testified as follows: "I do not know, only from hearsay. *Question*. Had you any conversation with him on the subject? *Answer*. Yes, sir. *Question*. Were you willing to abide by it? *Answer*. Yes, I had to do it. The President told me it was divided and I had to submit. *Question*. Did the President say so? *Answer*. Yes."

In the Congressional elections of 1858 Wendell distributed from two hundred and fifty to two thousand two hundred and fifty dollars in each of ten Congressional districts. "*Question*. If you had not been in receipt of the proceeds of the public printing, would you have contributed money, as you say you have done, in the various Congressional districts? *Answer*. I would not have been able to contribute so much. It was the profit I made out of the public printing that enabled me to contribute these amounts of money. The fact that I was in a public position known to be remunerative, induced frequent calls upon me, to which I responded. *Question*. I wish to know whether or not there was an implied or expressed understanding between you and any Executive officer of the government that you should make these contributions out of the proceeds of the printing, for political purposes? *Answer*. No, sir; none, except as to contributions I made toward the support of certain newspapers which the President saw fit to assign to me to support. *Question*. Did any of these Congressional candidates make demands upon you? *Answer*. Not demands. They were simple requests." Asked his motives in dispensing so much money, Wendell replied: "I looked upon it as a means of procuring from the Executive such work as was at his disposal." He spent thirty-eight thousand dollars to help elect Buchanan in 1856 and from thirty to forty thousand dollars in the spring of 1858 to put the English bill through Congress and thus end the Kansas question. This last was in the expectation that "in going in for it I would be entitled to the favorable consideration of the government in matters pertaining to my business." [1]

The Secretary of the Navy, acting "with the sanction of the President," was censured by a special resolution of the House of Representatives for corruption in his department. Coal, timber, and stores were purchased for the navy at outrageously high prices, and in both the Philadelphia and Brooklyn navy yards most disgraceful conditions existed. At the former yard it was a notorious fact that contracts were not let to the lowest bidder. In the following typical letter, imitated by all his rivals, a certain contractor presented his claims: "On the score of politics, which I have never before mentioned, I have greater claims upon the government than my competitors. Our shop at Bush Hill, Philadelphia, was the first institution in this country that raised the banner of Buchanan and Breckenridge. The day after the nomination we raised the standard, with two full length portraits of the President and of the Vice President, and at the election our shop furnished seven hundred and sixty-four votes for them. Notwithstanding the present monetary depression, we gave three hundred and twelve votes for the administration at the last election. We have supported the party with material aid by thousands of dollars, and worked hard, as any of the party in Philadelphia will testify."

In the Brooklyn yard patronage was divided between a few Democratic Congressmen of New York, and each laborer,

[1] For the Covode report, see *U. S. House Reports*, 36 Cong., 1 Sess.. No. 648.

who well knew to whom he owed his position, was sure of his place so long as his patron remained on intimate terms with the President. The constructive engineer, master plumber, and master block-maker represented one Congressman, the master painter another, the master spar maker, master blacksmith and the timber inspector another; each master selected the men under him and increased or decreased the force at will, subject only to the orders of his own master, the Congressman. The yard was a mere political machine. One representative testified: "The distribution of patronage by members of Congress was very deleterious on the purity of the elections; injurious to the workmen, in that it teaches laborers and mechanics to look to political influence for sustenance and support; that he himself had been besieged and beset by hundreds of claimants at his house and in his office." Occasionally the politicians fell into controversy with the masters, whom they had themselves placed in office.

One wrote: "Mr. —— tells me that you are to take men on on Tuesday. May I ask you to take him on and others whom I have asked you? I will have my proportion of men under you; if you do not give them, I will lodge claims against you. You have turned away all the men from my district but one already." Upon the removal of another, his sponsor wrote: "You may set it down as a fact that I will have you removed if you don't put that man on again."

An aggrieved Congressman wrote to the Secretary of the Navy that he could not get justice, that is, could not get jobs for the men in his district. "I appeal to you to vindicate my district from this unjust and partial discrimination. Mr. —— admits that he has not one man in his shop from my district"; in answer to which the secretary wrote to the yard in part as follows: "The department desires that a fair and liberal course be pursued toward Mr. ——'s district, and wishes you to inquire into and report on this matter." Thereupon "substantial justice" was done.

Those most strenuously recommended for places were generally very indifferent hands, who could find no employment elsewhere. The history of the yard was little else than a record of idleness, theft, insubordination, fraud, and gross neglect of duty, of testimonials and gifts of gold watches and diamond pins to the masters by forced contributions from the men, and the ever present dominance of politics. Not without significance was the employment in all the navy yards of the country on the eve of the Congressional elections of 1858 of four thousand more men than had been employed six months earlier.[1]

With the knowledge and tacit consent of the President, who frequently talked over the matter with him, according to one witness, political assessments were made on the men in the post office, custom house and navy yard in Philadelphia, and in 1856 seventy thousand dollars had been raised in this way. Naturalization frauds were also unearthed.

In the same net of calumnious charges the post-office department was involved by statements that tended to show that the appropriation of forty thousand dollars to print the post-office blanks was distributed to political friends, who reaped thirty thousand dollars in profits. This was the patronage that had without avail been offered to John W. Forney, anti-Lecompton Democratic member in the House of Representatives from Pennsylvania, for his vote on the Lecompton constitution, and the same was now keeping alive two Democratic papers.

The war department was attacked. A committee of investigation revealed the sale at Fort Snelling in Minnesota by the government, of a military reservation of eight thousand acres for ninety thousand dollars, or eleven dollars an acre. Notwithstanding the fact that the land, situated at

[1] For this report on the navy department, see *U. S. House Reports,* 36 Cong., 1 Sess., No. 621. December 1, 1857, 7113 men were employed in the navy yards, May 15, 1858, 6697, November 1, 1858, 10,038.

the junction of the Mississippi river with its most important tributary north of the Illinois, and almost certain to be the site of a large city, was worth far more than this, the partisan committee only dared to declare that the sale was "injudicious and improper" and had been conducted "without proper competition." The same department, seeking a site for a fort near New York City, bought for considerably over one hundred thousand dollars some marsh land on Long Island, abounding in fever and ague, which had been offered for sale for commercial purposes for less than fifty thousand dollars.[1]

Almost every branch of the national administration, including the President and a majority of his secretaries, were thus besmirched by the mud of partisan politics, particularly the President, to whom, directly or indirectly, most of the charges led. Seldom has a national Executive in a time of peace been so vehemently attacked. Cornelius Wendell would not be moved from his testimony that the President, whom he visited frequently, sometimes daily, personally knew of his operations. Republicans rejoiced openly at the success of their investigations. Their leading agency, the Covode Committee, reported no resolutions and framed no impeachment charges; such charges indeed had probably not been planned. But one hundred thousand copies of the report of the committee and thousands of copies of the reports of the other committees were circulated among the voters, till the newspapers were filled with material on "Old Buck's" corruption and the campaign orators furnished with abundant ammunition. The latter by no means neglected the opportunity. "Scoundrels," "rascals," "corruptionists," "bands of thieves and robbers" and similar epithets were hurled in scorn and derision at the discredited administration in endless repetition.[2] A fit candidate in

[1] The *Congressional Globe*, 36 Cong., 1 Sess., Vol. IV, App. p. 433.
[2] For a Bell-Everett treatment of Buchanan's corruption, see pp. 331–332.

every way to pit against this shocking corruption was "Honest Old Abe," against whom never a suspicion of dishonesty had been cast.[1]

The standards of the age in regard to the public service were beginning to crumble before the very machinations of party politics itself. The Democrats represented the spoils system then at the height of power and prestige, and were no worse than all about them. But the system inevitably led to evil conditions and had now caught in its clutches the chief magistrate of the nation as the leading victim. Certainly the charges against the administration were substantially true. The Republicans, on the other hand, for the purposes of partisan advantage unconsciously took a stand that looked to the coming reform of the civil service.

The writhings of Buchanan, like those of any victim of circumstances, were pitiable to behold. Following the Covode report he sent to the House another message of protest, which repeated the arguments of the former message on the same subject, and in a secret letter, since published, he wrote to the editor of the *New York Herald* to secure support for himself from that great paper. The whole effort of the committee was directed against himself alone, complained the President; they had examined every man, *ex parte*, who from disappointment or personal malignity could cast a shade upon the character of the Executive. "If this dragooning can exist, the presidential office would be unworthy of the acceptance of a gentleman. . . .   In performing my duties I have endeavored to be not only pure but unsuspected.   I never have had any concern in awarding contracts, but have left them to be given by the heads of the appropriate departments.   I have ever detested all jobs, and no man at any period of my life has ever approached me on such a subject.   The testimony of Wendell contains

[1] Undoubtedly the Weed-bossed Seward of Albany standards would not have made so strong an appeal in this respect to people as did Lincoln.

nothing but falsehoods, whether for or against me, for he
has sworn all round. . . . Do me what you may deem
substantial justice." [1]

Vastly more important than these charges of corruption
in the existing administration, were the charges of political
aggression, made against leading parties; that they had embraced entirely new principles unsanctioned by precedent in
the history of their respective parties, was mutually charged.

The Democratic party, in control of the government, was
rapidly committing the country to a policy of national expansion, which involved the acquisition as slave territory
of Cuba, Mexico, and possibly parts of Central and South
America, the extension of slavery to the territories of the
United States and to the free Northern states, and the reopening of the foreign slave trade. The words of Douglas
placed at the head of a prominent Southern paper, well
represented the dominant party: "We are bound to extend
and spread until we absorb the entire continent of America,
including the adjacent islands, and become one grand ocean-
bound Republic. I do not care whether you like it or not;
you cannot help it; it is the decree of Providence. This
country was set apart as an asylum for the oppressed of the
whole world." [2]

The attempt to acquire Cuba was a policy of long standing, more or less prominent in the annals of the country
from the first administration of George Washington. A
recent Buchanan presidential message in favor of the project repeated the old arguments of trade, commerce, and
geographical advantage, and a bill to place thirty million
dollars in the hands of the President to acquire the island,
though never passed, was urgently advocated by administration journals and followers in general. So acceptable

---

[1] *The Works of James Buchanan*, collected and ed. by John Basset
Moore, Philadelphia and London, 1908–1910, X, 434.
[2] The *Memphis Daily Appeal*, August 14, 1860.

was the policy that statesmen of all parties agreed that only one more Democratic administration was needed to add the island to the domains of the country, by fair means or foul. By "manifest destiny the Queen of the Antilles was gravitating towards the American shores."

To Mexico, however, more immediate attention was given in this presidential year, just as Cuba had held the more prominent place in the public mind during Buchanan's first years. The President's annual message, December, 1859, set forth the "unhappy condition of the disturbed Republic." After almost constant revolution since the late war with the United States, a new Mexican constitution had been formed in 1857, with General Comonfort as President. By a military revolution, which within a month's time overthrew the new government, the supreme power fell to General Zuloaga, who was in turn opposed by General Juarez; the former was a military adventurer, while the latter had legal claims to the presidency, based on the grounds that as Chief Justice of the Supreme Court he should accede to the chief magistracy during the absence of the regularly elected President. In spite of the recognition of Juarez by all civilized powers, including the United States, the rebel Zuloaga held out for some time, but finally transmitted his place to General Miramon, who was now in possession of the capitol at the City of Mexico, supported by the landholding, imperial church party, against the constitutional liberal forces of the people behind Juarez, entrenched at Vera Cruz. Hopeless anarchy and civil war prevailed.

Outrages of the worst description were committed. Though the two powers were nominally at peace with one another, the United States might as well have been at war with her neighbor. Important contracts with the citizens of the richer Republic, involving large expenditures, were defiantly voided by the Miramon government, the course of justice was interfered with, peaceful American citizens were expelled, and upon some forced contributions were levied. Many Americans Miramon arrested, some he executed. In April, 1859, three American physicians, who had been seized in the hospital at Tacubaya, while in attendance upon the sick and the dying of both sides, were speedily put to death without trial as well as without crime. Ormond Chase, a young American of courage and humanity, was arbitrarily executed at Tepic without even a conjecture on the part of his friends as to the cause of the arrest. "Other outrages," said the President to Congress, "might be enumerated, but these are sufficient to illustrate the wretched state of the country and the unprotected condition of the persons and the property of our citizens in Mexico." Claims were filed at Washington against the Southern Republic totalling ten million dollars.

The President recommended that a law be passed authorizing him, under such conditions as might seem expedient to Congress, "to employ a sufficient military force to enter Mexico for the purpose of obtaining indemnity for the past and security for the future." The present case, in the President's judgment, constituted an exception to the wise and settled policy of the United States not to interfere in the domestic concerns of foreign nations. Mexico was in a state of anarchy and confusion from which she could not extricate herself, nor could she prevent incursions of banditti into American territory; socially, commercially, and politically the United States had a far deeper interest in her fate than had any other nation. If we did not extend the helping hand, some other nation would, and thus at last, under circumstances of increased difficulty, we would be forced to interfere for the maintenance of the established American policy of the Monroe Doctrine. This earnest counsel Congress disregarded.

Thus foiled, the President took up the policy of a treaty with the Juarez faction, and early in January, 1860, he sent to the Senate for ratification a "treaty of transits and commerce" and a "convention to enforce treaty stipulations, and to maintain order and security in the territory of the Republics of Mexico and the United States." Under the terms of these documents there was guaranteed to this country peculiar trade advantages, the secure possession and enjoyment, free of duty and of Mexican control, of the Southern Tehuantepec route across Mexican territory from the Atlantic to the Pacific on the way to California and Asia, and of two other similar routes in the North. In order to insure the execution of the treaty, the United States was authorized to lend to the Juarez faction both land and naval forces, and in return she herself agreed to pay four million dollars, one-half of which was to go to Mexico and one-half to American citizens with claims against Mexico.

Two months later, while these treaties were pending in the Senate, and while the popular discussion of the various phases of slavery was already seething at white heat, the country was electrified by the news that the American squadron in the Gulf of Mexico had fired upon two Mexican vessels at Vera Cruz, that the fire had been returned, that blood had been shed and lives sacrificed. Were actual hostilities at hand? At last had the administration gained what many feared it was all along aiming at, — armed conflict for the coveted prize of more Mexican territory? It transpired that two steamers of the Miramon faction, besieging the Juarez forces at Vera Cruz, had been intercepted by the United States vessels and on being ordered in the middle of the night to display their colors had answered by a volley: the firing becoming general, three Americans were wounded, one mortally, while fifteen Mexicans were killed and ten wounded.[1]

[1] The two Mexican vessels were soon overpowered and towed to New Orleans, and there libeled as prizes in the courts of the United States, but the judge ruled that there was no actual conflict between the two countries and released the ships.

The incident itself was small, but the warm approval which it elicited from the Democratic press of the country was truly alarming. In a prominent editorial, headed "Manifest Destiny" the *Chicago Herald* declared: "It is becoming quite clear to men of sense that the United States can no longer refrain from taking a prominent and active part in the supervision and management of the affairs of our neighbors, the Mexicans. The utter incapacity of the Mexican people to govern themselves is no longer questionable. The interest of the civilized world would be subserved and the interests of Mexico and the United States would be infinitely benefited by a determined and bold protectorate on the part of the United States. Our relations with Mexico are necessarily of a character that renders her continued anarchy, confusion, and lawless violence no longer sufferable. However we might desire that our neighbors would save us this trouble, it is clear that our destiny draws us forward to the control and final absorption of Mexico." [1] "The sick man is at the last gasp, and to his funeral we must go, no matter whether we relish it or not," said the *New York Express.*[2] "There can be no more backing down," said *Frank Leslie's Weekly;* "our government has at last acted with the vigor becoming a great nation." [3]

Here was Democratic policy written spontaneously and indelibly in the administration press of the country, beyond the power of any quibbling party platform to add or to detract. Democrats of all factions were ready for the occupation and absorption of the sister Republic and believed that this would be speedily accomplished; Republicans, withholding approval, expected the same outcome.

Meantime the Mexican treaties of the President were hanging fire in the Senate, where finally they were defeated

[1] The *Chicago Herald*, March 10, 1860.
[2] The *New York Express*, March 20, 1860.
[3] *Frank Leslie's Illustrated Weekly*, March 31, 1860.

L

despite the support of the administration party and of such conservative papers as the *New York Times*. The Charleston convention, convening within six weeks of the Vera Cruz incident, never mentioned the subject, and was apparently as dead toward Mexico as toward the President himself. Territories already acquired were, in the judgment of the ruling statesmen of the party, a better immediate issue on which to fight the Republicans for the presidency than was the forcible acquisition of new regions. If, as was charged, Buchanan had procured the Vera Cruz incident and had brought the country to the verge of a foreign war, for the sake of throwing a new issue before the country and thus preventing the threatened split of his party on the domestic question, he signally failed. But as has already been observed, the burst of approval by Democratic papers of what was supposed to be impending annexation of Mexico, securely fixed the step as good Democratic policy.

A bullying, "big stick" attitude, with the approval of the party, had been displayed by the administration toward the South American Republics two years before the Mexican question became acute, in the dispatch to Paraguay of the greatest naval expedition in the country's history up to that time. In this poor and backward country of Paraguay in 1855 a sailor from the United States steamer *Water Witch*, while on a surveying expedition, had been killed by an attacking party of natives, and for the outrageous affront only a fleet of nineteen armed vessels, with two hundred guns and two thousand five hundred soldiers and marines, could exact adequate recompense and "achieve a happy effect in favor of our country throughout all that remote portion of the world."

With the same Democratic approval, William Walker, filibuster, "gray-eyed man of destiny," was now engaged in planting in a "glorious land of promise the institutions of the South." This policy, aimed at the independence of

Nicaragua and possibly of Honduras in Central America, held public attention throughout the fall months of the year, until Walker's capture by British intervention and his ensuing execution by the forces of Honduras, brought it to an inglorious end. At the same time the Italian Garibaldi was thrilling the world by his exploits in Sicily and Naples, and comparisons of the careers of the two men abounded. On the one hand was the Italian, noble, chivalrous, disinterested, and self-sacrificing, conquering kingdoms and despotisms only to dedicate them to liberty; on the other, the American freebooter and pirate, inferior, mischievous, large in promise, but without the qualities of leadership, attempting to fasten his clutches on a weak province in the interests of human bondage.

Yet the *Mobile Register*, a leading Southern paper, believed the success of Walker to be "of far more vital moment to the South than the suicidal policy of protection,[1] which sets the brains of so many on fire, and serves so many others as a pretext to gratify their personal ambitions. No territory that we can acquire through the Federal government can be of use to the South, and every friend of the South ought to resist such acquisitions. We have not negroes enough for our own use, much less to people new countries, and the slave trade cannot be legally opened for a good while yet. But the establishing, on the Southern frontier, of slaveholding Republics, encouraging and legalizing the importation of Africans, impairs no established financial interest of our own, and gives us natural allies, who may eventually, if deemed proper, be connected to us by close ties. This is the true Southern policy, and one well understood by those who have preserved their soberness of mind amid the senseless clamor which has caused so many of the American people to go mad." [2]

[1] That is, protection to slavery in the territories of the United States.
[2] Quoted in the *New York Times*, August 21, 1860.

The work of the secret order of the Knights of the Golden Circle, organized in 1854 and now actively bent on proslavery interference for Juarez in Mexico, was not without significance. Although the importance of the movement was assuredly exaggerated, it cannot be doubted that it existed in some form.

United States Senator Brown of Mississippi summed up to his constituents the Southern attitude as follows: "I want Cuba; I want Tamaulipas, Potosi, and one or two other Mexican states; and I want them all for the same reason; for the planting and the spread of slavery. And a footing in Central America will powerfully aid us in acquiring those other states. Yes, I want these countries for the spread of slavery. I would spread the blessings of slavery, like the blessings of the Divine Master, to the uttermost ends of the earth; and rebellious and wicked as the Yankees have been, I would even extend it to them." [1]

A severe criticism of this bold policy was voiced by Senator Crittenden of Kentucky. Once the government had striven to maintain amity and kindly relations with the states of South America and had succeeded. These states had come into the world as free nations under our auspices, the United States being their exemplar and protection; the good will of a whole continent was freely ours. Now this mighty fund of national strength, so nobly achieved, was giving way to suspicion and fear. Under a new policy the Washington government was searching the whole continent for little causes of offense and quarrel. A Yankee could no sooner go traveling abroad than somebody imposed on him, cheated him, or struck him and he came to the government with a claim. The Paraguayan chief, Topez, who was in nowise as formidable as a Cherokee Indian chief in this country, fired a gun at one of our ships, and stole some property of an American citizen, and lo! the country's largest armada

[1] The *Congressional Globe*, 36 Cong., 1 Sess., Vol. I, p. 571.

must be dispatched to obtain redress. This was both un-dignified and ridiculous.[1]

In their opposition, the Republicans revived the spirit of the Wilmot Proviso of Mexican War times, and laid stress on the inevitable spread of slavery consequent upon the proposed expansion. In the name of freedom only they were expansionists. Senator Seward confidently looked to the addition of British America, Russian America, and Spanish America to the United States, all united in a land of freedom; the men were then living, said the Senator, who would see this consummation.[2]

Up to this point in the program of expansion, Democrats of every stripe were in accord; they all coveted Cuba, Mexico, parts of Central and perhaps of South America, little questioning the desirability of such acquisitions.

Another step in the program involved the precise manner of the spread of slavery into the Western territories already acquired. The contest on this point between the Democratic factions, almost entirely of a historical character, has already been described;[3] between the Douglasites and the Republicans the fight was just as hot.[4] Douglas harked back to the American Revolution for the beginning of his great principle of self-government. "The dogma that a

---

[1] *The Life of John J. Crittenden*, by Ann Mary Butler Crittenden, Philadelphia, 1871, II, 176–177.

[2] The *New York Herald*, September 20, 1860; this is an extract from a speech delivered by the Senator at St. Paul, Minnesota.

[3] See pp. 92–101.

[4] Against the Breckenridge contention that Congress should pass a slave code for the territories it was pointed out more than once that such procedure by an act of Congress would simply be an exercise of the same power over the territories that the Republicans argued for. If Congressional legislation could protect slavery in the territories, would not that very act constitute a precedent for further Congressional action, this time forbidding slavery? There was no difference in the two acts. This argument disregarded the stand of the Supreme Court in the Dred Scott case.

citizen of the territories derives his power from Congress is
the old Tory idea that the citizens of the colonies derived
their power from the Crown. We exploded this idea in the
War of the Revolution, and the principle of popular sovereignty was born. We hold, therefore, that the citizen
does not derive power from Congress, for he has already
derived it from Almighty God." [1] The settler, going to a
territory, was entitled to as much self-government as the
English colonist. "You do not doubt but that the right of
self-government is an inherent right in North Carolina. If
it be an inherent right in this state, let me ask you, when you
emigrate to Kansas, at what point of time do you forfeit
that right? Do you lose all the sense, all the intelligence,
all the virtue you had, on the wayside, while emigrating to
a territory of the United States? . . . Those of us who
penetrated into the wilderness think that we know what
kind of laws and institutions will suit our interests quite as
well as you who never saw the country. . . . You cannot
convince us that we are not as good as our brothers, who
remain in the old states." [2]

The attractive power of these simple arguments was very
strong. Whether constitutional and legal or not, said the
New York Times, popular sovereignty in the territories as
to slavery had a strong hold on the masses; it satisfied the
instincts of nine-tenths of the liberty-loving people of the
North as a fair, just, and safe way of solving a hard problem.[3] The *New York Tribune* went so far as to suggest that
Congress allow the people of Dakota, Idaho, Arizona, and
Nevada to organize themselves as territories, elect their
own officials, and govern themselves through their own legislature, while a third leading Republican paper, the *Spring-*

[1] The *Springfield Tri-Weekly Republican*, July 23, 1860.
[2] The *Newbern Daily Progress*, September 5, 1860; this is from the
speech delivered by Douglas at Raleigh, North Carolina.
[3] The *New York Times*, June 26, 1860.

field Republican, believed that Congressional power over the territories, proclaimed as Republican doctrine in the party platform of 1856 but evaded in that of 1860, had ceased to be a test of true Republicanism. Many of the party deemed the principle unnecessary and unwise, and few had any idea that it would ever be carried out in actual practice.[1]

In their formal platform utterances on the subject the Republicans, far from openly opposing Douglas' position, contented themselves with a vague and half-hearted declaration that under the constitution, which guaranteed life, liberty, and happiness to all persons except when withheld by the due process of law, slavery could not legally and constitutionally be set up in the territories by any power. When over the veto of the territorial Governor the territory of Kansas at last excluded slavery from its midst, the whole Republican press applauded, forgetful for the moment of Congressional control; when in the territory of Nebraska a Governor's veto destroyed the territorial act to forbid slavery there, the same press rose up in indignation. Practically the Republicans wanted slavery to be forbidden in the territories but cared little by what power this was accomplished, whether by Congress or by the people of the territories themselves; the end and not the means was the important thing. Congressional control was a makeshift, a convenient weapon with which to oppose the possibility of the establishment of territorial slavery by the territory itself, which was always the lurking danger of popular sovereignty. This very opportunism was a tribute to the power of the Douglas principle.

A few Republican orators, but only a few, boldly attacked Douglas' position. Only by giving the blacks themselves a vote on their own enslavement could true popular sovereignty on the subject be secured; it was wrong everywhere

[1] The *Springfield Tri-Weekly Republican,* September 28, 1860.

to allow whites deliberately to enslave blacks. Let there be white and black sovereignty on the question, not white alone. It was blasphemy for Douglas to declare: "This government was made by white men, on the white basis, for the benefit of white men and their posterity forever, and should be administered by white men, and by none other whatsoever;" double blasphemy for him to say: "When the struggle is between the white man and the negro, I am for the white man; when it is between the negro and the crocodile, I am for the negro." To suppose that even popular sovereignty meant complete territorial control was an unmitigated and unadulterated sham, for over the territorial legislature stood the Governor's veto, over him his appointment and control by the President of the United States, and over all the Supreme Court; little was in the end really left to the people. Moreover, territorial slavery would inevitably lead to the extension of the conditions of social terrorism, which then obtained in the Southern states; freedom-loving whites would be hounded out; their free discussion throttled; their newspapers, their *Tribunes*, *Independents*, and *Posts*, debarred; their preachers' lips sealed. To fasten on the virgin soil of the West, the South as it existed in 1860, would be a blow to civilization and progress, to which no American should give sanction.[1]

Andrew Johnson, a Douglas United States Senator from Tennessee, turned the tables by asking what the Republicans would do with the blacks in the territories. Would they allow them to hold office, sit on juries, give testimony

---

[1] Early in the spring, in the House of Representatives at Washington, the Republicans by a trick forced the hand of the Democrats by bringing up for vote the question of forbidding by Congressional action a domestic institution of the West, namely polygamy. This bill passed the House by a vote of one hundred sixty to one hundred and forty-nine. If Congress possessed the power to forbid this territorial institution, why could it not also forbid slavery in the territories, another domestic institution?

in the courts, serve in the militia, and send their children to the public schools on an equal basis with white children? None could tell, and the Republicans would not answer.

From squatter sovereignty the contest extended to the question of loyalty to the Supreme Court, which had come suddenly to be the chosen agency of the Breckenridgeites to achieve the spread of slavery to the territories. Breckenridge praised and supported that tribunal for the Dred Scott decision, while Douglas, although forswearing this particular decision, still promised to obey when another was delivered.[1] Why thus did the Democracy turn its back on an unbroken record of more than a half century? A single decision in favor of slavery was the determining factor. Thomas Jefferson, the father of the party, who opposed the court almost from the time of his entrance into the cabinet of President Washington, said in 1810 : "But the opinion which gives to the judges the right to decide what laws are constitutional and what not, not only for themselves in their own sphere of action, but for the legislative and executive also in their spheres, would make the judiciary a despotic branch." To the end of his life in 1825 the great statesman led his party in violent opposition to the court. In 1832, President Andrew Jackson, the next great name in the history of the party, said in a presidential message : "If the opinion of the Supreme Court covered the whole ground in this case, it ought not to control the coördinate authorities of this government. The Congress, the Executive, and the Court must each for itself be guided by its own opinion of the constitution. Each public officer, who takes an oath to support the constitution, swears that he will support it as he understands it, and not as it is understood by others. It is as much the duty of the House of Representatives, of the

[1] This step was in advance of the Freeport doctrine, and was taken in the spring of 1860 in the Douglas convention platform. It was another "twist" of candidate Douglas, adept in the art of political shifting.

Senate, and of the President, to decide upon the constitutionality of any bill or resolution which may be presented to them for passage or approval, as it is for the Supreme Judges, when it may be brought before them for judicial decision. The opinion of the judges has no more authority over Congress than the opinion of Congress has over the judges; and in that point the President is independent of both. The authority of the Supreme Court, therefore, must not be permitted to control the Congress or the Executive when acting in their legislative capacities, but to have only such influence as the force of their reasoning may deserve."

Buchanan himself, who now praised the tribunal, while a Senator of the United States said to his fellow-senators in 1841: "But even if the judges had settled the question, I should never hold myself bound by their decision, whilst acting in a legislative capacity. Unlike the Senator from Massachusetts, I shall never consent to place the political rights and liberties of the people in the hands of any judicial tribunal. . . . The experience of all ages and countries has demonstrated that judges instinctively lean toward the prerogatives of government; and it is notorious that the Court, during the whole period in which he presided over it, embracing so many years of its existence, has inclined toward the highest assertion of Federal power." [1]

Every Democratic national convention previous to 1860 breathed the same spirit of hostility to the august tribunal. But at last, in a trice, because an important decision in their favor, the party turned into upholders of the court.

It was now the part of the antislavery party to revile the tribunal, which had turned so squarely against them. One

[1] This is a reference to Chief Justice Marshal. Roscoe Conkling, member of the House of Representatives from New York state, made a great speech on this subject; see the *Congressional Globe*, 36 Cong., 1 Sess., Vol. IV, App., p. 233.

of the Republican leaders, United States Senator Henry Wilson of Massachusetts, declared: "We shall change the Supreme Court of the United States and place men in that court who believe with its pure and immaculate Chief Justice, John Jay, that our prayers will be impious to Heaven, while we sustain and support human slavery." Senator Seward said: "Let the court recede. Whether it recedes or not, we shall reorganize the court and thus reform its political sentiments and practices and bring them into harmony with the constitution and the laws of the nation." Lincoln said: "If I were in Congress, and a vote should come up on a question whether slavery should be prohibited in a new territory, in spite of the Dred Scott decision, I would vote that it should." Senator Sumner said: "I am abound to disobey this act." [1]

Support of the Supreme Court of the United States was plainly a matter of political expediency.

Further still, in the development of their expansionist ideas, the slaveholders cast longing glances in the direction of the free states of the North and hoped sometime to be able to take their slaves there with impunity. Why not? It was recognized that a logical conclusion from the Dred Scott decision looked in that direction, for if the constitution with its guarantees of property rights fastened slavery on the territories, so also did it on the free states, where the same constitution was operative. Lincoln recognized this in the debates with Douglas. Only a definite judicial decision on the special point was needed to complete the revolution, and this was expected in the coming settlement of the Lemmon case in the national tribunal. Yet, with all this impending, it cannot be said that this matter was a clear cut issue in the campaign. Few Republicans in their public utterances

---

[1] For these references, see the *New York Herald*, October 9, 1860; for more material on Lincoln's position, see *Abraham Lincoln; Complete Works*, ed. by John G. Nicolay and John Hay, New York, 1894, I, 255.

referred to it, and Democrats never. Doubtless the former felt that they could win without the revolutionary slogan that the very liberty of their own states was at stake, and that the South, which was already committing itself to the extreme of secession, ought not to be further exasperated.

A reason for the desire for the repeal of the laws forbidding the foreign slave trade is now apparent. To reopen the trade would be to bring in thousands of fresh Africans and thus cap the climax of the whole imperialistic program. With Cuba, Mexico, and parts of Central and South America added to the domains of the United States as a great slave-holding Republic, with the Western territories and the Northern free states open to the institutions of slavery, there would be need of more blacks to fill the new places, to cultivate the new areas, and reduce them to a slavery status. There would be ample room for all the Africans who could be secured.

This vast scheme of slavery extension, now well developed and openly adopted by the Democratic party, was beheld by many with amazement, for its successful execution involved certain radical changes, that fairly laid the party open to the charge of aggression in having entirely altered its fundamental principles.

Only twelve years back, in 1847 and in 1848, the Democracy, in every free state but one, was in strong opposition to slavery in the territories to be acquired from Mexico. The Democratic legislature of Michigan resolved in 1847 : "That in the acquisition of any new territory, whether by purchase, conquest, or otherwise, we deem it the duty of the general government to extend over the same the Ordinance of 1787, with all its rights and privileges, conditions and immunities." The Democratic legislature of New Hampshire declared in the same year : "We are opposed to the extension of slavery over any such territory; and we also approve the vote of our senators and representatives in Congress in favor of the

Wilmot Proviso;" the same was passed in 1848, while in 1849 this legislature declared: "We are firmly and unalterably opposed to the extension of slavery over any portion of American soil now free." The Democratic legislature of Rhode Island, 1847, placed itself on record "against the acquisition of territory by conquest or otherwise, beyond the present limits of the United States, for the purpose of establishing therein slaveholding states." In 1847 the Democratic legislature of New York passed a resolution for an "unalterable, fundamental article or provision, whereby slavery or involuntary servitude, except as a punishment for crime, shall be forever excluded from the territory acquired or annexed" from Mexico; in Pennsylvania the same year the Democratic legislature put itself on record "against any measure whatever, by which territory will accrue to the Union, unless as a part of the fundamental law, upon which any compact or treaty for this purpose is based, slavery or involuntary servitude, except for crime, shall be forever excluded." The Democratic legislatures of Ohio, Connecticut, Illinois, and Wisconsin took the same position. In 1849 the Democratic state convention in Indiana resolved: "That the institution of human slavery is at variance with the theory of our government, abhorrent to the common sentiment of mankind, and fraught with danger to all who come within the sphere of its influence; that the Federal government possesses adequate power to inhibit its existence in the territories of the Union; that the constitutionality of this power has been settled by judicial construction, by contemporaneous exposition, and by repeated acts of Congress, and that we enjoin upon our senators and representatives in Congress to make every exertion, and employ all their influence, to procure the passage of a law forever excluding slavery from the territories of California and New Mexico." In 1849 the Democratic state convention of Massachusetts resolved: "That we are in opposition to slavery in every form and color, and in favor of freedom and free soil wherever man lives, throughout God's heritage. That as slavery does not exist by any municipal law in the new territories, and Congress has no power to institute it, the local laws of any state, authorizing slavery, can never be transplanted there; nor can slavery exist there but by a local law of the territories, sanctioned by Congress."

As was said by the Republicans, who brought all these Democratic resolutions to light, here was "pretty good Republican doctrine coming from high Democratic authority." How quickly the subservient Northern Democrats followed their Southern brethren away from freedom into proslavery ground! Through what a proslavery labyrinth of aggression had the Northern Democrats been led in twelve short years! Either to follow Breckenridge into the extreme professions of proslavery or to follow the milk and water declarations of Douglas, untouched by any moral enthusiasm for human rights, which might or might not mean slavery, to do either of these things was to take a step that was hardly thought of in the North in 1848.[1]

These Democratic resolutions, calling for the prohibition of slavery in the territories, distinctly named Congress as the agency through which the prohibition was to be accomplished. This reveals a second sense in which the slaveholders were working a revolution in general party principles. In demanding popular sovereignty on the subject of slavery in the territories or in planting themselves on the Calhoun-Yancey-Taney dogma, they were in either case getting away from Congressional control and were thus departing from previous Congressional practice. From 1787 to 1847 Congress, on at least eighteen different occasions, and during each Democratic administration, exercised power over the territories, giving them officers and giving or withholding

[1] For the Democratic resolutions, see the *Congressional Globe*, 36 Cong., 1 Sess., Vol. II, p. 2311.

approval to the acts of territorial legislatures. From 1823 to 1838 Congress five times approved of the laws of the territory of Florida and eleven times amended them. In Washington's first administration the Northwest Ordinance of 1787 was reënacted; in that of John Adams the same was reënacted for the newly organized territory of Indiana; in Jefferson's time the territory of Orleans was organized with slavery and certain restrictions, the cession of the Western lands of Georgia accepted with restrictions, and Governor St. Clair of the Northwest Territory dismissed from office for saying that an organized territory was without the control of Congress; Madison's administrations saw the arbitrary organization of the territory of Missouri by Congress, those of Monroe the passage of the Missouri Compromise with its Congressional restriction of slavery in the territories, unanimously approved by the President and his cabinet.[1] Under Jackson in 1836 a law was enacted that " no act of the territorial legislature, incorporating any banking institution, hereafter to be passed, shall have any force or effect whatever, until approved or confirmed by Congress," and under this law Jackson twice arrested the legislatures of Florida and Wisconsin. Van Buren's administration saw an act expressly retaining for Congress power over the laws of the territory of Iowa. Polk signed the act for the organization of the territory of Oregon, expressly forbidding slavery therein. With all these precedents the Democrats, following after the principles of the Dred Scott decision, were entirely out of harmony.[2]

[1] In 1848 in the Senate Calhoun denied that he had approved of the Missouri restriction while he had been a member of the Monroe cabinet; the Republicans later gave proof to the contrary. See the *Congressional Globe*, 36 Cong., 1 Sess., Vol. XIV, App., pp. 97 and 106.

[2] Buchanan was Polk's Secretary of State. In the Senate, 1860, Pugh of Ohio declared that Polk intended to veto the Wilmot Proviso, if that measure had passed the two houses of Congress; his message on the subject the President brought to the halls of Congress with him, and on it,

Again, on the question of the territorial slavery, the slave-holders were leading their party contrary to the established dogmas of the Supreme Court itself as these had been promulgated before the Dred Scott decision. In 1810 this court declared: "The power of governing and legislating for a territory is the inevitable consequence of the right to acquire and hold territory. Could this position be contested, the Constitution declares: 'Congress shall have power to dispose of and make all needful rules and regulations respecting the territory and other property belonging to the United States'; accordingly we find Congress possessing and exercising the absolute and undisputed power of governing and legislating for the territory of Orleans."[1] In 1828 the same tribunal laid down the following: "In the meantime Florida continues to be a territory of the United States, governed by that clause in the constitution which empowers Congress 'to make all needful rules and regulations.' Perhaps the power of governing a territory belonging to the United States, which has not, by becoming a state, acquired the means of self-government, may result necessarily from the facts that it is not within the jurisdiction of any particular state and is within the power and jurisdiction of the United States. The right to govern may be the inevitable consequence of the right to acquire territory. Whichever may be the source whence the power may be derived, the possession of it is unquestioned."[2]

though never an official document, he wrote a memorandum of his intention, and expressly denied the power of Congress over the territories. References on the power of Congress over the territories are, the *Congressional Globe*, 36 Cong., 1 Sess., Vol. I, pp. 302, 839; Vol. II, p. 1028; Vol. IV, App., p. 69. It cannot be said that Congress always exercised its power on the side of freedom, for it perpetuated slavery in the Western cessions of North Carolina and Georgia, in the territory of Orleans, and in Florida.

[1] Sere *vs.* Pilot, *U. S. Supreme Court Reports*, VI Cranch, 331.

[2] The American Insurance Company *vs.* 356 Bales of Cotton, *U. S. Supreme Court Reports*, I Peters, 510. See also the *Congressional Globe*, 36 Cong., 1 Sess., Vol. I, p. 304.

Finally, through their bold aggressions in the interests of slavery, the Democrats shattered their former devotion to the examples and precepts of "the fathers." The mighty party had progressed so far that it could no longer derive sanction and authority from its founder, Thomas Jefferson, and his compatriots, while, on the contrary, the hostile Republicans were going to these very sages for both aid and comfort. Never a Republican orator omitted reference to the strangeness of the spectacle. Douglasites and Breckenridgeites alike had gone astray. In this connection the following campaign document was very effective.

"'We hold these truths to be self-evident, that all men are created equal; that they are endowed by their Creator with certain inalienable rights, that among these are life, liberty, and the pursuit of happiness.'— *Declaration of Independence.*

"'I don't care whether slavery is voted up or voted down.' — STEPHEN A. DOUGLAS.

"'It is among my first wishes to see some plan by which slavery may be abolished by law.' — GEORGE WASHINGTON.

"'I don't care whether slavery is voted up or voted down.' — STEPHEN A. DOUGLAS.

"'Indeed I tremble for my country when I reflect that God is just, that his justice cannot sleep forever; that considering numbers, nature, and natural means only, a revolution of the wheel of fortune, an exchange of situation, is among possible events; that it may become probable by supernatural interference; the Almighty has no attribute which can take sides with us in such a contest.' — THOMAS JEFFERSON.

"'I don't care whether slavery is voted up or voted down.' — STEPHEN A. DOUGLAS.

"'We have found this evil, slavery, has preyed upon the very vitals of the Union, and has been prejudicial to the states in which it has existed.' — JAMES MONROE.

"'I don't care whether slavery is voted up or voted down.' — STEPHEN A. DOUGLAS.

M

"'Sir, I envy neither the head nor the heart of that man from the North who rises here to defend slavery on principle.' — JOHN RANDOLPH.

"'I don't care whether slavery is voted up or voted down.' — STEPHEN A. DOUGLAS.

"'So long as God allows the vital current to flow through my veins, I will never, never, never, by thought or word, by mind or will, aid in admitting one rod of free territory to the everlasting curse of human bondage. . . . Neither can I be induced by any earthly power to extend slavery over one foot of territory now free.' — HENRY CLAY.

"'I don't care whether slavery is voted up, or voted down.' — STEPHEN A. DOUGLAS."[1]

Some radical Southerners openly repudiated "the fathers" and proclaimed their own superior wisdom. Senator Wigfall used the following picturesque words : "I intend, Sir, to answer the twaddle about the fathers. There has been enough of that thing talked of. We are wiser than they were. We are the old men and they are the young men. I care not what their age or experience was. They organized this government, and the wisest man in that day could not tell how the thing would operate ; it was utterly impossible. We have the experience of seventy years. There are men now — I do not speak of myself — who have as much education, as much brains as they had. We have seen the experiment operating for seventy years. It is twaddle to talk about the wisdom of our ancestors, and every man knows it. Who is there that, at fifty years of age, would like to be bound by his judgment at twenty or twenty-five years ? What nation is there that is one hundred years old, that would consent to be governed by the wisdom of the past century ? What would be said of our arrogance and presumption if we were to pass a law here now that was not to be repealed for one hundred years ? . . . They legislated for themselves.

[1] The *New Haven Daily Palladium*, September 10, 1860.

We have to legislate for ourselves." Yancey, referring back to the Revolution, believed that the "old fogies of that day entertained opinions in relation to slavery which we of this day are unanimously agreed are not sound." [1]

At the beginning of the presidential campaign positive Democratic aggression was patent to all. The party was reaching out in every direction for more lands to conquer for human slavery, and in assuming this position it was breaking with Democratic principles of former days, with the declarations for freedom of the late forties, the uniform practices of Congress for the past half century, Supreme Court declarations with one important exception, and the advice and wisdom of the founders of the Republic. An entirely new page in the nation's history would be turned if the proposed schemes should be enacted into law. But before the end of the campaign more portentous aggression loomed over the horizon. This was secession from the Union, not yet a generally accepted policy, but a threat.

Arguments on the threatened secession abounded. The first contention of the Southerners in favor of the step hinged about the insidious dangers to slavery that would lurk in a Republican administration. Horace Greeley and other Republicans said that they would not touch slavery in the states, but would content themselves with attacking it in ways which were wholly constitutional; Southerners, on the other hand, believed that a Republican administration, no matter how faithful to the constitution, could not help undermining their institution. Under such a rule at Washington the whole fabric of slavocracy's imperialism would totter and fall as in a dream; Cuba, Mexico, and the more Northern of the South American states would recede from their grasp, the territories in the Western part of the United States together with the free Northern states would be forever

[1] The *Congressional Globe*, 36 Cong., 1 Sess., Vol. II, p. 1657; the *New York Times*, November 3, 1860.

dedicated to freedom, and new executive vigor would effectually curb the reviving slave trade. Freedom would intrench itself more firmly by carving out new free states in the Western country. The Supreme Court and the other courts of the United States would pass over to the control of antislavery, as vacancy after vacancy gave the new administration opportunities to elevate to the bench the partisans of freedom; there would be no more Dred Scott decisions, the Lemmon case would be lost to the South, and on the slave traders the extreme penalty of death would be imposed and the sentence carried out. Negroes, recognized as citizens, would be allowed to take up public land in the West, a privilege previously denied them; in the foreign consulates and embassies they would be received and welcomed as citizens and freely given passports, another privilege theretofore denied them. Skillful use of executive patronage would permeate the South, and with the appearance there of Republican postmasters and custom house officers an incipient Republican party would take root in the very land of slavery; for the temptations of office-holding to Southerners, who notoriously loved office, would be irresistible. Rescues of fugitives, general assistance in their favor, and defiances to the national fugitive slave law would multiply; practically no fugitives would ever be returned. More John Browns and Hinton Rowan Helpers, more attacks on slavery in the Border states, would be bound to follow; for, if these aggressions could happen under a Democratic régime, fully devoted to proslavery interests, how much more liable would they be with Lincoln in the presidential chair, working on the principle that the nation was bound to become all free or all slave, and with Seward in the Cabinet openly stating that slavery was bound to disappear and ought to disappear! Finally, in further plunder of the slaveholders, a high protective tariff would be passed by the national Congress, wholly in the interests of the North.

Thus would a Republican administration destroy the equality of the South in the Union, and ultimately reduce the states of that section to the condition of mere provinces of a consolidated despotism, to be governed by a fixed majority in Congress hostile to Southern interests and fatally bent on the ruin of Southern institutions. To acquiesce in such a fate "would be to emulate the infatuation of the Numidian king, who delivered his treasures, his arms, his elephants, and his deserters to the Romans and then renewed the war, after having needlessly deprived himself of the means of defense." [1] "The South will never permit Abraham Lincoln to be inaugurated President of the United States," declared a Southern writer; "this is a settled and a sealed fact. It is the determination of all parties in the South. Let the consequences be what they may, whether the Potomac is crimsoned in human gore, and Pennsylvania Avenue is paved ten fathoms deep with mangled bodies, or whether the last vestige of liberty is swept from the face of the American continent, the South, the loyal South, the constitutional South, will never submit to such humiliation and degradation as the inauguration of Abraham Lincoln." [2]

With irresistible felicity William L. Yancey summed up the Southern position at Cooper Institute in New York: "Who is more sovereign than the parties that have the reserved rights guaranteed to them? They have made this a government existing on the will of sovereign states, a compact between sovereign states, not made states by force, not made consolidated masses by the conquering march of a hero, with his army at his back and his sword thrown into the scale, where the will of the conquered is not consulted. That is not our form of government. Ours is a form of government

---

[1] The view of Hon. W. W. Boyce of South Carolina; see the *New York Herald*, August 13, 1860.

[2] The *New York Times*, August 7, 1860, quoting from the *Southern Confederacy* of Atlanta, Georgia.

that the people have willed. It is self-government. It is a
government where the states have willed to make a compact
with each other; and whenever that compact is violated,
who is there higher than the states? Who is more sovereign
than the parties to the contract, who have the reserved
rights guaranteed to them? There are rights reserved to
the states. The constitution itself guarantees them; and
there is the great right that rises above all, revolution, because it is the right of humanity, the right of civilization,
the right of an intelligent public opinion, the right of freemen, and that is, that when governments become oppressive
and subversive of the rights for which they were founded,
then, in the language of our fathers, they have the right to
form a new government. Governments should not be
changed for light or transient causes, but whenever the whole
property of an entire community is swept away by a policy
that undermines it, or deals it a death blow directly; when
the social relations of an enlightened and Christian people
shall be utterly destroyed by a policy which invidiously
undermines them, and produces inevitably a contest between
castes and races; when these rights are touched upon, and
the people see that the attack is coming, they will not wait
until the policy is clenched upon them. The very moment
their equality is destroyed in the government under the
constitution, then, in my opinion, it becomes the duty of
the state to protect its people by interposing its reserved
rights between the acts of the general government and its
people. And when it does that, if Abraham Lincoln, or any
other man who aids Abraham Lincoln or any other man in
the presidential office, shall undertake to use Federal bayonets to coerce a free and sovereign state in this Union
(I answer that question as an individual because it does not
involve my state), I shall fly to the standard of that state,
and give it the best assistance in my power. . . . But,
gentlemen, this is the time, this is the place, this almost the

hour for you to decide — what? That your constitution
and your government shall not be put to such desperate
straits. . . . Give us a fair showing. It is all we ask.
Give us an equal chance with you. It is all we ask. Trammel not our civilization and our industry with your schemes
of emancipation, your schemes of abolition, your schemes to
encourage raids upon us. Give us the showing we give you.
Hands off! Meet us in generous rivalry; and he who conquers in the strife is a conqueror indeed, because the victory
will be given to him as the just meed of superior sagacity,
superior intelligence, and superior virtue; and whenever
you get to be superior to the South in these things, gentlemen,
we will bow in reverence before you." [1]

The property argument for the aggressive step of secession
was of great weight. In 1850, with a cotton crop of 2,334,000
bales, 1,590,000 bales were exported; in 1859, with a crop of
4,019,000 bales, 3,021,000 bales were exported. In the same
interval home consumption of cotton jumped from 613,-
000 bales to 928,000 bales. Prices per pound, which in
the forties were only eight and nine cents, now averaged
twelve cents.[2] In 1850 in New Orleans good field hands sold
for from $800 to $1200, early in 1860 for from $2200 to $2500;
the increase in slave values in ten years was one hundred
per cent. Cotton, therefore, was a very valuable crop, the
negroes who cultivated it so valuable as to be well-nigh indispensable. This one source of prosperity was enormous,
was rapidly increasing, and would continue just as long as
slavery was secure — no longer. The ordinary instincts
of business prudence, which aim chiefly at self-preservation
and grow timid at the least flutter of insecurity and danger,
could dictate nothing else than getting away from the active

[1] See p. 301 for this speech in full.
[2] *The Cotton Industry, An Essay in American Economic History*, by
M. B. Hammond. (Publications of the American Economic Association.)
New York and London, 1897, App. I.

source of agitation and trouble. Under the same circumstances every large business interest would embrace secession. The four million slaves, said Yancey, were worth, at Virginia prices, two billion eight hundred million dollars; the vast property demanded to be let alone, and with a Republican administration at Washington it would not be let alone.

The following bombastic sentiments could be duplicated from contemporaneous utterances a hundred times, so commonly held were its sentiments and arguments for secession. Cotton was king, and rather than be deprived of it Europe would surely rush to its defense and aid secession. "Is it possible, aside from this statistical view of it, to say what cotton has done for mankind? Has any man yet attempted to estimate the influence, moral, political, and physical, which that delicate and beautiful plant exercises on the destinies of man? Silent and unseen, yet all powerful and universally pervasive, its influence may not inaptly be compared to the light of the sun. . . . So, abstract our cotton crop from commerce, and behold, if you can, without a shudder of horror, the fearful picture. Verily, there would be curses of despair on 'Change, and wailings in the palaces of the world's merchant princes. Aye, and worse than this, there would be wailings in the cabins of the poor, and cries of strong men and suffering women and starving children would ascend together; remorseless crime would stalk forth from its dark cells, and soon the midnight air would be frozen with the cry of 'murder,' and the stars in the vaults of Heaven would be eclipsed in the conflagration of cities whose people were fed and clothed with cotton. Great Britain alone is estimated to have two million employees in her cotton factories. Add to this number those who are dependent on these employees for subsistence, and we have by estimation, not less than six million souls in the British Empire whose meat and drink and clothing and shelter come of this cotton! It is literally their life's blood. Without but one year's supply of cotton from these factories, and *horresco referens!* Fancy, if you can, this vast multitude of gaunt and desperate men, with the lean and bony fingers of famine throttling their suffering wives and helpless babes, rushing through the land and crying for bread. Never since the Egyptian mothers tore their hair and smote their breasts over the prostrate forms of their first-born after the dread visitation of the Angel of Death, has such a wail gone up to the throne of God as that which would pour into the ears of the British Government. It could not stand six months. No, sir; not all the bayonets that won at Waterloo; not all the guns that blew up the ramparts at Sebastopol, could stop the wild fury of these desperate men, with death alike behind and before them. Where would be Liverpool? and where Manchester and her kindred cities, whose swarming thousands literally breathe an atmosphere of cotton? The everlasting clang of their vast machinery, the roar of their snorting engines, and the busy hum that marks so much industry, would be forever hushed; the stillness of death would reign in the streets, or the silence would be fearfully broken by the shouts of a raging and lawless mob. Their desolation could not be more complete were the plowshare guided over their foundation stones, and salt, the emblem of utter barrenness, sown in the blackened furrow! . . .

"Does any man imagine that I exaggerate the importance of cotton and its fabrics? If so, let him examine the statistics for himself. Let him examine the British press, and the writings of the leading economists on the subject. A learned writer in *Blackwood's Magazine*, referring to this subject, says: 'With its increased growth (that is, of cotton), has sprung up that mercantile navy, which now waves its stripes and stars over every sea, and that foreign influence which has placed the internal peace, we may say, the subsistence of millions in every manufacturing country in Europe, within the power of an oligarchy of planters.' The *London Econo-*

mist, on the same subject, holds the following language:
'The lives of nearly two millions of our countrymen are dependent on the cotton crops of America; their destiny may
be said, without any kind of hyperbole, to hang upon a
thread. Should any dire calamity befall the land of cotton, a
thousand of our merchant ships would rot idly at dock; ten
thousand mills must stop their busy looms; ten thousand
mouths would starve from lack of food to feed them!' "[1]
The same reliance on King Cotton, the same hopes, were
staked on its influence in the Northern states. Continuing,
the speaker last quoted said: "In the United States the
effect would only be less dreadful, because we have greater
resources for feeding our more widely spread population, and
because there are fewer of our people engaged in manufacturing. But no sane man can doubt that it would be frightful
to contemplate. If a little temporary derangement of our
financial condition could produce such distress and terror
throughout the land as was witnessed through the pressure of
1857, what would be the effects were this four million, five
hundred thousand bales of cotton, forming two-thirds of all
that we export to foreign countries, suddenly to fail us?
Grass would grow in the streets of many a lovely New
England village; and many a haughty trader, who now
dwells in a marble palace, would come down to the dust of
poverty and humiliation, dragging with him all that was
lovely and delicate in his household. The source of three-
fifths of all your wealth and prosperity being gone, the strikes
which now disturb your business and alarm your capitalists
would be tinged with revolution and stained with blood.
The misery and suffering which would sweep through the
land, with all their attendant evils, would be such as make
you regard your Lawrence tragedies [2] and present social

---

[1] The *Congressional Globe*, 36 Cong., 1 Sess., Vol. II, p. 1160–1161.
This is from a speech by Vance of North Carolina.

[2] The fall of the Pemberton mills of Lawrence, Massachusetts, is here
referred to; many operatives were killed.

difficulties as indeed but a merciful visitation. The imperial city of New York would be shaken to the center. Not only the great traffic in cotton, but her entire trade with the South, would be cut off. We could not trade there; for without our cotton we would have little to trade with. Many a great mercantile house would be closed, and the names of its partners paraded in the lists of bankruptcy. Great clipper ships would rot at their wharves and the worm of decay would eat into their timbers, for lack of that cotton and its fabrics, with which their holds were once so richly freighted. The white sails of our vast merchant marine, equal to any in the world, would no longer 'float in every breeze under the whole heavens,' but general ruin and dismay would pervade all ranks and classes of men."

The North and all Europe, said another, were more interested than the South that the cotton crop should be supplied uninterruptedly. Entrenched behind the universal want of the civilized world, the South was holding all countries under bond to keep the peace. Neither the Northern states nor Europe dared disregard cotton; nay! Europe did not dare to permit the North to disregard it.

The high tariff, to which the North was committed, constituted another secession argument. England, as the great manufacturing and trading rival of the Northern states, would avail itself of the offer of free trade in a new Southern Confederacy, go in there, win that market away from the Northern states, and protect it. Secession and free trade would give the English manufacturers a chance to crush the Yankee competitors.

In an independent Southern Republic the patent laws of the United States could be broken and patents stolen with impunity; debts due the hated Northerners could be repudiated.[1]

---

[1] The *New York Times*, October 30, 1860, quotes the *Charleston Mercury* at length on this point.

The Northwestern states, which were more closely identified with the South than with the North, would follow the South into secession, for the magnificent river that flowed through their limits joined the two sections, the Northwest and the South, in stronger bonds of unity than could possibly be established between the East and the West by the "mere hooks of steel," — the railroads.

Contrariwise, there were Southern arguments against secession. That which would now seem the strongest argument against the movement, namely, the expense, the extra taxation involved, seems scarcely to have been considered. A careful search of the Southern press nowhere reveals that the point was emphasized, for it is found in only scattered references.[1] Doubtless the great determination of the slaveholders, their passionate excitement, their prosperity and their reliance on King Cotton for speedy foreign aid, would in part explain this unexpected turn. Some were deterred by the expected certainty of a servile insurrection after secession. The only consideration that at any moment prevented such an uprising was the belief of the negroes that the whole power of the central government would be brought to bear against them. "Fancy four million blacks, with their tropical blood, intermixed with the more nervous blood of their masters, boiling in their veins, with the memory of a lifetime of oppression urging them on, maddened by the desire for gratification of their long-smothered revenge, and with the full consciousness that they must triumph or meet a fate far worse than death, — fancy these men, animated by

---

[1] This observation applies only to the period of the presidential campaign; later in the controversy, the fear of taxation may have loomed larger in the South. One difficulty as to internal taxation in the South was pointed out, the struggle that would inevitably ensue between the mountainous antislavery sections and the proslavery seaboard sections on the subject of taxation of slaves. This was already a burning question in the local politics of Virginia and North Carolina. It was expected that this controversy would wax warmer after secession.

this spirit, engaged in a life or death struggle with the whites of the South, and you have a picture of what must occur in every Southern state if they resolve to destroy the only safeguard which they now have — the Union of the states." [1]

Secession would be unwise, it was urged in other quarters, in so far as it would increase the antislavery spirit of the North and cause the Northern supporters of the South to disappear. It was urged, too, that there was an element of impracticability in such a movement, because one secession involved others; from the proposed Southern Confederacy itself, first one state might withdraw, then another and another, until but one was left. From what could that single state withdraw? Only confusion, eternal bickerings between states, could result. [2] What right to secede from the Union had Florida and Louisiana, purchased and brought into the Union by the common treasure? What right had Texas, bought with the blood of the soldiers of all the Union?

The question as to when and how to carry secession into effect was often considered; should it be precipitated after the election of Lincoln, after his inauguration, or after some overt act of hostility to the South by his administration? What constituted an overt act? and how should secession be accomplished, — by one state after another, by a number of states acting together, or by a convention of them all? It came commonly to be agreed that the affronted states should effect secession while Buchanan was still in office, for it was believed that as President he would not raise his hand in opposition, whereas it was feared that Lincoln would offer strenuous opposition. [3]

[1] The *New York Herald*, August 1, 1860, quoting from the *Chicago Democrat*.

[2] This idea was drawn from a letter written by Thomas Jefferson, January 1, 1796.

[3] This sentiment as to President Buchanan was repeatedly expressed in the South.

The attitude of the four political parties on the subject of secession may easily be traced.

No party, North or South, either through its platform or through the utterances of its candidates, openly avowed secession; but in the South, the home of disruption, where out of three political parties, two were openly and aggressively for the Union, one at least was lukewarm in its union professions. This was the Breckenridge Democracy, and its candidate may speak for himself.

"All over the country the charge of disunion is made against me by anonymous writers and wandering orators. Their whole stock in trade is 'disunion, disunion.' Their continual cry is that this man and his party are attempting to break up the Union of the states. We say, how can principles be sectional or disunionist which are based strictly upon the constitution? And the large number of young gentlemen who are ringing bells,[1] with tongues as long and heads as empty as the bells which they are ringing, cry 'disunion, disunion.' From sources yet more eminent comes the information that I and the political organization with which I am connected, are laboring for a disruption of the Confederacy. I do not reply now to what Mr. Douglas says all over New England, in Virginia, and wherever he goes, because it is quite natural for a gentleman as much interested as he to think that any man who opposes his principles must be a disunionist. Indeed, by his declarations we must all be disunionists in Kentucky, for he declares that those who assert that territorial legislatures have no power to exclude slave property, and that Congress should interfere for its protection, are disunionists, and that

[1] This is a sarcastic reference to the fact that the supporters of Bell and Everett took to ringing bells as a campaign demonstration. This was common among the Bell men both in the North and in the South. In New York State, where the Bell and Everett party, by fusion, sold out to the two Democratic factions, Republicans followed the Bell and Everett processions, ringing bells and crying "Auction, auction!"

is what the whole legislature of Kentucky said last year. In my own state, where, I trust, my character and antecedents are known, one of the oldest and most eminent of our public men has not said that I was a disunionist, but has intimated that I am connected with an organization whose bone and body are disunion. . . . The man does not live who has power to couple my name successfully with the slightest taint of disloyalty to the constitution and the Union. . . . Now, if it be true that I am not a disunionist, and if it be true that the political principles I advocate are not disunionist principles, but the principles of the constitution, is it not rather hard to establish disunion on sound men with constitutional principles? That, gentlemen, would seem to exhaust the subject, — sound men with constitutional principles, which principles I have announced in the form recognized in American politics, to be asserted by means of the ballot box." [1]

The ardent Union parties of the South, the Bell-Everetts and the Douglasites, after these pusillanimous words, which were all that the candidate dared to speak in answer to definite questions as to how he stood on the subjects of secession and Federal coercion of states,[2] gave themselves no rest; their cue was to force the Breckenridgeites out into the open and convict them of their true secessionist sentiment, and they gave themselves to the attack with unwonted vehemence. Secession was hurled at the Southern Democracy from every side. Candidate Breckenridge's sentiments were vague and hollow; they did not glow with frank love of the Union; the speaker hedged. He who was not openly and ardently for the Union, was against it. Moreover, hot-headed, out-and-out secessionists in every Southern state belonged to the

---

[1] The *New York Herald*, September 6, 1860. This paper here gives in full one of the very few political speeches Breckenridge delivered in the campaign. The place was Lexington, Kentucky, Breckenridge's home.

[2] See pp. 180–181.

Breckenridge party, and to their words, always in evidence, appeal was made.

Several sensational documents revealed Yancey's position with merciless precision. That great leader, the soul of the Breckenridge party, questioned by many a Northern audience in the height of the campaign, persistently refused to tell in the crisis, one way or the other, what were his sentiments as regarded secession; it was a question for his state to decide after the election, and he would go with his state.[1] But in the months immediately preceding the presidential campaign he had often expressed himself on the subject in words as eloquent as any campaign speech, and newspaper readers came to know the record by heart, so often was it laid before them by the hostile press.

Welcoming the Southern commercial convention in Montgomery, Alabama, May, 1858, he used the following words: "I must be allowed, at least on my behalf, to welcome you, too, as but the foreshadowing of that far more important body, important as you evidently will be, that, if injustice and wrong shall continue to rule the councils of the dominant section of the country, must, ere long, assemble on Southern soil, for the purpose of devising some measure by which not only your industrial, but your social and political relations, shall be placed on the basis of an independent sovereignty, which will have within itself a unity of climate, a unity of soil, a unity of production, and a unity of social relation; that unity which alone can be the basis of a successful and permanent government." Within a month's time he wrote to James S. Slaughter in regard to prompt resistance to the next Northern aggression: "It must come in the nature of things. No national party can save us; no sectional party can even do it, but if we could do as our

---

[1] See his words in New York, pp. 322–328. In this speech, he did allow himself to declare against coercion of a state by the national government to prevent secession. For the answer in Baltimore, see p. 215.

fathers did, organize committees of safety all over the Southern states, and it is only in them that we can hope for any effective movement, we shall fire the Southern heart, instruct the Southern mind, give courage to each other, and at the proper moment, by one organized concerted action, we can precipitate the cotton states into a revolution." In Montgomery, Alabama, a few weeks later, he organized a lodge of the "League of the United Southerners," in the preamble of whose constitution ran these words: "And believing further that it is the duty of the South to use all proper means to sustain her rights within the Union, with a view to being justified before the world in resuming the powers she has delegated to the general government, in the event she fails to obtain justice in the Union, we organize ourselves under the following constitution." The motto of the society, of which numerous branches were formed, was "A Southern Republic is our only safety." A month or so later, explanatory of the Slaughter letter, he wrote to Roger A. Pryor, an editor of Richmond, Virginia, and later fire-eating member of the national House of Representatives: "It is equally true that I do not expect Virginia to take any initiative steps toward a dissolution of the Union, when that exigency shall be forced upon the South. Her position as a Border state and a well-considered Southern policy (a policy which has been digested and understood and approved by the ablest men in Virginia, as you yourself must be aware), would seem to demand that when such a movement takes place, by any considerable number of the Southern states, Virginia and the other Border states should remain in the Union, where by their position and their counsels, they could prove more effective friends than by moving out of the Union, and thus giving the Southern Confederacy a long abolition hostile border to watch. In the event of the movement being successful, in time Virginia and the other states that desired it, could join the Southern

N

Confederacy and be protected by the power of its affirmance and its diplomacy."

"*We shall fire the Southern heart, instruct the Southern
mind, give courage to each other, and at the proper moment,
by one organized concerted action, we can precipitate the cotton
states into a revolution.*" These eloquent, damning words
of Yancey would not down; they were never denied; and
by the common consent of the nation, they were associated
with the Breckenridge party, as its very heart and soul.[1]

A leading Bell-Everett speaker named a list of twenty-six
leading public men in the South, including members of the
United States Senate, the United States House of Repre-
sentatives, governors of states and ex-governors, all of them
Breckenridge men and all openly in favor of disunion
if Lincoln were elected.   In this list were the Hon. Jefferson
Davis of Mississippi, the Hon. L. M. Keitt of South Caro-
lina, the Hon. Mr. Curry of Alabama, the Hon. J. T.
Morgan of Alabama, the Hon. J. L. Orr of South Carolina,
the Hon. R. B. Rhett of South Carolina, the Hon. William
L. Yancey of Alabama, Governor J. J. Pettus of Alabama,
Ex-Governor McRae of Florida, Governor Perry of Florida,
Ex-Governor McWillie of Mississippi, the Hon. Reuben
Davis of Mississippi, the Hon. Roger A. Pryor of Virginia,
Governor Gist of South Carolina, and the Hon. Mr. Boyce
of South Carolina.[2]

These attacks on Breckenridge by the Southern Unionists
were accompanied by definitely formulated announcements
of a different policy.

---

[1] For the above quotations and many others, see the *Newbern Daily
Progress*, Newbern, North Carolina, August 16, 1860, and the *Memphis
Daily Appeal*, July 19, 1860.   At Charleston, on the evening of the secession of the Alabama delegation, addressing crowds in the street, Yancey
said : "Perhaps even now the pen of the historian was nibbed to write
the story of a new revolution," at which three cheers for a new Southern
Republic were proposed and given with a will.

[2] See the Bell-Everett attack of Brownlow on the secession of the
Breckenridge party, pp. 336–340.

Bell's adhesion to the Union was accompanied by an appeal to moderation and compromise, which were "the characteristics of the constitution itself." His words of former days were spread broadcast. "The middle or moderate party," he said in Congress in 1832, in discussing the tariff of that year, "is never in much esteem with the extremes of either side, but it has always found its support in the good sense and moderation of the great body of the people." In 1835 in a speech in Nashville he said: "As long as moderation and the spirit of conciliation shall preside over the administration of the Federal government, any faction which shall seek to divide the Union, either by rousing a sense of injustice and inequality in the action of the government in one section, or by seizing upon the delicate and inflammable question of slavery in the other, can always be shorn of its strength and defeated of its purpose, without the slightest convulsive sensation in our system. . . . The real danger to our system, as in every other system of free government, is in violent party action of the government. A proscribed and disregarded minority, respectable for its numbers, its talents, and even for the virtues of many of its members — for violence is never the exclusive attitude of any one party — such a minority is always tempted in resentment for its real or imaginary wrongs, in redress for its violated privileges as American citizens, in being deprived of all participation in the government, compelled to obey laws and be the subjects of a policy prescribed and directed exclusively by their opponents, such a minority, I repeat, is constantly tempted to seize upon every vexed and irritating question, to make common cause with the spirit of fanaticism itself, in an effort to right, or at all events, to avenge, their injuries. This is the danger of our system." [1]

[1] The *National Intelligencer*, September 20, 1860; here is published a campaign tract of the Bell-Everett party, and the sentiments, copied in the text above and taken from this tract, represent, therefore, the position of the party in the crisis of 1860.

Sometimes the Bell men grew violent and forsook their moderation. Before an excited crowd in Knoxville, Tennessee, where Yancey was defending his principles, W. G. Brownlow and four other Bell supporters asked the speaker what he would do if Lincoln were elected, and Yancey responded by another question: "Who are you in favor of for President?" The Bell men admitted their allegiance and Brownlow, as their spokesman, declared: "When the secessionists go to Washington to dethrone Lincoln, I am for seizing a bayonet and forming an army to resist such an attack, and they shall walk over my dead body on their way." Yancey replied that he would not individually secede but would follow his state. "If my state resists, I shall go with her, and if I meet this gentleman (pointing to Brownlow), marshalled with his bayonet to oppose us, I'll plunge my bayonet to the hilt through and through his heart, and feel no compunction for the act, and thank my God that my country has been freed from such a foe. This man, forgetful of his nativity, has uttered fratricidal sentiments of hostility toward the men of the South, who differ from him upon their view of their rights, and the time and the manner in which they should be asserted and supported, but who, if they err in judgment, err on the side of patriotism and through their devotion to their native land." [1]

Douglas' program of unionism, which was much more positive than that of Bell, culminated at Norfolk, Virginia, where the head of the Breckenridge ticket handed Douglas a paper with two questions on it. The first question ran: "If Abraham Lincoln be elected president of the United States, will the Southern states be justified in seceding from the Union?" "To this I answer emphatically, no. The election of a man to the presidency by the American people, in conformity to the constitution of the United States, would not justify any attempt at dissolving this glorious

[1] The *New York Times*, September 29, 1860.

confederation. Now I will read to you the second question and answer it. 'If they, the Southern states, seceded from the Union upon the inauguration of Abraham Lincoln, before he commits an overt act against their constitutional rights, will you advise or vindicate resistance by force to their secession?' (Voices of Bell men were heard crying 'No, no, Douglas.') I answer emphatically that it is the duty of the President of the United States, and all others in authority under him, to enforce the laws of the United States as passed by Congress and as the courts expound them. And I, as in duty bound by my oath of fidelity to the constitution, would do all in my power to aid the government of the United States in maintaining the supremacy of the laws against all resistance to them, come from what quarter it might. In other words, I think the President of the United States, whoever he may be, should treat all attempts to break up the Union, by resistance to its laws, as Old Hickory treated the nullifiers in 1832. The laws must be enforced, but at the same time be it remembered, it is the duty of every citizen of every State, and every other functionary, to preserve, maintain, and vindicate the rights of every citizen and the rights of every state in the Union. I hold that the constitution has a remedy for every grievance that may arise within the limits of the Union." Yet he believed in the right of revolution against an oppressive government; the President of the United States he would "hang higher than Haman" if he transcended his power. "I am for putting down the Northern abolitionists but am also for putting down the Southern secessionists, and that too by an exercise of the same constitutional power. I believe that the peace, harmony, and safety of this country depend upon destroying both factions.[1]

[1] The *New York Herald*, August 27, 1860. For the answer at Raleigh, North Carolina, to the same questions, see pp. 294–296. For Yancey's answers, see pp. 322–328.

These words are of refreshing frankness compared with the craven position of candidate Breckenridge on the same subject,[1] or the milk and water utterances of candidate Bell.[2] Yet, on the morality of slavery, Douglas was the one who hedged.[3]

At Baltimore, Douglas delivered the following words: "Nor can they screen themselves under the pretext that this would be making war on sovereign states. Sovereign states cannot commit treason — individuals may. . . . When a citizen of Vermont arrays himself against the constitution and the laws by resisting the marshal in the execution of the fugitive slave law, we do not allow the violator to screen himself under the sovereignty of Vermont, but we punish the violators of the law wherever we find them. . . . Secession means revolution. It is only another word for the same meaning. I hold to the inherent right of revolution, whenever the evils of civil war and revolution are less than those of obedience to law. It is upon that principle only that Washington, Jefferson, Franklin, and Adams justified their conduct in seceding from the British Empire. When they seceded they did not skulk behind the pretended sovereignty of the colonies. They avowed that the evils of resistance were less than those of submission. They looked the gallows in the face, and like brave men dared all the consequences of their acts, though the halter awaited their necks had they failed."[4]

Douglas believed that his own section of the Northwest would never countenance secession. "You go into one of our new settlements in Kansas, Nebraska, Illinois, or any of them, and there you will find that a North Carolinian has settled down by the side of a Connecticut farmer, with a Virginian next to him, a New Yorker, a South Carolinian

---

[1] See pp. 174–175.   [2] See p. 179.   [3] See p. 184.
[4] The *Newbern Daily Progress*, Newbern, North Carolina, September 14, 1860.

and representatives of every state around him, the whole union being represented on the prairie by the farmers who have settled on it. In the course of time the young folks in the community begin to visit, and in a short time a North Carolinian boy sees a Yankee girl he likes, and his prejudices against her people begin to soften. In a few years, the Carolina and the Connecticut people are united, the Virginian and the Pennsylvanian, the Yankee and the slaveholder, are united by the ties of marriage, and friendship and social intercourse; and when their children grow up, the child of the same parents has a grandfather in North Carolina and another in Vermont; and that child does not like to hear either of those states abused; . . . and he will never consent that this union shall be dissolved, so that he will be compelled to obtain a passport and get it viséed to enter a foreign land to visit the graves of his ancestors. . . . Do you think that a citizen of Illinois will ever consent to pay duties at the custom house when he ships his corn down the Mississippi to supply the people there? Never on earth. We shall say to the custom house gate-keepers that we furnish the water that makes the great river, and we will follow it throughout its whole course to the ocean, no matter who or what may stand before us." [1]

The opportunity to take this strong Union stand, Douglas certainly welcomed. Yet as is often the case with patriots, patriotism now "paid." As early as the Charleston convention it had been observed that a certain amount of secession sentiment in the South would benefit Douglas in the North without hurting him in the South. It would enable him to appeal to Union sentiment in every state against hated traitors, and would afford him a new issue to talk about, to him who of all candidates needed it. His "gur-reat pur-rinciple" of popular sovereignty was getting

---

[1] The *Newbern Daily Progress*, Newbern, North Carolina, September 5, 1860; from a speech by Douglas at Raleigh, North Carolina.

to be an old story; people had heard enough of it; and yet he was not fit to discuss before either Southern or Northern audiences the subject of slavery. The very logic of popular sovereignty demanded that he be neutral here; necessarily "I don't care whether slavery is voted up or voted down" became his position. In the midst of the greatest moral upheaval of his country's history, he stood almost alone as the only public man who did not and would not commit himself on the issue of the right or wrong of African slavery. If on the stump he was asked point blank as to his slavery professions, he bluffed and abused his inquirer and never answered. In a small town in Ohio the previous year, when an old man asked him the fatal question, Douglas proceeded to descant on popular sovereignty; "You are not answering my question, Mr. Douglas; I know all about that; but what is your opinion — is slavery a moral or political evil?" "You may thank me that I do not rebuke you for your impertinence," shouted Douglas in confusion, while the friendly and excited audience quickly completed the questioner's discomfiture. Practically the same incident was repeated the next year at Bangor, Maine.

But over and over again Douglas repeated his Union professions, and challenged Breckenridge to come out and answer in turn the Norfolk questions on secession and coercion. These questions had already been propounded and Douglas' instantaneous and courageous reply recorded before Breckenridge arose to deliver his Lexington speech. But, as all recognized, Breckenridge could not display an ardent attachment to the Union and at the same time head his ticket. His position was delicate. If he stood forth too prominently for the Union, and favored coercion of seceding states by the Washington government, he would offend the radical secessionists of the extreme South; on the other hand, if he openly embraced secession, he would injure his cause in the Border states. Answer Douglas, therefore, he could not, and to cover his position he and his party tried to turn the tables and to reveal secession among the Southern Douglasites.

This Breckenridge retaliation upon Douglas met with some success, for many Southerners, loyal to Douglas in this campaign of 1860, had uncomfortable records in past secession movements to be brought to light. Said the Douglas vice presidential candidate, Herschel V. Johnson, as the Governor of Georgia in 1856, to the legislature of the state: "I therefore recommend you to provide by law for the calling of a state convention, in the event of the rejection of Kansas"; he then believed that disunion was at hand and he was friendly to the movement. "The election of Fremont," wrote Johnson in 1856, "must drive the Southern states to dissolution." Governor Robert C. Wickliffe of Louisiana, who helped at Baltimore to make the Douglas platform, as the Governor of his state had sent a secessionist message to his legislature. Ex-Governor Winston of Alabama, a Douglas elector, in 1857 wrote to his legislature: "We have everything to gain and nothing to lose by disrupting every tie that binds us to the Confederacy." Pierre Soulé, an ardent Douglas man of Louisiana, was ardent for secession in 1850. J. P. Hambleton, the editor of the *Atlanta Confederacy*, strong for Douglas, was red-hot for secession and war. Alexander H. Stephens, Douglas elector in Georgia, in Congress said: "Whenever the government is brought in hostile array against me and mine, I am for disunion, openly, boldly, fearlessly, for revolution. When that day comes, if ever it does, 'down with the government' will be my motto and watchword." Miles Taylor of Louisiana, the chairman of the Douglas national committee, in an address to the people of the United States, said: "Thank God, no disunionists support Douglas and Johnson," but as a member of Congress he had openly spoken disunion sentiments. Breckenridge papers, issue after issue, kept up the merciless exposure, while they sanctimoniously clothed themselves in the garments of Unionism. The charge was even circulated that Douglas had invited Yancey to become his running mate on the ticket as candidate for the vice presidency.[1]

The Breckenridge retort to Bell may almost be anticipated, for it centered about the non-committal attitude of the Constitutional Union Party on the great questions of the day. Bell's platform, which called merely for "the constitution of the country, the union of the states, and the enforcement of the laws" as the only true political principles, was too short and indefinite. Whose interpretation of the constitution was meant, that of Washington and Madison, of Calhoun, Yancey and Taney, or of Douglas? What laws would be enforced, those of freedom or those of slavery? The conflict of opinion could not be settled by ignoring it. As well advise the tempest to be calm as to attempt to mollify an aroused community into abandoning claims which it believed to be just and essential to its welfare. No real vital beliefs on slavery, the great question of the day, could be found in the record of either Bell or Everett; from the very necessities of their position they were straddlers. If asked to specify his opinions, either with great propriety could reply in words attributed to Sir Robert Peel: "When that question is made to me in a proper time, in a proper place, under proper qualifications, and with proper motives, I will hesitate long before I will refuse to take it into consideration." [2]

Could a party whose leaders refused to commit themselves definitely on slavery, be trusted in its professions of Unionism? In Congress Bell had been on every side of the

---

[1] For all of the quotations given here and very many more, see the *Western Kentucky Yeoman*, September 28, 1860. While the Breckenridgeites here and there may have questioned Douglas' devotion to slavery, this attack on Douglas was not a prominent one.

[2] See pp. 256–257 for Carl Schurz's treatment of Bell.

slavery question. He identified himself with Slade and John Quincy Adams in favor of the abolition petitions of the thirties and the forties, opposed House rule 21, which forbade the reception by the House of petitions to abolish slavery in the District of Columbia, in the states or in the territories, and he opposed the annexation of Texas and the ensuing Mexican war; during the debates on the compromise measures of 1850 he turned and fought the Wilmot Proviso principle and praised slavery; turning again, he fought the Kansas-Nebraska measures, and finally ended by being mentioned at the Republican convention at Chicago as a suitable Republican candidate for the presidency.'

Now in his presidential campaign, Bell allowed his Southern supporters to praise slavery and to proclaim far and wide extracts from his utterances, carefully selected from the proslavery portion of his record. At the same time, his Northern supporters in Massachusetts, the home of Everett, the vice presidential candidate, stoutly denied any sympathy or connection with slavery. To this position was the party finally reduced, supporting slavery in one section and denying that support in the other. Gradually the antislavery record of Everett was developed, how in the thirties he had subscribed to the statement that "slavery was a social, political, and moral evil" and had never retracted; how he had approved the main line of Charles Sumner's speech for which the proslavery Brooks had assaulted the Senator, and how finally, in his home in Cambridge, Massachusetts, he sent his children to the public schools, where negroes were admitted. This revelation of the record of Bell and Everett on slavery, and the two-faced nature of their campaign, was relied upon to counteract and weaken their Union appeal.

By the Republicans, secession was seldom made an issue; they ridiculed the Southern braggadocio, joked about it, but almost never took it up in earnest debate. This doubtless proceeded from deliberate purpose, for had the universally recognized predominant party, surely destined to win the election, opposed the Southerners argument for argument on this point, then inevitably in self-defense the Southerners would have stiffened in their position, and secession would have been rendered still more certain. Such a campaign by the Republicans would also have served to frighten their own supporters, many of whom would consider long before casting a ballot for Lincoln if persuaded that that ballot would hasten secession and civil war. Surely thousands of Republican votes were cast without the least expectation that war would result. Up to the election, a serious Republican argument against disruption can scarcely be found. A few hot-heads in Congress, under provocation, proclaimed that they would coerce the disunionists into remaining in the Union; a campaign speaker now and then mentioned the subject; a few said (to employ a phrase later used by Horace Greeley in this connection), "Let the erring sisters go in peace." But that is all.

To Mayor John Wentworth of Chicago, as to thousands of others, the cry of secession was but "the old game of scaring and bullying the North into submission to Southern demands and Southern tyranny." [1] "It reminds me of the story of the doctor," said a Congressman on the floor of the House of Representatives at Washington; "a quack doctor was called to see a man who was attacked with some sort of disease or other, I do not know what, and the doctor did not know either; but he told his patient that he would give him a certain medicine that would throw him into fits, and he said that he was 'Hell on fits.' So with these Democratic politicians before a presidential election. They always try to give the country some sort of medicine that will throw it into fits. They are 'Hell on fits.' They are now at work trying to throw the country into fits, and they are succeeding pretty well." Senator Hale of New Hampshire told the

[1] The *New York Herald*, August 1, 1860.

story of a division in a Connecticut church, with one deacon on one side and one on the other. The preacher preached harmony and all were moved. Full of emotion Deacon Jones went to Deacon Snow. "Deacon Snow, we must have union." "Good," said Deacon Snow, "we must." "Well," continued the former, "there is but one way to get it, Deacon Snow." "Brother, what is it?" "Well, you must give in, for I cannot." This was exactly the attitude of the South. There were irreconcilable differences of opinion between the two sections and the South said, "You must give in, for we cannot; you are used to it and we are not." [1]

Snapping his fingers in scorn at the slaveholders, Seward shouted, at St. Paul, Minnesota: "For the first time in the history of the Republic the slave power has not even the power to terrify or alarm the freeman, so as to make him submit, and scheme, and coincide, and compromise. It rails now with a feeble voice, as it thundered in our ears for twenty or thirty years past. With a feeble and muttering voice they cry out that they will tear the Union to pieces. (Derisive laughter.) Who's afraid? (Laughter and cries of "no one.") They complain that if we do not surrender our principles, and our system, and our right, being a majority, to rule, and if we will not accept their system and such rules as they will give us, they will go out of the Union. Who's afraid? (Laughter.) Nobody's afraid; nobody can be bought." [2]

After secession was an accomplished fact, the North took up the subject seriously and for the first time debated its constitutional aspects.[3]

[1] See Carl Schurz's humorous treatment in New York of practically the same subject, pp. 270–271.

[2] The *New York Herald*, October 18, 1860.

[3] In the South the constitutional aspects of secession were a matter of debate in the Bell-Everett and Breckenridge campaign; but this debate did not become general in the nation till the Republicans took it up after secession was an accomplished fact.

The aggressions of the slaveholders, which have now been passed in review, seemed a never ending theme in popular discussion. All were familiar with the indictment. The last count, secession, was of the most immediate importance in the campaign, although the others were not forgotten, territorial aggrandizement, aimed at peaceful neighboring nations, at the newly organized territories, and at the freedom of the Northern free states, insistent demands for a legalized foreign slave trade, renunciation of professions of freedom made in past years, departure from the previous practices of the government, the new attitude of the Supreme Court, and shipwreck of the party traditions of loyalty to "the fathers."

But the opponents of the slaveholders were not behind in taking a new and aggressive position; and the very existence of the Republican party, built up in six short years out of the conscious desire of a multitude of people to destroy slavery, is proof of the charge.

The grounds for this incontrovertible statement cannot be found in the formal declarations of the platform of the Republican party, for that document was piously worded to disclaim any intended attack on state institutions; as little may it be found in the cunning strategy of the majority of campaign orators, for these planted themselves squarely on their platform in concealing their real intentions. The record of daily events disclosed Republican policy. Northern newspapers embodied it, and not the party platforms; the spontaneous words and acts of individual men in their actual contact with slavery, and not the deceptive utterances of the politicians. An enumeration of the leading factors involved in the popular discussion readily suggests itself; the John Brown raid and the stupendous wave of enthusiastic approval called forth in countless ways by that event; Hinton Rowan Helper's *Impending Crisis* and the ensuing struggle over the speakership in the House of Representatives; the bitter debates of the Senate and the House; the unsparing presentation of the evils of slavery in the Republican press; the responsive sympathy of Sunday Schools and Churches for blacks in· distress; the moblike resistance to the Fugitive Slave Law and the rescue of fugitive slaves; the enactment of the personal liberty laws in the various state legislatures; the repugnance of courts to convict and punish the stealers and rescuers of the fugitives; the refusal of the Northern governors to give up offenders to the South under writs of extradition; the popular terrorism practiced on Southerners traveling quietly in the North with their slaves; the outcome of the Lemmon case in the courts of New York; the prominence in the Northern press of the alleged kidnapping cases in the Border states; the burning indignation at the foreign slave trade, at the government's lukewarm attitude in regard to the suppression of the trade, and at the demand in the South for its reopening; the sympathy for the free negroes; the fierce denunciation of slavery by religious bodies and by the religious press; the division and strife in the great national charitable societies. These things all had but one meaning, and that was that the Northern people were mightily opposed to slavery and stood ready to strike it mortal blows. This was the inexorable logic of daily events,[1] and it was the genuine Republican doctrine. None could deny it.

That this interpretation is fair and true, the testimony of many bold spirits goes to prove. John Wentworth, Mayor of Chicago and editor of the *Chicago Democrat*, wrote: "A scheme may be devised and carried out which will result in the peaceful, honorable, and equitable emancipation of all the slaves, . . . the states must be made free . . . the work will be one of time and patience, but it must be done."[2] William H. Seward, when asked how long the "irrepressible

---

[1] See Chap. IV.
[2] The *New York Herald*, August 1, 1860.

conflict" would last, replied: "So long as the wrong exists, and right and reason are left free to combat it. I hold that slavery is wrong, and myself and those who think with me, are in a conflict with those who think slavery right. There are but two sides to the question." [1] In a fiery speech in Lansing, Michigan, he declared: "I will favor, as long as I can, within the limits of constitutional action, the decrease and diminution of African slavery in all the states." [2] At St. Joseph, Missouri, speaking of freedom, he said: "But it is going through; it is bound to go through. As it has already gone through eighteen of the states of the Union, so it is bound to go through all of the other fifteen. It is bound to go through all of the thirty-three states of the Union, for the simple reason that it is going through all the world." [3]

In his own way, Horace Greeley was as representative a Republican as William H. Seward. He wrote: "Believing slavery to be a flagrant violation of the inalienable rights of man, a burning reproach to the country, an enemy to prosperity and progress in art, intelligence, and civilization, I mean to labor for its eradication from my own and all other countries, so long as I live. But recognizing the right of each state to regulate its own domestic concerns, I stand ready to forego and desist from all political action respecting slavery from the moment the slave states disclaim all intention, forego all efforts, to extend their peculiar institution beyond their own limits. Thenceforward I will oppose slavery in Virginia or elsewhere exactly as I oppose intemperance or gambling there — not otherwise." [4] Again he wrote: "We pray God in his own good time, to make an end of it everywhere, and would gladly, gratefully, have the time come in our day. . . . We all rejoice at every evidence

---

[1] The *New York Herald*, August 27, 1860.
[2] The *New York Herald*, September 8, 1860.
[3] The *New York Tribune*, October 1, 1860.
[4] The *New Haven Daily Palladium*, October 24, 1860.

from time to time afforded that the fabric of human bondage totters to its fall. But if you ask us to undertake the overthrow of slavery in the states, we will answer you, we will each do whatever is within his power to put a speedy end to slavery; but we citizens of New York or New England have no power over the laws of Virginia or Alabama. We will do our best, whenever opportunity shall be afforded us, to convince the citizens of these states that they ought to abolish slavery within their respective states." [1]

The *New Haven Daily Palladium* believed and hoped that "a speedy abandonment of slavery as an industrial institution would come in good time." The radical program of Sumner's "Barbarism of Slavery" was spread before thousands as a Republican campaign document, while Sumner himself, Hale, Burlingame, Giddings, Lovejoy, and C. M. Clay were spreading the same teachings. One of the party's most popular campaign speakers, Carl Schurz, a young German emigrant of thirty-one years of age and himself a member of the Republican national committee, stood forth boldly in the slave city of St. Louis and in a great speech manfully pleaded with the slaveholders to give up their slaves and join the ranks of antislavery; the animus of the party behind the speech cannot be doubted. [2] The standard bearer of the party, Abraham Lincoln, "always hated slavery as much as any abolitionist," and through the medium of his famous senatorial convention speech, which was in wide circulation as a campaign document, he was day after day declaring to multitudes that the contest between slavery and freedom would go on till the nation was entirely free or entirely slave; and he believed that freedom would win.

The Democratic interpretation of the Republican posi-

---

[1] The *New York Independent*, September 27, 1860.
[2] The members of the national committee read and approved of this speech before it was delivered. See Appendix for the speech in full.

o

tion is not without weight in this connection. The Democrats persistently "saw the nigger peeping through the fence." Witness their campaign transparencies and mottoes. In a great procession of fusionists in New York City one transparency pictured a farm scene. H. G. was in front and a negro and Abe were sitting on rails. H. G., shabbily dressed, as was his wont, and with the *Tribune* in hand, says: "Vote our ticket — we are not abolitionists until Old Abe is elected." A cunning Yankee eyes him and replies: "I see the nigger peeping through the fence." A second scene represented a corner of fence rails. Abe was astride the rails and beneath him in a lurking attitude was a greasy, wooly negro; H. G. was in front, with pants stuck in his boots and *Tribune* in his pocket; he waved away the attention of a good-looking man who pointed with his cane to the nigger and chuckled: "I see the nigger peeping through the fence." Round about were the words: "Lincoln on the fence, the nigger on the fence, the nigger under the fence, the nigger on the wood pile." [1]

[1] Others of these transparencies were as follows: First, there was a truck covered with flags and devices and drawn by gayly caparisoned horses. "Weighed in the balance" said the inscription. Old Abe was on the center of a beam, suspended by a pivot. On one end was a very fat negress, and on the other was H. G., falling from his position. Over the negress was the scroll, "Guess I'se the heaviest, Massa." The battered hat of the philosopher was on the ground, marked *Tribune*. Second, a small truck was drawn by a jackass and occupied by two people, one representing the well-known editor, dressed in white hat and drab coat, the other a negress; the man was paying loving attention to the negress. The whole was labelled, "The effect of the irrepressible conflict." Third, there was a boat at the head of which was Abe with the flag "Discord," and H. G. at the stern holding the tiller and the *Tribune*. Between the two sat the amalgamationists, a thick-lipped negro embracing a white girl; a fellow darkey exclaims, "I'se looking at you, Sambo," and Sambo chuckles, "Yah, yah." The boat is labelled "Steamer *Abe Lincoln*, Captain Greeley, for the Mormon settlement, November 7, 1860." The prow of the boat touches the land and is met by Jonathan who says, "Look here, Old Abe, you can't land that crowd here," and Abe replies, "Why Jonathan, these are my principles," and H. G. says "Colored

This testimony of the Democracy and of the leaders of the Republican party accords well with the evidence of daily events in revealing Republican aggression. The party hoped to destroy slavery, and this was something new in a large political organization.

While both Republican and Democratic aggression were powerful and, for the most part, sectional movements, secession, on the one hand, sprang from the carefully thought-out plans and programs of definite leaders, whereas antislavery arose, without leadership, from the spirit of an unnumbered multitude of common people. Each denied its own aggression, and each affirmed that of the other. The slaveholders pointed out that their measures were the logical outcome of the constitutional principles held by Yancey and other leaders in 1848 and even earlier, and that those were the real aggressors who in more recent years adopted antislavery as their political principle. Republicans appealed to the changes in the Democratic party practices and principles to fasten the blame on that party and affirmed that the true act of aggression was the rapid conversion of an entire party to the proslavery principles originally held by only a handful. Removed from the heat of the conflict, the present generation regards the rival contentions with impartiality and as its just verdict must declare that each party was acting upon principles developed practically simultaneously, that each was guilty of aggression and that each, from its own point of view, was justified in its aggression. Assuredly the secessionists were justified in their step. They believed that slavery was right — it does not matter for the moment how they arrived at this conclusion; with this assumption in their minds, no other course than secession from the Union for the protection of their vast property

folks have preference of staterooms"; one of the party says "Free love and free niggers will certainly elect Old Abe if he pilots us safe." See the *Liberator*, November 2, 1860.

was possible. In the Union, then or very soon thereafter, with the triumph of the antislavery Republicans bent on universal freedom, their millions and billions invested in slaves were sure to be swept away. To remain in the Union and suffer that fate would have been weak and reprehensible in the extreme. The only possible chance for safety lay in getting away from their Republican brethren into a government of their own. The Republicans, too, were justified in their course. As antislavery, freedom-loving men, they were appealed to in their moral natures, and were swept along by a great and irresistible wave of moral sympathy. Thus the infinite pathos of the ensuing civil war. Both sides were right! Neither could have given in and have remained true to itself. The North was right in opposing slavery, the South was right in seceding from the Union in its defense. That the rest of the world in 1860 outside the Southern states believed, and all the world now believes, slavery a moral wrong, does not alter the fact that in 1860 the South deemed it a moral right.

A topic of interest to contemporaries, because of supposed partisan advantage, concerned the existence or the non-existence of a concerted conspiracy on the part of the slave-holders to break up the party conventions of the year in order later to break up the Union. If it could be shown that the slaveholders went into the Charleston convention for the express purpose of breaking it up and rendering the election of Lincoln more certain, as well also as to afford to themselves a pretext for secession, then the movement and its sponsors, at the moment, would be discredited. For the men of that day loved their party, especially the Democrats who had been triumphant in so many contests. To these men treason to their party was most base; few crimes worse. Accordingly the Douglasites spared no opportunity to confront the slaveholders with conspiracy charges and to rake up all the related facts possible.[1]

[1] See pp. 176–178.

William L. Yancey loomed up as the arch conspirator, and his words, already quoted,[1] seconded by the equally determined words of scores of lesser lights, would seem amply to prove the plot against the Union, as charged by Douglas, Bell, and many others. But the evidence does not show that these men went into the Charleston convention to wreck that body and the Democratic party, in order to ride over the ruins into the dissolution of the Union, although the opposition constantly made this charge; with present knowledge this can never be proved. It cannot be affirmed at what moment the self-confessed disunionists decided when was the time to strike, — before the Charleston convention, during that convention, or after it. Nor is this knowledge exceedingly important, for if the Southern statesmen were far-sighted enough to realize that a rupture of the Charleston convention would aid them in achieving secession from the Union, they are to be commended for their foresight. Certainly, by the time of that convention the intentions of the Republicans as to slavery and the probability of Republican success in the coming presidential election, which would furnish the justification of secession, were plain to all the world. All is fair in love and war, and most of all in politics. If the rupture of the convention was the simplest step toward accomplishing the disunion determined upon, Yancey and his followers are not to be condemned.[2]

Subsidiary topics found a place in the Republican program; in the campaigns of the other parties, though not altogether in their platforms, they were completely disregarded. These were the tariff, internal improvements, the Pacific railroad, the Pacific telegraph, and the homestead act. In the House of Representatives at Washington, scores

[1] See pp. 176–178.
[2] On pp. 115–116 the opinion is expressed that Yancey did not disrupt the Charleston convention for the ultimate purpose of disrupting the Union.

of speeches were made in favor of a protective tariff, particularly by members from Pennsylvania and New Jersey, and a tariff bill was passed in that body, but was immediately smothered in the Democratic Senate; the Republican convention at Chicago strongly indorsed the policy;[1] and in the campaign minor references to it were made in public speech. But beyond this the economic doctrine of protection to industries received little recognition. Both branches of the Democracy were in opposition. Even here, however, candidate Douglas did not miss a chance to twist. He who in 1855 had said: "I am a free trade man to the fullest extent we can carry it, and at the same time collect revenue enough to defray the expenses of the government. In other words I am for no other kind of a tariff than a revenue tariff," as a candidate for the presidency in 1860, while speaking in Pennsylvania, praised the protective policy. It was the Keystone state and New Jersey with large iron interests, that were mainly responsible for the prominence of the question.

The doctrine of internal improvements by the general government was brought to the front by the strong message of President Buchanan vetoing an act to appropriate $55,000 from the national treasury to improve St. Clair Flats in Michigan between Lakes Huron and Erie, and by the opposing platform declaration of the Republicans in favor of such improvements. The word "regulate" in the constitutional clause giving Congress power "to regulate commerce with foreign nations, and among the several states and with the Indian tribes," said the President, who adhered to strict construction of the constitution, did not mean to create but rather to rule that which was already created. "What a vast field would the exercise of this power open for jobbing and corruption. . . . Members of Congress, from an

---

[1] As the platform was read to the convention, more applause was given to the tariff plank than to any other.

honest desire to promote the interests of their constituents, would struggle for improvements within their districts, and the body itself (Congress) must necessarily be converted into an arena, where each would endeavor to obtain from the treasury as much money as possible for his own locality. The temptation would prove irresistible. A system of log-rolling (I know of no word so expressive) would be inaugurated, under which the treasury would be exhausted, and the Federal government be deprived of the means necessary to execute those great powers clearly confided to it by the constitution for the purpose of promoting the interests and vindicating the honor of the country." Let Michigan herself, with the consent of Congress, provide for the desired improvement by levying tonnage duties on passing commerce; that great state should "cease to depend on the treasury of the United States." He admitted that the government concerned itself with such improvements as lighthouses, buoys, beacons and public piers, but this was only after a secession of land for the purpose had been obtained from the states.[1]

In spite of this admirable message, which revealed the President at his best, strong public sentiment was crystallizing in favor of the opposite view of the powers of the government, and with this the Republicans identified themselves. Surely the historian must record that Buchanan as a prophet has been vindicated.

In the minds of the people, of all the various public improvements then proposed, a railroad to the Pacific seemed the most desirable; party conventions, Democratic (of both factions) and Republican alike, united in the demand. The West was calling for the undertaking in the belief that it would aid them in the conquest of the country and in the general spread of population; the East was moved by considerations of commercial gain. Horace Greeley, in an

[1] *U. S. Senate Executive Documents*, 36 Cong., 1 Sess., No. 6.

almost forgotten book,[1] summed up the arguments. The arrivals and departures by sea at the port of San Francisco told their own story. Many more traveled westward

SAN FRANCISCO

	ARRIVALS	DEPARTURES
1849	91,415	
1850	36,462	
1851	27,182	22,946
1852	66,988	22,946
1853	33,232	30,001
1854	47,531	23,508
1855	29,198	22,898
1856	28,119	22,747
1857	22,990	16,902

overland, 60,000 in 1854, 12,000 in 1857, and 30,000 in 1859; some traversed the plains eastward. In all, 50,000 people were annually crossing the continent one way or the other, and nine-tenths of these would travel by the cheaper and quicker railroad, if only the opportunity were afforded. Moreover, with the railroad two and three times as many would set out as did actually set out without it; if the railroad had existed in 1850, two million Anglo-Saxons would at that very time be on the Pacific coast. The author considered the output of gold which averaged fifty million dollars per year for the previous ten years, or five hundred million in all. In return for all this outflow of treasure, millions of dollars worth of silks, jewelry, spices, drugs, etc., were coming to the coast in traffic that always sought the quickest route. Some of the government mail subsidy of a million and a half dollars for service over the Isthmian route could be secured for the new road, as well as the six million per year then expended for transportation of soldiers and munitions of war

[1] *An Overland Journey from New York to San Francisco in the Summer of 1859*, by Horace Greeley, New York and San Francisco, 1860.

westward; Mormon patronage also could be counted upon. Along the route, population and trade would be stimulated. Greeley thought that in all a trade of $17,000,000 per year could be diverted to the road, a sum that would be vastly increased by the new trade sure to be opened in the Pacific with Asiatic countries. The road would increase the efficiency of the army, render the mails more sure and frequent, and advance the cause of education in general.[1] Despite all the well-known practical difficulties of construction, a railroad to the Pacific was indispensable; it would be worth more to the country than a dozen Cubas.

Even President Buchanan went beyond the bounds of strict construction of the constitution in favor of the enterprise, and declared that it might well be looked upon as an aid in guarding the Pacific coast from foreign enemies and as such could be undertaken by the national government under the war power of Congress. Many Southerners also, for the moment, cast aside strict construction ideas, although it was generally for a Southern Pacific for which they gave their voice; they could never be brought to assist the Republicans in favor of the Northern route.

The same interests sought a telegraph to the Pacific, and in the two houses of Congress there was the same sectional clash of opposing sides, the same inability to agree on details.[2]

The strongest of the minor issues advanced by the Republicans embraced the subject of a homestead act, by which it was sought to attract settlers to the West through cheap public lands. As a result of the panic in 1857 and the re-

[1] One argument, later of importance, does not seem now to have been prominent; such a connection with the Pacific regions would tend to prevent the possible secession of those regions from the Union.

[2] A typical Western paper, the *Topeka Tribune*, ridiculed this project; the Indians would cut down the wires, the prairie fires would burn the poles, and to guard the line from these evils would require the services of thousands of men.

sulting hard times there was hardly any other topic in the whole West worthy of political discussion; a homestead policy was stronger than any party.[1] Men in their ruin were seeking the aid of the government. The Nebraska legislature passed an act relieving the settler's homestead and twenty acres of land for a certain period from all attachment, levy, or sale, provided the settler himself lived on the land. "Come to Nebraska," said the *Nebraska City News*, "snap your fingers in the face of your creditors; strike out a bold path for the West and for Nebraska; here be men again, and secure for yourselves farms, homes, and a liberal competency for life, then like honest and honorable men pay off all just and honorable demands upon you, here and elsewhere." [2]

While the whole West, irrespective of party, Democrats and Republicans, Douglas men and Lincoln men, called for the proposed national bounty, the Republicans seemed to make the more consistent appeal to propitiate the sentiment. Aside from the opposition in the Senate of the vice presidential candidate, the party was practically united for the measure; Republican votes, in previous years, had stood by it in time of defeat; Republican senators and representatives arranged the details of the Homestead Act of 1860, which the Democratic President vetoed. The Democratic record was much less welcome. Douglas, as a western man, had always worked for free homesteads, but three times in eight years Democratic votes had defeated the bill in the Senate, and crowning all was the veto message of the Democratic President. Only personally, therefore, and not on the record of his party, could Douglas meet the Republican appeal to the western voters.

---

[1] This was the opinion of Horace Greeley, expressed in a letter, dated Davenport, Iowa, early in 1860. See the *Democrat and News*, Davenport, Iowa, September 27, 1860.

[2] *The Nebraska City News*, Nebraska City, Nebraska, January 21, 1860.

A special argument for free homesteads, in addition to the economic considerations usually urged, was the antislavery contention of the Republicans, who favored filling the West with hard-working, independent, free soil settlers, to win the section for freedom. Small independent owners would people the country faster than would large slaveholders; posted in all the West, they would hem in slavery in the Southern states, surround it "by a cordon of fire," and contribute to the final destruction of the system by rendering its expansion impossible. Nor were the Southerners unconscious of the force of this reasoning, for defense of slavery led them to oppose the homestead policy from the very beginning; in their efforts they brought both the Whig and the Democratic parties over to their side, and not till the new Republican party was born on the antislavery issue did free homesteads secure adequate political recognition.

Buchanan's veto message represented the opposition. By strict construction of the constitution it was impossible for Congress to give public lands away to individuals; "to dispose of" did not mean "to give away" — such a degree of control over the territories Congress did not possess. To those who paid one dollar and twenty-five cents for their western lands, had then settled them and constructed roads, established schools, and laid foundations of prosperous communities, it would be unfair to allow others to come in and settle by their side on very cheap or free lands; to the old soldiers of former wars, who had been paid in part for their services by warrants on the public lands, the measure would be unfair, for the value of their warrants would decrease, if others were allowed to acquire equally good lands at a cheaper rate; the measure would be unfair in its discrimination in favor of agriculturists as against artisans and laborers, and unfair to the old states as compared with the new; and finally, as an inducement to secret and lawful agreements in taking up land, the act would really lead to an increase of speculation rather than to the destruction of speculation, as was claimed by its supporters. Public speculation it would indeed kill, but the hidden agreements would multiply. Finally, it would diminish the government revenue.[1]

Fortunately for the country this view of James Buchanan on free homesteads was soon to be overthrown.

Although these less important issues were entirely subordinate to the great slavery issue, they still represented distinct needs in certain localities, as in the West where the Mississippi valley was in a critical period of development. After a decade of rapid growth, during which the section drew more attention to itself, it was now in a position in national politics, where Congressional action seemed destined to make or mar the record. The prominence of the West in national life was now assured.

[1] *The Works of James Buchanan*, collected and ed. by John Basset Moore, Philadelphia and London, 1908–1910, X, 443.

CHAPTER VIII

LEADERS AND CONDUCT OF THE CAMPAIGN

INCONTESTABLY Stephen A. Douglas was the greatest figure on the contemporary political stage, the true giant of the times; more attention was given to him by campaign speakers and newspapers than to any other American. Forty-seven years of age, in the prime of physical manhood, and of uncommon native powers of intellect, he well represented the vigor of will and the pushing restlessness characteristic of Americans. Short of stature, with broad full chest, massive head and face lined with care and thought, with severe expression, and with a voice loud and clear, he was a powerful campaign speaker. His wit was shrewd, his tongue ready, while his good nature extended even to recklessness. Although of no general culture, he could master a subject quickly; he was always able to command his knowledge, and remarkable clearness of statement characterized his every utterance. His personal magnetism before an audience was commanding. But his tastes were low and his manner vulgar, and both in Washington and in the West his intimates were of the bar room. He took no account of the moral element in politics and made no appeals to it. Few men thoroughly trusted him, few, if any, shed tears over his defeat. He was a trickster, whose next move no one could predict. While Lincoln was swept into power on the crest of a mighty wave of moral sentiment, which he always recognized and served, the morally deficient

Douglas obstinately turned his face and was overwhelmed.[1]

In illustration of Douglas' unbridled ambition for the presidency, the following story was told. Before the Democratic convention of 1856 William L. Marcy gave "a dinner to the candidates." In good humor and satire, with the charm of social intercourse for which he was famous, Marcy took up in order the names of his guests and discussed each one's chances for the nomination. He ended without mentioning Douglas and the latter broke in, "Well, Governor, what do you think of my chances?" "Beg pardon, Mr. Douglas, that reminds me of a story. When I was a boy in my native town in Massachusetts, standing by the roadside one day, a horseman at full speed, his steed foaming at the mouth, suddenly drew up and asked the distance to the next town. 'Ten miles,' came the reply. 'And how long will it take me to get there?' demanded the excited horseman. 'Why, look here, my good friend, if you ride any way decent, it will take just about two hours, but if you go like hell and damnation, you will never get there.'" Whereat Douglas got the laugh.

No ambitious man was ever more censorious, egotistic, and condescending. "When a man tells me he will vote for me if nominated, wonderful condescension indeed!" he said in the Senate; "vote for me if nominated! As if such a man could for a minute compare records with me in labor for the Democratic party!" At Newark, New Jersey, he used the following language: "I confess that my ambition — my individual choice — would be to retain my seat in the

---

[1] At an out-of-doors reception in Rhode Island, Douglas stood with a big cigar in his mouth, supporting himself with a heavy cane in one hand, while with the other he shook the hands of the people. At a reception in the hotel parlor in Norwich, Connecticut, in the presence of refined and elegantly attired women, careful of the cleanliness of their gowns as these swept the floor, he stood with his cigar in his mouth, coarsely spitting on the floor.

Senate, in preference to the presidency, and if elected I shall deem that I make a sacrifice in accepting it rather than you by the change of place. If, therefore, I consent to accept your votes, I shall do it on the express condition that I render you quite as great a favor by receiving them as you do by giving them. I don't want the office unless for your good and mine, and the good of our children and their posterity."

His campaign tour of the country was the most sensational in the history of the country to that time. Practically every state, with the exception of several in the South, and practically every large city, outside of Charleston, South Carolina, heard him; for over two months he spoke continuously. sometimes delivering a score or more of speeches in a day, The severe and dignified Washington could not be imagined traveling from state to state, haranguing crowd after crowd, flattering, cajoling, joking, handshaking, to win a few votes. John Adams and Thomas Jefferson were politicians who coveted office, but neither could make a speech. Even Henry Clay, prince of canvassers, was silent when a candidate, except to write a few letters. Jackson and Harrison made several speeches in their own states; candidates Cass and Scott essayed speech-making, but with unhappy results, and Fillmore and Buchanan belittled themselves by a few speeches. Fremont in 1856 was silent. But Douglas now spoke everywhere, before all kinds of audiences and without formal preparation. Many indiscriminate questions on the most important subjects he answered offhand, as at Norfolk on the subjects of secession and coercion. Often he evaded. His bravery was ready for everything.

Artemus Ward, then a young newspaper man connected with the *Cleveland Plaindealer*, characterized Douglas as follows: "Mister editor: — I seez my quil to inform the public, through the medeum of your column, of the great addishun I have gest made 2 mi grate metropoliticion sho bizness, and darin slak rope & gimnastic Surkus. Last nite I had an intervu with Stephen A. Duglas, the renouned politikal ambidexter & proprioter and Cheef Kloun of the grate popler suvrenty sho. Mr. Duglas is generally kald the littil jiant from his havin performed the grate feet of wakin the hole length of Mason's and Dixon's close line, the dred scot decisshun in one hand and his hole popler suvrenty sho in the uther; and also for pulin up the grate tree kald the Missourie Kompromise, which was first planted in 1787 by Thomas Gefferson & uthers, and set out again in 1820. Mr. Duglas puld up this tre and the constitushun with it and plaist them under his feat.

"But I was goin on to sa that he haz bin travlin thru the estern & suthern stats performin his triks and speekin his pees. The way he takes um in with his popler suvrenty game is not slo. He holds out a bil to the peple, and sez, ther's popler suvrenty — there's the grate prinsipul. At first tha think tha see it; but when tha look a littil sharper it vandishes like the du on the oriental kornstalk when the noonda sun rises in the east on a thunderin hot da in the middle of Juli; it kant be found nowhere. The folks sum times git mad and korner him in a tite plase, but he is tarnal smaul and kan krawl thru a mity littil hole. But tha sa he did wun gratc trik at one plais — he ate an ox and 20,000 klams.

"As soon as I herd of his arrival in town I went to pay him a vizit. I found him in the sho room speakin his pees. I thawt I would not be very formal, and sez I, haven't ye got that pees larnt yit? Sez he, yes — but thers sum of the doktrin the peple dont bleeve and I have to alter it occashunaly to sute the plase. Says I, how doo yu like the sho bizness? Sez he, it dont pa. Says I, my sho is dooin a stavin bizness. He groned and a tere started in his i, and says he, I thowt I shood make a good deal out of mi popler suvrenty; but, sez he, it has spilt the hul sho; the pepel begin to see thru it; and tha sa it is a humbug. Sez i, what are yu gooing to doo with it? Sez he, as soon as I have yused up my posters and advertisements, I shal thro it overborde.

"Sez i, Duglas, whattle yu tak for yur popsovrenty? Sez he, ile sel it cheep. I told him I diddent no how too manig his triks; but I wood go into partnership with him in the sho biznes. Sez he, its a bargin. I then axt him what he thawt of takin along some darkies 2 sing songs and dans the hornpipe. Sez he, I wunt have ennything to do with the nigger bizness agin; it dont pa. He sed he went into the nigger bizness in 1854 and had ben goin down hil ever sins; he said it had nerly rooincd him. The littil jiant then performed on the slak rope and chin the greest pole and spoke his pees on the top. One of Abe Lincoln's rales was next browt in, and Duglas was set on and rode owt thru the bak dors. Duglas is about 5 feet hi, and a thunderin grate man for wun of his size. I maid a frenological examinashun of him. Hee is a man of tremendous power. His kaves are huge. His bump of humbugging is as big as a goos eg. Conseenchusness is caved in. Hede make a furst rate crier in the sho bizness; his bump of telin yarns aint smawl. Duglas and I have kompleted our program for our nu sho. We call it the nu yunion sho, greest pole surkus together with uther alarmin and darin feets.

"Duglas wil perform the grand dubble and single handed game of popler suvrenty. This game can be seen best with the ize shet. But I must klose. We are gooing Westward ho in a fu daze. Yurs in haste, Artemus Ward, Jr. pee es. Duglas seze give popler suvrenty a good blo in the paper." [1]

Abraham Lincoln, fifty-one years old, was an unknown. His words, acts, his career, were followed in the daily press once, where those of the Little Giant were mentioned a hundred times. "Who is Abraham Lincoln?" queried the Democrats in derision, as they recalled the earlier query, "Who is James K. Polk?" "We will return James K. Polk

[1] The *New Haven Daily Palladium*, October 23, 1860.

P

to the convention that discovered him," came back the answer with appropriate application. In the long list of dark horses from 1840 to 1860, including Harrison, Polk, and Taylor, none was darker than Lincoln. He was an uneducated man, a vulgar village politician, without experience worth mentioning in the practical duties of statesmanship, said the Democratic *New York Herald;* a third-rate western lawyer, continued the same paper, poorer even than poor Pierce, without the ability to speak good English grammar, hackneyed, illiterate.[1]

After studying Lincoln's picture in *Harper's Weekly,* the editor of the *Charleston Mercury* wrote as follows: "A horrid looking wretch he is, sooty and scoundrelly in aspect, a cross between the nutmeg dealer, the horse swapper, and the night man, a creature 'fit evidently for petty treason, small stratagems and all sorts of spoils.' He is a lank-sided Yankee of the uncomeliest visage, and of the dirtiest complexion. Faugh! after him what decent white man would be President?"[2] "It is humiliating, if not disgusting," said the same paper, "to see a party in this country putting forward a man for the presidential chair, once occupied by Washington and Jefferson, whose only achievements have been that he split a few hundred rails in his early life, and at a later period villified the armies of his country while fighting her battles on foreign soil."[3]

The *Houston Telegraph,* of Houston, Texas, thus described him: "Lincoln is the leanest, lankest, most ungainly mass of legs and arms and hatchet face ever strung on a single frame. He has most unwarrantably abused the privilege, which all politicians have, of being ugly, and when he unfolds his everlasting legs and arms and rises to speak, his unique countenance, expressive of the most complete equanimity,

---

[1] The *New York Herald*, May 19 and 22, 1860.

[2] The *Charleston Mercury*, June 9, 1860.

[3] The *New York Herald*, July 24, 1860, quoting the *Charleston Mercury*.

the auditor will feel inclined to beat a most precipitate retreat; but a few moments dispell the illusion and he finds
himself listening eagerly to a most profound and concise
reasoner, the dry details of political controversy being relieved
by flashes of genuine wit.   His forensic utterances are characterized by an earnestness of manner, and apparent honesty,
to which he is mainly indebted for his success in carrying
with him the popular feeling." [1]

That these criticisms and jibes went home to the Republicans is evidenced by the rapid appearance in the party press
of scores of descriptions of the candidate's home life and of
his manners and habits.   His refraining from tobacco and
liquors; his refusal to entertain with whisky and insistence
on ice water, when at his home the Republican committee
officially informed him of the nomination; the plain, rather
bare looking parlor in the modest frame house, the customary
little table in the center of the room, and on it the silver-
plated ice water pitcher, Bible, and photographs; all these
things were noted.   "Truth constrains us to say that 'Honest Abe' is not a handsome man; but he is not so ill-looking
as he has been represented.   'Handsome is that handsome
does,' however, is a sensible adage," declared the *New York
Tribune*.   The *Worcester Spy*, Worcester, Massachusetts, believed that its candidate had a "strong, manly, cordial,
winning look, which attracts every one," [2] while the *Albany
Evening Journal* insisted that no one could rise from a half
hour's conversation with Mr. Lincoln without being agreeably
impressed alike with his voice, manner, expression, and personal appearance.

After the nomination Lincoln remained quietly at his home
in Springfield, Illinois, made no important political utterances, and wrote no letters on political topics that found
their way into the papers.   This he did with the approval

[1] The *New York Tribune*, June 12, 1860.
[2] The *New Haven Daily Palladium*, June 5, 1860.

of many of the Republican leaders, including, among others, William Cullen Bryant.[1] In conversation with a reporter of the *New York Herald* he declared that in response to invitation he would like to go into the South and discuss political issues, but that he was dissuaded from such a course by the fear of ill-treatment. This was a sad confession for a presidential candidate — that there were some states which he dared not enter ; could anything better indicate the sectional nature of the Republican party ? queried the *Herald.*

Douglas, who knew his adversary well, entertained for him perfect respect and always referred to him in the highest terms. Lincoln's Mexican war record was attacked by the Democrats with some effect, his futile but famous "spot resolutions" were ridiculed, and his vote that that war was "unnecessary and unconstitutionally commenced" was denounced.[2]

A westerner thus described John C. Breckenridge : thirty-nine years old, Vice President of the United States ; a splendid young fellow distinguished as an orator and as a statesman ; of infinite tact, courage, and popularity ; his good fortune is a proverb ; whatever he touches turns to gold.[3] John Bell, sixty-three years old, was a timid politician of the metaphysical school, with his face turned toward both the North and the South ; his mind was never made up.

William H. Seward may be set over William L. Yancey as a popular leader. By far the most prominent Republican speeches of the campaign were those of Seward, delivered on a long tour through New York, Pennsylvania, Ohio, Indiana, Michigan, Wisconsin, Illinois, Kansas, and Missouri. Every

[1] *The Life and Works of William Cullen Bryant*, ed. by Parke Goodwin, New York, 1883–1884, II, 142.

[2] The "spot" resolutions called upon the President to communicate to the House of Representatives at what spot the Mexican war began ; the House never acted on the resolutions.

[3] The *Fayette and Union Telegraph*, Connersville, Indiana, February 24, 1860.

speech was fresh, without repetition of former utterances, and far outclassed the ordinary stump speech in fervency of utterance, literary quality, elevation of thought, and great enthusiasm on the part of the auditors. Still some sentiments ran through them all, the "irrepressible conflict," to which the orator now returned after his ill-judged apostasy when seeking the presidential nomination,[1] the evil effects of slavery, the necessity of curbing the slave-holders in the territories and in the states, the absurdity of secession, the manifest destiny of the United States to absorb all the continent, and the transference of political power from the East to the West. It was as the oracle of the party that Seward spoke. Lincoln, the orator scarcely mentioned, and when he did condescend to refer to the candidate, it was done curtly. Returning homeward Seward's party reached Springfield, Illinois, where the proud, haughty, domineering New Yorker never left the railroad car. Far from it. But Abraham Lincoln, humble American, one in a large crowd, came to the depot and nudged his way through the crowd to Seward's car and into it; Seward rose, shook hands with the visitor, introduced him to the members of the little party, then again sat down! There was no conversation. Finally, to relieve the situation, Seward made a short speech to the people and Lincoln found his way out of the car as best he could.[2] Every second of the time the easterner's attitude of mind was evident — he felt that he was superior to Lincoln and did not try to conceal it. Admirers of both men could wish that the incident had never happened. Why did Seward choose to humiliate Lincoln? Why did he not defer to his formally designated leader, render him homage as the party's candidate, and pay him a social visit in his home?

[1] See pp. 119–120.
[2] One account had it that the Seward party left the car and proceeded a few feet from it; then, for some reason which was not given, returned to the car.

Personal conceit and pride furnish the only explanation. The Senator was not satisfied with being universally named as the next Secretary of State; he judged that the first place was rightfully his. In this connection a comment of the *New York Herald* is most illuminating. Lincoln, in his general unfitness, would require some one to run the government for him, and Seward, who saw this and coveted the place for himself, was giving his support to the ticket, faint as it was, to win the substance if not the honors of power, dominance over the inferior man's mind. Deprived of the nomination, he nevertheless sought the post of the real President. What a startling and prophetic utterance, in view of the attitude of Seward toward his master at the beginning of the coming administration ! [1]

William L. Yancey was the "Great Precipitator," the "Seward of the South." Early in life he served a state prison sentence for murder of a kinsman, then became a successful editor, member of the state Senate of Alabama and of the United States House of Representatives; he had favored nullification in Jackson's time, and since 1848 had been a secessionist of the extreme type. In his oratory he displayed great powers as a logician, skill in making the worse appear the better reason, and infinite tact in dealing with an audience; he possessed humor and sarcasm, and unusual pride in his position as the leader of the Southern movement. No man ever put the arguments of the South more powerfully.

Late in the campaign, in order probably to shatter the belief that the slaveholders really desired the election of Lincoln and to make it evident that he was doing all in his power to ward off abolitionism, he made a speaking tour

[1] The *New York Herald*, August 16, 1860. The reader should here recall Seward's memorandum to the President, entitled "Some thoughts for the President's consideration, April 1, 1861," in which he mildly suggested to Lincoln that the latter was not fit to be at the executive head of the government and that he should turn this task over to him, Seward. The document is given in full in Hart's *Contemporaries*, IV, 293.

through nearly all the large cities of the North, where, because of curiosity to see and hear the archconspirator, a respectful welcome was always accorded him.   Many questions were asked him.   "But suppose Old Abe is elected? what are you going to do about it?" some one asked him at Baltimore.   "I suppose you live in a slave state, my friend?" "I do," came the answer.   "Well, then, just let me ask you a question by way of clearing the ground, and when you answer, I will answer you."   "Ask on."   Yancey then asked the questioner what he would do if, after Old Abe was elected, another John Brown were to invade Virginia at the head of five thousand men, poison all the wells, set fire to all the houses, cities, and towns, murder all the women and children, set free all the negroes, rob all the banks, drive out all the whites, and take possession of the whole state.   He finished and waited in triumph for the reply.   It was instantaneous. "We'd stop him before he got to all that."   At the timely answer one irrepressible burst of laughter greeted the orator, in which the latter was forced to join to save himself.   This secession issue, in all the Northern cities, he uniformly evaded, and his evasions, in a land where Douglas' honest stand was very popular, undoubtedly lost Breckenridge many votes.[1]   At Boston, when confronted by three cheers for Douglas, he regained control of the audience by calling for three cheers for the Constitution and the Union.   At Cincinnati he shouted with fervor that free speech was not denied in the South and boldly challenged any man to affirm and prove the contrary; the denial was immediately forthcoming, but proof was sharply demanded and when this was not instantaneously at hand, the tricky orator emerged in a triumphant blaze of oratory.

At Boston he declared: "You go with your labor where you please."   A voice: "No, sir, we can't go South."   Yancey: "Yes, sir, you can go South.   There isn't a man among

[1] See pp. 322–325 for his answer in New York.

you who is not welcome if he doesn't come to steal our nig-gers. We have plenty of Northern men in our city; they do not try to steal our property, or to incite rebellion, and they stay. But let any one come with a lighted torch to this magazine under us, to blow us up and to destroy our society, we would be less than men if we did not hang him to the highest tree."

The newspapers of the next morning, reporting this Boston utterance, told also of a young Boston school-teacher, who by invitation had gone to Alabama to take charge of an academy. After remaining at his post but one day, a sermon by Henry Ward Beecher and a letter from Charles Sumner were found in his trunk; ducking in the pond was at once administered, and then the culprit had to leave. The story was culled from the Southern papers themselves. Said the *Richmond Despatch*, at about the same time, concerning the fate of three Northerners in Orange Court House, Virginia: "On Saturday night they were waited upon by a committee of armed citizens and marched at the point of the bayonet to the depot, while the "Rogues' March" was played, as be-fitted the occasion. Here they were compelled to get on the cars." The *Charleston Mercury* reported: "Served him right. A man named William S. McClure, hailing from the state of Maine, was on Saturday last, by order of the Vigi-lance Committee, whipped by a negro at Grahamville for tampering with slaves in that vicinity. McClure was then placed on the cars of the Charleston and Savannah Railroad and arrived in this city yesterday and given in charge of the Mayor who will ship him by the first conveyance to the North." Lurid tales came out of Texas, how a Northern colporteur, with Bibles, religious books, histories, school-books, and atlases, was arrested, flogged, and finally hung and burned for having with him a copy of the *Impending Crisis;* how more John Browns were at work there, rousing the slaves to insurrection, burning towns, and spreading universal terror; and how finally three Northern preachers were hanged.

These reports from the Lone Star state and some from the other Southern states may have been exaggerated for campaign purposes, but there can be no doubt that in a majority of instances the accounts of the persecutions of Northern men in the land of slavery were true; they were believed in the North by the masses of the people, who looked upon them not so much as political buncombe, but rather as the natural continuation of the similar attacks that undeniably characterized the Southern reaction after John Brown's raid. Scarcely a local community in any free state lacked a hero, who by bitter personal experience had learned the lesson of Southern despotism. Thus the masses of the Northern people, in their daily following of current events, in their daily reading of the small local press, and in their daily village conversation and reflection saw clearly one phase at least of slaveholding society at more or less close range; and they were coming to despise the Southerners as more cruel, arbitrary and despotic than even the terrible Mexicans or the bloodthirsty Austrians in Italy.

By these home facts many a Northern audience and many a Northern newspaper shrewdly parried Yancey's eloquent appeals; his oratory, rhetoric, skillful reasoning, and fervid appeals to brotherhood, nationality, and the constitution fell flat.

Yancey's leading theme was the impending danger to slavery. "Suppose the Republican party gets into power, suppose another John Brown raid takes place in a frontier state, and suppose Sharp's rifles and pikes and bowie knives and all the other implements of warfare are brought to bear on an inoffensive people, and that Lincoln or Seward is in power, where will there be a force of United States marines to check that band? Suppose that is the case — that the frontiers of the country will be lighted up by the flames of midnight arson, as in the case of Texas, that our towns are burned, that the peace of our families is disturbed, that poison is found secreted throughout the whole country, in order that it may be placed in our springs and in our wells; with arms and ammunition placed in the hands of this semi-barbarous people, what will be our fate? Where will be the United States Marshals to interfere? Where will be the dread of this general government that exists under this present administration? Where will be the fear of Federal officers to intimidate or to prevent such movements? Why, gentlemen, if Texas is now in flames, and the peace of Virginia is invaded now, under this administration, and under the present aspect of things, tell me what it will be when a higher law government reigns in the city of Washington? Where then will be our peace, where our safety, when these people are instigated to insurrection, when men are prowling about this whole country, knowing that they are protected by an administration that says that by the constitution freedom is guaranteed to every individual on the face of the earth? Can you expect any people of spirit or courage, and true to themselves, to their firesides, and to their families, can you expect such a people to render allegiance to the Constitution, permitted to be trampled under foot knowingly by this higher law government? Can you expect the people of the South to give such a government their assent? " [1]

No former President or presidential candidate had any prominence in the campaign, neither Van Buren, Tyler, Fillmore, Scott, nor Pierce; Fremont was entirely out of the public mind. Even President Buchanan himself was a solitary figure.[2] Without indorsement by either faction of his party and openly accused of corruption by the opposition,

[1] The *New York Herald*, September 22, 1860.

[2] Pierce in 1856 was indorsed by the Democratic national convention at Cincinnati as "true to the Democratic principles and therefore true to the great interests of the country," and "unqualified admiration" was expressed for his "measures and policy."

the President was fast losing his friends, the *Springfield Republican* even going so far as to aver that in the memory of those then in middle life no President left office with so few friends.   Those who elected him, now reviled and neglected him.   He was represented as old and infirm, rapidly losing his intellectual powers, overwhelmed by the magnitude of the responsibilities devolving upon him, and extremely eager to quit office.   Repeatedly he declared against a second term. In the spring, speaking to a large company of newspaper editors then visiting Washington on an excursion, he said: "The duties of the presidency are severe and incessant.   I shall soon retire from them; and if my successor shall be as happy in coming in as I will be in going out, he will be one of the happiest men in the world.   (Laughter.)   While I was Minister to England a distinguished nobleman once said to me, 'Mr. Buchanan, if I were to judge from your newspapers, I should infer that the different candidates for the presidency were the greatest rascals in America.'   (Laughter and cheers.)   I replied that it did look so; but it was really only a way we had of talking about each other at election time.   (Hearty laughter and applause.) . . . I shall not desire to draw a single breath beyond the existence of this, our beloved Union." [1]

In the course of the summer the President made a political speech in Washington, which, as it was generously reported, appeared to be very eloquent.   But his voice on the occasion was weak, almost piping, in striking contrast to his strong voice of former days in the Senate; as he went on, he gradually weakened and could hardly be heard.   He spoke from notes and, while speaking, frequently withdrew into the White House to sip water.   Occasionally he was interrupted by some one in the crowd calling out, "Go it, old man" and other inappropriate expressions, which he would notice by leaving his sentence and saying, "Well, you may say, my

[1] The *Washington Constitution*, May 10, 1860.

friend, that I am an old man," and at that the crowd would laugh and jeer.[1]

By Democrats as well as Republicans Henry Clay was reverently remembered for his dashing leadership, his great statesmanship, his oratory, and the love of his fellow-men, and parties vied with one another in claiming devotion to his principles. Occasionally the "Godlike Webster" was on men's lips, but little attention was paid to that statesman's views and still less personal affection for him expressed. The same with John C. Calhoun, whose cold and unconquerable logic was sometimes called to mind, but never his personality; much of the credit for his views was reaped by his successor, William L. Yancey.

Next to Seward the most popular man in his party but with qualities very different from those of the distinguished Senator, was Horace Greeley, editor of the *New York Tribune*. During the Republican national convention in Chicago admiring crowds constantly attended him, and at the party's ratification meeting in New York City, the night after the election, he was acclaimed with mighty cheers as the hero of the meeting, the greatest Republican present. "Of all men in the nation who have aided forward the auspicious result, no other man has done more than he," said Theodore Tilton, chairman of the meeting; "never flowed nobler blood in any man's veins than beats in that man's heart." By common consent the *New York Tribune* was ranked with the *New York Herald* and the *New York Times*, the greatest American newspapers; the *Weekly Tribune* confessedly had a more widespread circulation than any other paper, enjoying as it did a large sale in every country district of the North; on the editorial pages of these daily and weekly editions, with a literary brilliancy and wit which

---

[1] This was the President's only public participation in the campaign. For the description of the strange and pathetic scene, see the *New York World*, July 14, 1860.

to this day still appeal to a reader as the most pleasurable of all contemporary utterances, he aroused, informed, and guided public opinion to a remarkable degree, and always left a lasting impression for human liberty. Uncouth in manners and appearance but of big heart and mighty brain, he was by common consent the newspaper champion of Black Republicanism, a typical Yankee.[1]

In the conduct of the campaign one factor ever present in the minds of the leaders of all parties was the possibility that the election might fall into the House of Representatives through a failure of the people to elect. As soon as the disruption of the Charleston convention loomed up as a possibility, the charge was made that the South was preparing to bring about this result through a split in their own party and the consequent creation of a strong third party; thus an election by the people would be prevented, in which contingency the national House alone could decide the issue. This, it was charged, was the chosen method for disrupting the Union, for the tumultuous House might well fail to settle a majority vote on one of three candidates for the presidency, the Senate might fail to unite on one of two candidates for the vice presidency, and there then would be no government. The Constitution made no provision for such a contingency.[2]

---

[1] In his eulogy Tilton went on: "Sixteen years ago, on the third night after the election of 1844, he (Greeley) was sitting in his office awaiting the returns from St. Lawrence County, which were to decide for the state and the nation. The river boat *Empire* brought down the figures; crowds were gathered on the pier watching her approach. The *Tribune* office was deserted by all but one man, and that was its editor. He sat alone in his office till a messenger broke in upon him with the adverse news. He read the message and then burst into tears. Well, they were manly tears. But on Tuesday night last the same man was sitting in his office, and as hour after hour only brought better and better news, the expression on his face grew into brighter smiles."

[2] There were fourteen Democratic states in the House, fifteen Republican and one American; Kentucky was divided five to five, Maryland

In solemn language the Republicans appealed to the people to elect the Republican candidates and prevent strife in the House. In an election in the House much would depend on how the speaker used his power of appointment of committees and his other patronage.[1] Disputes would arise as to how each state delegation should decide its vote, whether by plurality, majority, unanimously, or even by a minority vote; the law was silent here and precedent was not binding. Among the members excitement would run high, for they would be fresh from the passions and the excitement of the presidential contest before the people. The bare choice of a speaker had roused them to fury; many had then gone armed; threats of violence had been freely uttered; blows had been given and more than once it had seemed that the country might be on the verge of anarchy. Yet, aside from the moral effect of victory, the only thing at stake was the appointment of committees and of fifteen or twenty minor officials. How would it be when the presidency was the prize, with its control of eighty millions of the public money annually and the appointment of thirty thousand public officials, absolute veto on legislation, control of treaties and foreign relations, and the general pilotage of the Republic? Could any public man desirous of peace, contemplate without horror the scenes that would probably result? No one

---

three to three, and North Carolina four to four; in Illinois an anti-Lecompton Democrat held the balance of power. The Constitution said that Congress should provide for vacancies in the presidency and in the vice presidency, occasioned by removal, death, resignation, or inability to serve; and in 1792 Congress declared that in the absence of both the President and vice president the president *pro tempore* of the Senate should succeed to the presidency, and after him the speaker of the House. But this was not applicable to a failure to elect. If in this contingency Congress ordered a new election, a point would be strained.

[1] Some said that the possibility of the House election was one of the elements that embittered the speakership contest in the House the previous winter; to gain the speakership was but a step in the struggle for the prize of the presidency, which it was predicted would be awarded by the House.

could suppose that the men who now threatened to break up the Union if Lincoln were elected, would allow him to be elected by the House, if menaces, blows, daggers, and pistols could prevent it.   A contest would be inevitable, and as it went on, citizens by the thousand would gather in Washington, street fights would ensue, the House would be invaded, and civil war might be precipitated at once.[1]

The House failing to elect, the Senate might quickly proceed to choose the Breckenridge vice presidential candidate, Lane, as Vice President, who then would become President. The claim was made that the choice really lay between Lincoln and Lane.   Or the Senate might fail to make any selection.[2]

In addition to these possibilities in the manipulation of a Congressional election of the President and Vice President, another possible way to beat Lincoln was through fusion of parties, and in New York, Pennsylvania, New Jersey, Rhode Island, and perhaps one or two other states, this was accomplished.   As arranged by a special fusion committee in New York, that state's thirty-five members in its electoral college were to be divided, in case the Democrats won the election before the people, eighteen for Douglas, ten for Bell, and seven for Breckenridge.   Similarly, in other states there was the gentlemen's agreement of fusionists that if it appeared that Douglas would win in a state electoral college, then the fusionist electors of that state were to vote for him, and for Breckenridge if it appeared that he was to be the winner. The liability of confusion and dispute in the arrangement was obvious; how it would work in actual practice was not explained.   To such an extent are the electoral colleges of the states mere customary institutions.

[1] The *New York Times*, October 8, 1860.

[2] Henry J. Raymond frequently spoke on this subject; David Dudley Field devoted an entire speech to it in Philadelphia.   Almost every Republican speaker sounded the alarm, "Lincoln or Lane!"

The lack of sincere political principle displayed by the parties entering into these bargains and agreements did not escape comment. Where were true Democratic principles? was sneeringly inquired of what was contemptuously styled the "Dry Goods Electoral Ticket," and who was its authorized expositor, Douglas, Breckenridge, or Bell? The Republicans were the only party that stood for moral principle. To Douglas' personal credit be it added that he openly repudiated fusion, though the partial success of the movement would seem to make it appear that he privately consented.

Jefferson Davis is authority for the statement that both Bell and Breckenridge, in order to unite the divided forces opposed to Republicanism, agreed to withdraw if only Douglas would do the same, but that the Illinoisian steadfastly refused his consent. Such an attitude would accord with Douglas' well known characteristic of persistency.[1]

The spoils system, in that heyday of its power and prestige, was used unsparingly against Douglas and for Breckenridge. "Heads off!" like the relentless cry of an avenging fury, seemed to pursue every Douglas man in office. "The President told me," Douglas said over and over again in his speeches, "that if I did not obey him and vote to force the Lecompton constitution upon the people of Kansas against their will, he would take off the head of every friend I had in office."[2] Buchanan denied this, although habitually acting with the motives attributed.[3] Douglas custom officials in Boston, Albany, Troy, and Burlington, Vermont, were removed, also postmasters faithful to Douglas in Memphis, Tennessee, Salem, Massachusetts, Woodstock, Vermont, in three small towns in Indiana, in Columbus, Ohio, Albion,

[1] *The Rise and Fall of the Confederate Government*, by Jefferson Davis, New York, 1881, I, 52.
[2] The *New York Semi-Weekly Evening Post*, September 15, 1860.
[3] The *Washington Constitution*, September 7, 1860.

New York, and Rutland, Vermont. This prostitution of public office was taken as a matter of course by the public as well as by the President.[1] Without the least suggestion of condemnation, a leading paper declared that in the event of the success of the Republicans there would be the biggest sweep in offices since the time of Jackson; Harrison and Taylor had died too soon to effect many removals of the entrenched Democrats, but Lincoln was expected to make an absolutely clean sweep and all were ready.[2]

The most unique and original popular feature of the campaign were the Republican marching clubs, the Wide Awakes. Late in February at the beginning of the short campaign previous to the spring state election, Cassius M. Clay, a stanch Republican from the slave state of Kentucky, visited Hartford, Connecticut, to deliver a partisan address. Excitement ran high. To do escort duty from the depot a number of young Republicans, some of them not yet voters, volunteered their services, and borrowing torches from the fire company house and protecting their coats by glazed capes, with their quickly improvised torchlight procession they made the most interesting political demonstration ever seen in the city. Within a week a regular company of Wide Awakes of fifty members was formed; soon there were hundreds of members in the one city and many clubs over the

[1] *The Works of James Buchanan*, collected and ed. by John Basset Moore, Philadelphia, and London, 1908–1910, X, 460. In the letter denying the conversation with Douglas, in which the latter charged that the President had threatened to take off the heads of the Douglas men in office, Buchanan said: "Besides I have not removed one in ten of his friends, and not one of his relatives. Even among those of his friends who have rendered themselves prominently hostile to the measures of the administration, a majority still remain in office." This surely is an indirect admission that the President was to some extent using his patronage against Douglas. See the *Washington Constitution*, September 7, 1860.

[2] The *New York Herald*, October 12, 1860. *The Executive Journal of the United States Senate* discloses the fact of many removals from office by the President at this time.

whole state; within four weeks two thousand Wide Awakes from the surrounding towns attended the dedication of a lodge for the first society and took part in a great parade, while within a few months four hundred thousand members were enrolled in the numerous societies in every state of the North. The idea spread like wildfire.

The preamble of the constitution of the unique organization ran as follows: "We, the undersigned, young men of the city of Hartford, desirous of securing the ascendency and perpetuity of the principles of the Republican party, and the election of its candidates for office, and to all places of honor and trust in the government, do hereby explicitly declare our devotion to the Constitution and the Union, our opposition to interference with slavery in the states where it now legally exists, and our unqualified and unalterable determination to resist by all constitutional means its further extension and pledge ourselves to use all honorable means for the success and triumph of the Republican party, and of the election of its candidates to office." There were regular weekly meetings, and military drill, but no secret meetings or grips or pass words; in the marching the officers carried lanterns, the private members torches.[1]

Harper's Weekly published a two-page picture of the demonstration of the society in New York. Fifth Avenue was a blaze of light from the torches, lanterns, and fireworks, and crowded with fifty thousand people to witness the parade; from the city alone there were five thousand Wide Awakes in line, five thousand more from Connecticut, Rhode Island, and even Maine. Among the mottoes and transparencies were the following: "Free soil, free speech, and free men;" "Free Homesteads;" "The United States is rich enough to give us all a farm;" "Eternal Vigilance is the price of liberty;" "The Union must be preserved — Jackson;" "The territories must be free to the people;"

[1] The *New York Herald*, September 19, 1860.

"Free soil for freemen."   To the *Liberator*, the parade of the society in Boston was the most imposing political demonstration ever witnessed in that city.   Ten thousand men were in line, including seven thousand horsemen.   Some of the transparencies were : "Free labor and free men all over God's heritage;" "The Pilgrims did not found our empire for slavery;" "Plymouth Rock, the corner stone of a free Republic;" "No more slave territories."   Two hundred negroes had as their banner, "God never made a tyrant or a slave;" along with a company of thirty-eight negroes went the banner, "Liberty throughout all the world."   Mottoes at Batavia, New York, were : "Opposition to the extension of slavery in the territories;" "Protection to American industries;" "Equal privileges for all citizens;" "Homesteads for all actual settlers;" "River and harbor improvements;" "Do not destroy that immortal charter of liberty, the Declaration of Independence;" "Champions of freedom."   At Syracuse, New York : "The Republican platform : to man, his birthright; to labor, freedom; to him that wants to labor, work and independence; to him that works, his dues;" Douglas was pictured riding on the black horse of the South, and the white horse of the North, the horses part, and with one hand pointing to the Dred Scott decision and the other to popular sovereignty Douglas cries : "Oh! my platform;" a plantation scene, with an overseer, whip in hand, was placarded : "Bad for America;" "Protection to American Industries;" "Abraham Lincoln does care whether slavery is voted up or voted down;" "Lincoln and free homesteads."   At Springfield, Illinois : "Pass the homestead bill and that will settle the slavery question;" "Illinois railmakers will fence in the niggers;" "Free labor elevates, slave labor degrades;" "United we stand, divided we fall;" "Followers of Henry Clay, the man who did care;" "Old Abe, one of Hammond's mudsills;" "That 160 acres we must have;" "We do care whether slavery is voted up or voted down."

The procession at this great meeting in Springfield was unique. It stretched for eight miles and was many hours in passing Lincoln's home; thousands were on foot, on horses, and in wagons. One hundred and three wagons carried twelve hundred persons from the surrounding towns. In imitation of the overland travelers to the far West, the farmers had fitted up their wagons with bedding, cooking utensils, and food, and bringing the whole family had come in from miles around; the custom dated back to 1840. In each delegation there was generally one wagon gayly decorated and filled with young ladies, clad in white dresses; there were couples of ladies and gentlemen on gayly caparisoned horses, there were flatboats and schooners, and finally a woolen mill making clothes in the procession and bearing the inscription: "Protection to American Industries." [1]

The Democrats did not dare to copy the magnificently successful society of the Republicans, but they had their marching clubs known under various names, such as the "Ever Readys," "Little Giants," "Invincibles," "Douglas guards," etc. The following were displayed at Washington, D.C., as Breckenridge mottoes: "Democracy is good for all;" "Let millions join in the loud refrain, 'Hurrah for Breckenridge and Lane';" "No rail party or union splitters;" "Cuba must be ours;" "Iron bands shall soon unite the Atlantic with the Pacific;" "Breckenridge, the man of destiny." In the fusion parade in New York, participated in by thirty thousand marchers and requiring three hours to pass a single point, were the following: "No North, no South, no East, no West;" "The Whole Union;" "The Union must and shall be preserved;" "Black Republicans at war with every principle of the constitution;" "We want none but white men at the helm;" "United we stand, di-

[1] The *Weekly Illinois State Journal*, Springfield, Illinois, August 15, 1860.

vided we fall;" "No rail splitter can split this Union;" "Too late for the Black Republicans to alter the constitution;" "We want a statesman, not a rail splitter as president;" "The Union and the Constitution;" "We will defend the Union or die in the last ditch;" "Down with the Black Republican flag of Disunion;" "No niggers are allowed in this club;" "I see the nigger peeping through the fence;" "Billy Seward and his three aunties, Aunty Mason, Aunty Rent, and Aunty Slavery." [1] Douglas mottoes at St. Louis read: "We will march to the music of the Union;" "Popular sovereignty, the great bulwark of American Independence;" "We are opposed to all sectional parties;" "The Union must. and shall be preserved;" "Douglas, the great defender of the rights of the people." At the Douglas parade in Belleville, Illinois, there were the usual decorated wagons, bands of music and flaming banners. One wagon was a model of the ship *Constitution*, twenty feet long, fully rigged and manned by thirteen boys; another bore officers and soldiers of the war of 1812, a third the heroes of the battle of Buena Vista. Three different towns were represented by delegations of thirty-three ladies on horseback, each clad in blue skirt and white waist, and with a brown straw hat trimmed in red, white, and blue, to typify the sisterhood of the states. [2]

Southerners affected to construe the existence of the Wide Awakes into a military menace to their section; the military discipline practiced, the order, the drill, and the marching, were only in preparation for the defense of Lincoln's inauguration and of the North in general, when it came to blows. [3]

---

[1] The *New York Herald*, October 24, 1860.

[2] The *Daily Missouri Republican*, August 23, 1860. *The same*, October 2, 1860, contains a take-off on the names of the Republican candidates, arranged thus,

Ham lin	Hum bug
Lin coln	Bug bear.

[3] The *New York Times*, September 29, 1860, quoting the *Charleston Mercury* and the *Richmond Enquirer*.

Late in the campaign appeared the Southern imitation, the Minute Men, a society that extended rapidly in many states. The constitution of one of these societies at Edgefield, South Carolina, ran in the preamble as follows: "We, the undersigned, citizens of South Carolina, in view of the impending crisis necessarily incident upon the election of a Black Republican to the presidency of these United States, and in view of our duties to our section, ourselves, and our dearest interests, which must fall in the event of the triumph of Northern fanaticism, hereby form ourselves into an association, under the name and style of Minute Men, and we do further solemnly pledge 'our lives, our fortunes, and our sacred honor' to sustain Southern constitutional equality in the Union, or failing that, to establish our independence out of it." [1]

In the Democratic papers the emblem of that party was a rooster. The elephant of the Republicans was not yet prominent, though in the West at least the idea was not unfamiliar to the party leaders. At the head of the column of Republican news one western paper pictured an elephant and the inscription, "Clear the track." [2] The streets of the cities in all sections were strung with banners and likenesses of the different candidates. Pole-raisings and flag-raisings were common. The present charges as to the corrupt use of money in a presidential campaign were practically unknown, as was also campaign violence. Occasionally a marching club would be set upon by rowdies; a Republican newspaper in Missouri was forcibly suppressed; but such acts were few.

Contemporaries seemed to agree in the judgment that the campaign was not exceedingly exciting and they were correspondingly surprised. The *New York World* deemed it the tamest presidential contest since the second election

[1] The *New York Herald*, November 5, 1860.
[2] The *Weekly Illinois State Journal*, August 15, 1860.

of Monroe; the *New York Evening Post* spoke of the calm and quiet of it; Greeley declared it was not so noisy as the campaigns of 1840 and 1856. Reasons for this were obvious. Enthusiasm for human liberty, which in 1856 convulsed the public mind and turned preachers into campaign speakers, was indeed as strong as ever, but with the assurance of victory, revolutionary methods to arouse the public mind were no longer necessary. So truly was it a contest of principle, that offensive personalities, which usually lead to excitement, were comparatively conspicuous for their absence. Harrison was attacked as a coward and as a dotard, Clay was accused of every crime in the decalogue, Pierce was held up to ridicule as a white-livered coward, Scott as a poor general, cruel, and corrupt, Fremont as guilty of every crime; but little of this now attached to Lincoln, Douglas, Breckenridge, or Bell; indeed, President Buchanan's character was blackened more than that of any of the candidates. The factional fight of the Democrats led the partisans of that party to train on one another the guns that otherwise they might have leveled at the Republicans.[1] It was not a man-worshipping struggle. Probably a majority of the Republicans wanted another candidate; they loved Lincoln now, but they had learned to love him for his principles before they were taught to love him for himself. In some campaigns, admiration for a hero had been the guiding motive, but now it was love of principle. The campaign had not been waged on any of the supposed defects of the opposing candidates as leading issues. The Republicans could say to all the candidates, "We have done you no harm before the people;" public life had been fought, not personal integrity and worth. No party said, "The opposing candidate is unworthy, therefore give us the election." Greeley

---

[1] The *New York Independent*, August 2, 1860; the *New York World*, August 12 and 23, and September 26, 1860; the *New York Semi-Weekly Evening Post*, August 1, 1860.

believed that there had been as many campaign speeches in 1860 as before from 1789 to 1860. It was preëminently a campaign of education. Many men spoke every day for two or three months; ten thousand set speeches were made for Lincoln in New York State alone, fifty thousand throughout the Union. There was a very general enlistment of the mercantile or capitalist class in the fusion and Democratic cause, for the men of property and business were afraid of disunion and of the financial loss that it might entail. This fear grew as the day of the election drew near, until by November 6 all the conditions were prepared for the sudden precipitation of a financial panic, if any untoward result was declared at the polls. The attitude of the commercial classes was a salient feature of the situation, as nothing like it had existed since the bank contest of the thirties. There had been more exciting, enthusiastic, and demonstrative campaigns, but none in which a larger number of men took a more sober interest, none in which the public mind was better educated.[1]

How the vote would go never once seemed in doubt. Throughout, the Republicans were sanguine of success, the Democrats discouraged and expecting defeat. In August early fall state elections took place in North Carolina, Arkansas, Texas, Missouri, and Kentucky, unimportant except as indicating the bitterness of the struggle in the slave states between Bell and Breckenridge; plainly as the campaign progressed the Constitutional Unionists became stronger and stronger in the South and would push the Breckenridge Democracy very hard in the final contest. September elections in Vermont and Maine confirmed the Republicans in their hopes, and October elections in Pennsylvania, Ohio, and Indiana sealed everything as a great and sweeping Republican victory. North and South alike now conceded the success of Lincoln. At Cedar Rapids,

[1] The *New York Tribune*, November 8 and 9, 1860.

Iowa, hearing of the October results, Douglas is said to have remarked to his secretary: "Mr. Lincoln is the next President. We must try to save the Union. I will go South." [1]

Lincoln received 1,857,610 popular votes, Douglas 1,365,967, Breckenridge 847,953, and Bell 590,631; in the electoral colleges there were 180 votes for Lincoln, 12 for Douglas, 39 for Bell, and 72 for Breckenridge. Fusion was defeated in New York by 47,000, in Pennsylvania by 75,000, and in Rhode Island by 5000; in New Jersey, where the fusionists won, they were not loyally supported by the Douglasites, so that the result there was three electoral votes for Douglas and four for Lincoln. [2] In the Southern states Lincoln received 17,000 votes in Missouri, 1300 in Kentucky, 3800 in Delaware, 2300 in Maryland, and 1900 in Virginia, not a vote in all the remainder of the South. Almost as meager was the Breckenridge Northern vote, 2400 in Illinois, 1000 in Iowa, 900 in Wisconsin, 12,000 in Indiana, 11,000 in Ohio, 16,000 in Connecticut, 6000 in Massachusetts, 21,000 in New Hampshire, 6000 in Maine, and 200 in Vermont. Some states were very close. Douglas won Missouri by 429 over Bell, Bell Virginia by 358 over Breckenridge, Breckenridge Louisiana by 2400 over Bell, Breckenridge Maryland by 700 over Bell, Lincoln California by 650 over Douglas, and Lincoln Oregon by 260 over Breckenridge. Of the large cities, New York went against Lincoln for fusion by 30,000, Philadelphia for Lincoln by 1000, Chicago for Lincoln by 5000, and St. Louis for Lincoln by 700. [3]

---

[1] *The History of the Rise and Fall of the Slave Power in America*, by Henry Wilson, Boston, 1872–1877, II, 699–700. According to Wilson, Douglas in the early summer in New York conceded Lincoln's election privately to his Republican friends.

[2] That is, the Douglasites voted for their own three men on the fusion ticket, but refused to vote for the four representing the other parties to the fusion; undoubtedly, many of the Douglas men scratched the names of the four and voted rather in favor of the Lincoln electors.

[3] These figures are taken from the *New York Tribune Almanac*.

William Cullen Bryant, poet and editor of the *New York Evening Post*, amid marvelous enthusiasm at the New York jubilee meeting, celebrated the Republican triumph by the following notable speech: "My friends, great motives have called us together this evening. We are assembled to celebrate an important moral and political victory, one of the most important, it seems to me, that has ever been achieved. The youngest of those who now listen to me may live to the middle of the next century, and yet never witness an election so pregnant with great results as that which has been held. We now stand upon the battlefield of the great contest, while around us and before us lie the carcasses of the slain. At our feet, conquered, lies that great oligarchy which has so long held the South through submission and fear, and has ruled the North through the treachery of Northern men; and has tyrannized equally over both. You, my friends, animated by the generous impulses of your time of life, have aided to deal the terrible blow that has stretched the creature on the earth. It lies before us, horrible and ghastly, with its head severed from its huge trunk, and with all its members dissevered; lifeless and dead it now lies there, and from that death there is no resurrection. A new era is now inaugurated, the old order of things has passed away, never, we hope, to return. A new order of things is begun, and there will be no more attempts to force by blood and violence, upon the peaceful inhabitants of an unoffending territory, a barbarous institution, which they indignantly repel and utterly abhor. There will be no more attempts to wrest from their owners any neighboring territory for the purpose of despotism, and no more attempts to revive that thing, accursed of God and man, the execrable slave trade. There will be no longer any daring violations and defiances of the law by which that execrable traffic is prohibited. There will be no more attempts to purchase members of Congress, and buy of them enactments of laws which their own consciences disapprove. For the part which you have taken in the inauguration of this new system your own conscience must applaud you. You have not listened to the mean and selfish suggestions of interest, or to the counsels of craven and abject fear, and have put your hearts into the contest and into your acts, as your consciences have dictated, and your own consciences will furnish you a sufficient reward. And I exhort you, whenever you are tempted by sordid self-interest, or by the counsels of cowardice, to swerve from the dictates of conscience and the law of duty, to remember how you have acted on this occasion, and let that remembrance strengthen and confirm your virtue. I have been long an observer of public life, but never in public life; and never have I seen any course of right steadily pursued without public opinion coming round to that course and crowning those that pursued it with glory and triumph. This cloud, which now bursts with fertilizing showers over the whole land, I remember many years since, a little speck in the firmament, no bigger than a man's hand; slowly it enlarged itself, and then with greater rapidity, until it now fills the whole heaven, shedding down abundance over the hills and thirsty valleys, till the dry fields are filled with abundant moisture; and you, my friends, will now reap the harvest of liberty and peace." [1]

[1] The *New York Tribune*, November 9, 1860.

APPENDIX A

THE PARTY PLATFORMS[1]

I. REPUBLICAN PLATFORM

"*Resolved*, That we, the delegated representatives of the Republican electors of the United States, in convention assembled, in discharge of the duty we owe to our constituents and our country, unite in the following declarations : —

"1. That the history of the nation, during the last four years, has fully established the propriety and necessity of the organization and perpetuation of the Republican party, and that the causes which called it into existence are permanent in their nature, and now, more than ever before, demand its peaceful and constitutional triumph.

"2. That the maintenance of the principles promulgated in the Declaration of Independence and embodied in the Federal constitution — 'that all men are created equal; that they are endowed by their Creator with certain unalienable rights; that among these are life, liberty, and the pursuit of happiness; that, to secure these rights, governments are instituted among men, deriving their just powers from the consent of the governed' — is essential to the preservation of our republican institutions; and that the Federal constitution, the rights of the states, and the union of the states must and shall be preserved.

"3. That to the union of the states this nation owes its unprecedented increase in population, its surprising development of material resources, its rapid augmentation of wealth, its happiness at home, and its honor abroad; and we hold in abhorrence all schemes for disunion, come from whatever source they may; and we congratulate the country that no Republican member of

[1] These platforms are taken from *A History of the Presidency*, by Edward Stanwood, Boston and New York, 1898.

Congress has uttered or countenanced the threats of disunion so often made by Democratic members, without rebuke and with applause from their political associates; and we denounce those threats of disunion, in case of a popular overthrow of their ascendency, as denying the vital principles of a free government, and as an avowal of contemplated treason, which it is the imperative duty of an indignant people sternly to rebuke and forever silence.

"4. That the maintenance inviolate of the rights of the states, and especially the right of each state to order and control its own domestic institutions according to its own judgment exclusively, is essential to that balance of power on which the perfection and endurance of our political fabric depends; and we denounce the lawless invasion by armed force of the soil of any state or territory, no matter under what pretext, as among the gravest of crimes.

"5. That the present Democratic administration has far exceeded our worst apprehensions, in its measureless subserviency to the exactions of a sectional interest, as especially evinced in its desperate exertions to force the infamous Lecompton constitution upon the protesting people of Kansas; in construing the personal relation between master and servant to involve an unqualified property in person; in its attempted enforcement, everywhere, on land and sea, through the intervention of Congress and of the Federal courts, of the extreme pretensions of a purely local interest; and in its general and unvarying abuse of the power intrusted to it by a confiding people.

"6. That the people justly view with alarm the reckless extravagance which pervades every department of the Federal government; that a return to rigid economy and accountability is indispensable to arrest the systematic plunder of the public treasury by favored partisans; while the recent startling developments of fraud and corruptions at the Federal metropolis show that an entire change of administration is imperatively demanded.

"7. That the dogma that the constitution, of its own force, carries slavery into any or all of the territories of the United States, is a dangerous political heresy, at variance with the explicit provisions of that instrument itself, with contemporaneous exposition, and with legislative and judicial precedent; is revolutionary in its tendency, and subversive of the peace and harmony of the country.

"8. That the normal condition of all the territory of the United States is that of freedom; that as our Republican fathers, when they had abolished slavery in all our national territory, ordained that no person should be deprived of life, liberty, or property without due process of law, it becomes our duty, by legislation, whenever such legislation is necessary, to maintain this provision of the constitution against all attempts to violate it; and we deny the authority of Congress, of a territorial legislature, or of any individual, to give legal existence to slavery in any territory of the United States.

"9. That we brand the recent reopening of the African slave trade, under the cover of the national flag, aided by pervasions of the judicial power, as a crime against humanity, and a burning shame to our country and age; and we call upon Congress to take prompt and efficient measures for the total and final suppression of that execrable traffic.

"10. That in the recent vetoes, by their Federal governors, of the acts of the legislatures of Kansas and Nebraska, prohibiting slavery in those territories, we find a practical illustration of the boasted Democratic principle of nonintervention and popular sovereignty, embodied in the Kansas-Nebraska bill, and a demonstration of the deception and fraud involved therein.

"11. That Kansas should of right be immediately admitted as a state under the constitution recently formed and adopted by her people and accepted by the House of Representatives.

"12. That, while providing revenue for the support of the general government by duties upon imports, sound policy requires such an adjustment of these imposts as to encourage the development of the industrial interests of the whole country; and we commend that policy of national exchanges which secures to the working men liberal wages, to agriculture remunerating prices, to mechanics and manufacturers an adequate reward for their skill, labor, and enterprise, and to the nation commercial prosperity and independence.

"13. That we protest against any sale or alienation to others of the public lands held by actual settlers, and against any view of the free homestead policy which regards the settlers as paupers or suppliants for public bounty; and we demand the passage by

Congress of the complete and satisfactory homestead measure which has already passed the house.

"14. That the Republican party is opposed to any change in our naturalization laws, or any state legislation by which the rights of citizenship hitherto accorded to immigrants from foreign lands shall be abridged or impaired; and in favor of giving a full and efficient protection to the rights of all classes of citizens, whether native or naturalized, both at home and abroad.

"15. That appropriations by Congress for river and harbor improvements of a national character, required for the accommodation and security of our existing commerce, are authorized by the constitution, and justified by the obligations of government to protect the lives and property of its citizens.

"16. That a railroad to the Pacific Ocean is imperatively demanded by the interests of the whole country; that the Federal government ought to render immediate and efficient aid in its construction; and that, as a preliminary thereto, a daily overland mail should be immediately established.

"17. Finally, having thus set forth our distinctive principles and views, we invite the coöperation of all citizens, however differing on other questions, who substantially agree with us in their affirmance and support."

II. DEMOCRATIC PLATFORM (DOUGLAS)

"1. *Resolved*, That we, the Democracy of the Union, in convention assembled, hereby declare our affirmance of the resolutions unanimously adopted and declared as a platform of principles by the Democratic convention at Cincinnati in the year 1856, believing that Democratic principles are unchangeable in their nature when applied to the same subject matters; and we recommend as the only further resolutions the following : —

"Inasmuch as differences of opinion exist in the Democratic party as to the nature and extent of the powers of a territorial legislature, and as to the powers and duties of Congress, under the Constitution of the United States, over the institution of slavery in the territories, —

"2. *Resolved*, That the Democratic party will abide by the

decisions of the Supreme Court of the United States on the questions of constitutional law.

"3. *Resolved*, That it is the duty of the United States to afford ample and complete protection to all its citizens, whether at home or abroad, and whether native or foreign.

"4. *Resolved*, That one of the necessities of the age, in a military, commercial, and postal point of view, is speedy communication between the Atlantic and the Pacific states; and the Democratic party pledge such constitutional government aid as will insure the construction of a railroad to the Pacific coast at the earliest practicable period.

"5. *Resolved*, That the Democratic party are in favor of the acquisition of the island of Cuba, on such terms as shall be honorable to ourselves and just to Spain.

"6. *Resolved*, That the enactments of state legislatures to defeat the faithful execution of the fugitive slave law are hostile in character, subversive of the Constitution, and revolutionary in their effects.

"7. (Added at the Baltimore convention.) *Resolved*, That it is in accordance with the interpretation of the Cincinnati platform that, during the existence of the territorial governments, the measure of restriction, whatever it may be, imposed by the Federal Constitution on the power of the territorial legislature over the subject of the domestic relations, as the same has been, or shall hereafter be, finally determined by the Supreme Court of the United States, should be respected by all good citizens, and enforced with promptness and fidelity by every branch of the Federal government."

III. DEMOCRATIC PLATFORM (BRECKENRIDGE)

"*Resolved*, That the platform adopted by the Democratic party at Cincinnati be affirmed, with the following explanatory resolutions: —

"1. That the government of a territory organized by an act of Congress is provisional and temporary; and, during its existence, all citizens of the United States have an equal right to settle with their property in the territory, without their rights, either of person

R

or of property, being destroyed or impaired by congressional legislation.

"2. That it is the duty of the Federal government, in all its departments, to protect, when necessary, the rights of persons and property in the territories, and wherever else its constitutional authority extends.

"3. That when the settlers in a territory, having an adequate population, form a state constitution, the right of sovereignty commences, and, being consummated by admission into the Union, they stand on an equal footing with the people of the other states; and the state thus organized ought to be admitted into the Federal Union, whether its constitution prohibits or recognizes the institution of slavery.

"4. That the Democratic party are in favor of the acquisition of the island of Cuba, on such terms as shall be honorable to ourselves and just to Spain, at the earliest practicable moment.

"5. That the enactments of state legislatures to defeat the faithful execution of the fugitive slave law are hostile in character, subversive of the constitution, and revolutionary in effect.

"6. That the Democracy of the United States recognize it as the imperative duty of this government to protect the naturalized citizen in all his rights, whether at home or in foreign lands, to the same extent as its native-born citizens.

"*Whereas*, one of the greatest necessities of the age, in a political commercial, postal, and military point of view, is a speedy communication between the Pacific and Atlantic coasts,

"*Therefore be it resolved*, That the Democratic party do hereby pledge themselves to use every means in their power to secure the passage of some bills, to the extent of the constitutional authority of Congress, for the construction of a Pacific railroad from the Mississippi River to the Pacific Ocean, at the earliest practicable moment."

IV. Constitutional Union Platform

"*Whereas*, Experience has demonstrated that platforms adopted by the partisan conventions of the country have had the effect to mislead and deceive the people, and at the same time to widen the political divisions of the country by the creation and encouragement of geographical and sectional parties, therefore, —

"*Resolved*, That it is both the part of patriotism and of duty to recognize no political principle other than the Constitution of the country, the union of the states, and the enforcement of the laws, and that, as representatives of the constitutional Union men of the country in national convention assembled, we hereby pledge ourselves to maintain, protect, and defend, separately and unitedly, these great principles of public liberty and national safety, against all enemies at home and abroad, believing that thereby peace may once more be restored to the country, the rights of the people, and of the states reëstablished, and the government again placed in that condition of justice, fraternity, and equality, which, under the example and Constitution of our fathers, has solemnly bound every citizen of the United States to maintain a more perfect union, establish justice, insure domestic tranquillity, provide for the common defense, promote the general welfare, and secure the blessings of liberty to ourselves and our posterity."

APPENDIX B

REPUBLICAN SPEECH BY CARL SCHURZ, ST. LOUIS, MISSOURI, AUGUST 1, 1860 [1]

"MR. PRESIDENT AND GENTLEMEN: To deny the existence of an evil they do not mean to remedy, to ascribe to paltry causes the origin of great problems they do not mean to solve, to charge those who define the nature of an existing evil, with having originated it, these are expedients which the opponents of reformatory movements have resorted to since mankind has a history. An appeal to ignorance or timidity is their last hope, when all resources of logic and argument are exhausted. The old comedy is repeated again and again.

"The assertions that the great contest between free and slave labor has no foundation in fact, that the origin of the slavery controversy is to be found in the fanaticism of a few Northern abolitionists, and that those who speak of an 'irrepressible conflict' are to be made responsible for its existence, these form the argumentative staple of those who possess either not sagacity enough to discern, or not courage enough to state facts as they are.

"In investigating the causes of the great struggle which has for years kept the minds of the people in constant uneasiness and excitement, I shall endeavor to act with the most perfect fairness. I will not indulge in any denunciations. I shall impeach the motives of no one. I shall not appeal to prejudice or passion. I invite you to pass in review the actual state of things with calmness and impartiality.

"It is one of the best traits of human nature that we form our first opinions on matters of general interest from our innate sense of right and wrong. Our moral impressions, the dictates of our consciences, the generous impulses of our hearts, are the sources

[1] From a contemporary pamphlet; *Yale University Political Pamphlets*, Vol. 17.

from which our first convictions spring. But custom, material interest, and our natural inclination to acquiesce in that which is, whether right or wrong, that *vis inertiæ* which has brought so much suffering upon humanity, are apt to overrule the native instincts of our moral nature. They are sicklied over by the pale cast of calculation; the freshness of their impelling power is lost, and questions essentially moral are imperceptibly changed into questions of material interest, national economy, or political power.

"The people of the South have evidently gone through that process in regard to the institution of slavery; they have become accustomed to identify its existence with the existence of Southern society, while even a large majority of the people of the North were rather inclined to silence their moral objections to it, and to acquiesce, until its immediate interference with matters of general interest gave a new impulse to their native antipathy. Although I am not ashamed to confess, that the moral merits of the question would alone have been more than sufficient to make me an antislavery man, yet I will confine myself to a discussion of its practical effects, in order to make myself intelligible even to those who do not sympathize with me. This is the first time that I have had the honor to address a meeting in a slave state, and even now I owe the privilege of expressing my opinions freely and without restraint to the circumstance that, although in a slave state, I stand upon the soil of a free city, and under the generous protection of free men. (*Applause.*) Must I call a privilege what ought to be universally respected as the sacred birthright of every American citizen? Ask any slaveholder who may be present in this vast assembly whether he does not deem it wrong and unjustifiable that I, an antislavery man, should be permitted to give a public expression of my views in a slave state? whether he would not be in favor of silencing me by whatever means within his reach? whether I would not be silenced at once in a strong slaveholding community? I do not mean to blame him for it. Let us give him a fair hearing. The slaveholder will state his political views substantially as follows: 'On the point of astronomy, or chemistry, or medicine, you may entertain whatever opinion you please; but we cannot permit you to discuss the relation of master and servant, as it exists here in the slave state, for in doing so you would endanger our safety and under our social system. Our condition is such that the slightest movement of insubordination once started, is apt to grow with uncontrollable rapidity; we have, therefore, to guard against everything that may start it; we cannot allow free discussion of the subject; we have to remove from our midst every incendiary element; we cannot be expected to tolerate opinions of persons among us that are opposed to the ruling order of things. Whenever a mischievous attempt is made, we are obliged to repress it with such energy and severity as to strike terror into the hearts of those who might be capable of repeating the attempt. Our condition requires the promptest action, and if, in cases of imminent danger, the regular process of the courts is too slow or uncertain, we are obliged to resort to lynch law in order to supply its deficiencies.

"'Moreover, we must adapt our rules and customs of government to the peculiar wants of our social organization. In order to be safe, we must intrust the government in its general administration as well as in details to those who, by their own interests, are bound to be the natural guardians of the system. Hence our safety requires that the political power in our states should be put into the hands of the slaveholders; and where we have no law to that effect, custom upholds the rule.

"'In order to put the political ascendency of those who are most interested in the preservation of slavery upon a solid basis, we must put down everything that would produce and foster independent aspirations among the other classes of society. It would not only be insane to educate the slaves, but highly dangerous to extend to the great mass of poor white nonslaveholders the means of education; for in doing so we might raise an element to influence and power whose interests are not identical with those of the slaveholder. This is our policy of self-preservation, and we are bound to enforce it.'

"Sir, I mean to be just to the slaveholders, and, strange as it may sound, as to the propriety of their policy, I agree with them. Having identified their social existence with the existence of slavery, they cannot act otherwise.

"It is necessity that urges them on.   It is true that slavery is
an inflammable element.   A stray spark of thought or hope may
cause a terrible conflagration.   The torch of free speech or press,
which gives light to the house of liberty, is very apt to set on fire
the house of slavery.   What is more natural than that the torch
should be extinguished, where there is such an abundance of ex-
plosive material?

"It is true, that in a slaveholding community the strictest
subordination must be enforced, that the maintenance of established order requires the most rigorous, preventive, and repressive
measures, which will not always allow of the strict observance of
the rules of legal process; it is equally true that the making and
the execution of the laws can be safely intrusted to those who,
by their position, are bound to the ruling interest; true that popular education is dangerous to the rule of an exclusive class; true
that men must be kept stupid to be kept obedient.   What is more
consistent, therefore, than that the fundamental liberties should
be disregarded whenever they become dangerous; that the safeguards of human rights in the administration should be set aside
whenever the emergency calls for prompt and energetic action;
that the masses should be left uneducated, in order to give the
slaveholding oligarchy an undisputed sway?   In one word, that
the rights, the liberties, and the security of the individual should
have to yield to the paramount considerations of the safety of
the ruling interest?   All this is true; and accepting the premises,
all these necessities exist.   You seem startled at this proposition
and ask, what is the institution that demands for its protection
such measures?   The slave states are by no means original in
this respect.   Look at the kingdom of Naples, where the ruling
power is governed by similar exclusive interests, and acts on the
same instinct of self-preservation; does it not resort to the same
means?   You tell me that the principles underlying our system
of government are very different from those of the kingdom of
Naples, and that the means of protection I spoke of run contrary
to the spirit of our institutions.   Indeed, so it seems to me.   What
does that prove?   Simply this: That a social system which is
in antagonism with the principles of democratic government, cannot be maintained and protected by means which are in accord-

ance with those principles; and, on the other hand, that a social system that cannot be protected by means that are in accordance with the democratic principles of our government, must essentially be in antagonism to those principles. It proves that the people in the slaveholding states, although pretending to be free men, are, by the necessities arising from their condition, the slaves of slavery. That is all.

" But I am told that the slave states are sovereign, and may shape and govern their home concerns according to their own notions, subject only to the Constitution of the United States. Granted. But the necessities of slavery do not stop there. The slave states are members of a Federal family, and as the King of Naples in his foreign policy is governed by his peculiar interests, so is the policy of the slave states in our Federal affairs governed by their peculiar necessities.

"I hear much said of the aggressive spirit of the slave power, but I am inclined to acquit it of that charge, for all its apparently aggressive attempts are no less dictated by the instinct of self-preservation, than the most striking features of its home policy.

"Let us listen to the slaveholder again. He says: 'What will become of the security of our slave property, if inside of this union a slave may finally escape from the hands of his master, by simply crossing the line of his state? But the fanatical antislavery spirit prevailing in the free states, will avail itself of every facility the common legal process affords, as the trial by jury and the writ of habeas corpus, to aid the fugitive in his escape. We are, therefore, obliged to demand such legislation at the hands of the general government, as will remove these obstacles thrown in the way of the recapture of our property, and oblige the citizens, by law, to assist us in the re-apprehension of the fugitive, so the trial by jury and the writ of habeas corpus will have to yield, and the good old common law principle, that in all cases concerning life and property the presumption be in favor of liberty, goes by the board. This may seem rather hard, but is it not eminently consistent?'

"The necessities of slavery do not stop there. Let us hear how the slaveholder proceeds. ' In order to obtain such legislation from our national councils, it is necessary that the prejudices against slavery existing in the free states be disarmed. It is impossible that the slave interest deem itself secure as long as a violent agitation is kept up against it, which continually troubles us at home, and exercises upon the national legislature an influence hostile to slavery. We are, therefore, obliged to demand that measures be taken to stop that agitation.' Nothing more natural than that. The right of petition, held sacred even by some despotic governments, must be curtailed. Post office regulations must prevent the dissemination of antislavery sentiments by the newspapers. Even in the free states willing instruments are found, who urge the adoption of measures tending to suppress the very discussion of this question. Laws are advocated in Congress (and that 'champion of free labor' Douglas, takes the lead), making it a criminal offense to organize associations hostile to slavery, and empowering the general government to suppress them by means of a centralized police. (*Loud cheers.*) This may seem somewhat tyrannical, but is it not eminently consistent? (*Applause.*)

"But in order to succeed in this, slavery needs a controlling power in the general government. It cannot expect to persuade us, so it must try to subdue and rule us. Hear the slaveholder : 'It is impossible that we should consider our interests safe in this union, unless the political equilibrium between the free and the slave states be restored. If the free states are permitted to grow and the slave states stand still, we shall be completely at the mercy of a hostile majority. We are, therefore, obliged to demand accessions of territory out of which new slave states can be formed, so as to increase our representation in Congress, and to restore the equilibrium of power.' Nothing more sensible. The acquisition of foreign countries, such as Cuba and the Northern states of Mexico, is demanded ; and, if they cannot be obtained by fair purchase and diplomatic transaction, war must be resorted to ; and, if the majority of the people are not inclined to go to war, our international relations must be disturbed by filibustering expeditions, precipitating, if possible, this country into wars, thus forcing the peaceable or cheating the enthusiastic into subserviency to the plans of the slave power. You may call this piracy, disgracing us in the eyes of the civilized world. But can you deny that slavery needs power, and that it cannot obtain that power except by extension?

"So, pressed by its necessities, it lays its hand upon our national territories. Time-honored compacts, hemming in slavery, must be abrogated. The Constitution must be so construed as to give slavery unlimited sway over our national domain. Hence your Nebraska bills and Dred Scott decisions, and slave code platforms. You may call that atrocious, but can you deny its consistency?

"'But,' adds the slaveholder, 'of what use to us is the abstract right to go with our slave property into the territories, if you pass laws which attract to the territories a class of population that will crowd out slavery? if you attract to them the foreign immigrant by granting to him the immediate enjoyment of political rights? if you allure the paupers from all parts of the globe by your preëmption laws and homestead bills? We want the negro in the territories. You give us the foreign immigrant. Slavery cannot exist except with the system of large farms, and your homestead bills establish the system of small farms, with which free labor is inseparably connected. We are, therefore, obliged to demand that all such mischievous projects be abandoned.' Nothing more plausible. Hence the right of the laboring man to acquire property in the soil by his labor is denied; your homestead bills voted down; the blight of oppressive speculation fastened on your virgin soil, and attempts are made to deprive the foreign immigrant in the territories of the immediate enjoyment of political rights, which in the primitive state of social organization are essential to his existence. All this in order to give slavery a chance to obtain possession of our national domain. This may seem rather hard. But can you deny that slavery for its own protection needs power in the general government? and that it cannot obtain that power except by increased representation? and that it cannot increase its representation except by conquest and extension over the territories? and that with this policy all measures are incompatible, which bid fair to place the territories into the hands of free labor?

"This is not all. Listen to the slaveholder once more: 'Our states,' he tells us, 'are essentially agricultural producing states. We have but little commerce, and still less manufacturing industry. All legislation tending to benefit the commercial and manufacturing interests principally, is therefore to our immediate prejudice. It will oblige us to contribute to the growth and prosperity of the free states at our expense, and consequently turn the balance of political power still more against us.   We are, therefore, obliged to demand that all attempts to promote, by Federal legislation, the industrial interest, be given up.'   Nothing more logical.   The system of slave labor has never permitted them to recognize and develop the harmony of agricultural, commercial, and industrial pursuits.   What is more natural than that they should seek to give the peculiar economic interest in which their superiority consists, the preponderance in our economical policy?   Hence their unrelenting opposition to all legislation tending to develop the peculiar resources of the free states.

"Here let us pause.   Is there nothing strange or surprising in all this?   You may call it madness, but there is method in this madness.   The slave power is impelled by the irresistible power of necessity.   It cannot exist unless it rules, and it cannot rule unless it keeps down its opponents.   All its demands and arts are in strict harmony with its interests and attributes; they are the natural growth of its existence.   I repeat, I am willing to acquit it of the charge of wilful aggression; I am willing to concede that it struggles for self-preservation; but now the momentous question arises, how do the means which seem indispensible to the self-preservation of slavery agree with the existence and interests of free labor society?

"Sir, if Mr. Hammond of South Carolina, or Mr. Brown of Mississippi, had listened to me, would they not have been obliged to give me credit for having stated their case fairly?   Now, listen to me while I state our own.

"Cast your eyes over that great beehive, called the free states. See by the railroad and the telegraphic wire every village, almost every backwoods cottage, drawn within the immediate reach of progressive civilization.   Look over our grain fields, but lately a lonesome wilderness, where machinery is almost superseding the labor of the human hand; over our workshops whose aspect is almost daily changed by the magic touch of inventive genius; over our fleets of merchant vessels, numerous enough to make the whole world tributary to our prosperity; look upon our society where by popular education and the continual change of condition the dividing lines between ranks and classes, are almost obliterated; look upon our system of public instruction, which places even the lowliest child of the people upon the high road of progressive advancement; upon our rapid growth and expansive prosperity, which is indeed subject to reverses and checks, but contains such a wonderful fertility of resource, that every check is a mere incentive to new enterprise, every reverse but a mere opportunity for the development of new powers.

"To what do we owe all this? First and foremost, to that perfect freedom of inquiry, which acknowledges no rules but those of logic, no limits but those that bound the faculties of the human mind. (*Cheers.*) Its magic consists in its universality. To it we owe the harmony of our progressive movement in all its endless ramifications. No single science, no single practical pursuit exists in our day independently of all other sciences, all other practical pursuits. This is the age of the solidarity of progress. Set a limit to the freedom of inquiry in one direction and you destroy the harmony of its progressive action. Give us the Roman inquisition, which forbids Galileo Galites to think that the earth moves around the sun, and he has to interrupt and give up the splendid train of his discoveries and their influence upon all other branches of science is lost; he has to give it up, or he must fight the inquisition. (*Cheers.*) Let the slave power or any other political or economic interest tell us that we must think, and say, and invent, and discover nothing which is against its demands, and we must interrupt and give up the harmony of our progressive development, or fight the tyrannical pretension, whatever shape it may assume. (*Loud cheers.*)

"Believing as we do, that the moral and ideal development of man is the true end and aim of human society, we must preserve in their efficiency the means which serve that end. In order to secure to the freedom of inquiry its full productive power, we must surround it with all the safeguards which political institutions afford. As we cannot set a limit to the activity of our minds, so we cannot muzzle our mouths or fetter the press with a censorship. (*Applause.*) We cannot arrest or restrain the discussion of the question, what system of labor or what organization of society promotes best the moral and intellectual development of man.

(*Loud applause.*)   We cannot deprive a single individual of the privileges which protect him in the free exercise of his faculties, and the enjoyment of his right, so long as these faculties are not employed to the detriment of the rights and liberties of others. Our organization of society resting upon equal rights, we find our security in a general system of popular education which fits all for an intelligent exercise of those rights.   This is the home policy of free society.   This policy in our Federal affairs must necessarily correspond.   Deeming free and intelligent labor the only safe basis of society, it is our duty to expand its blessings over all the territory within our reach ; seeing our own prosperity advanced by the prosperity of our neighbors, we must endeavor to plant upon our borders a system of labor which answers in that respect.   Do we recognize the right of the laboring man to the soil he cultivates and shield him against oppressive speculation ? Seeing in the harmonious development of all branches of labor a source of progress and power, we must adopt a policy which draws to light the resources of the land, gives work to our workshops and security to our commerce.   These are the principles and views governing our policy.

"Slaveholders, look at this picture and at this.   Can the difference escape your observation ?   You may say, as many have said, that there is a difference of principle, but not necessarily an antagonism of interests.   Look again.

"Your social system is founded upon forced labor, ours upon free labor.   Slave labor cannot exist together with freedom of inquiry, and so you demand the restriction of that freedom ; free labor cannot exist without it, and so we maintain its inviolability. Slave labor demands the setting aside of the safeguards of individual liberty, for the purpose of upholding subordination and protecting slave property ; free labor demands their preservation as essential and indispensible to its existence and progressive development.   Slavery demands extension by an aggressive foreign policy; free labor demands an honorable peace and friendly intercourse with the world abroad for its commerce, and a peaceable and undisturbed development of our resources at home for its agriculture and industry.   Slavery demands extension over national territories for the purpose of gaining political power.

Free labor demands the national domain for workingmen, for the purpose of spreading the blessings of liberty and civilization. Slavery, therefore, opposes all measures tending to secure the soil to the actual laborer; free labor, therefore, recognizes the right of the settler to the soil, and demands measures protecting him against the pressure of speculation. Slavery demands the absolute ascendency of the planting interest in our economical policy; free labor demands legislation tending to develop all the resources of the land, and to harmonize the agricultural, commercial, and industrial interests. Slavery demands the control of the general government for its special protection and the promotion of its peculiar interests; free labor demands that the general government be administered for the purpose of securing to all the blessings of liberty, and for the promotion of the general welfare. (*Great applause.*) Slavery demands the recognition of its divine right; free labor recognizes no divine right but that of the liberty of all men. (*Loud cheers.*)

"With one word, slavery demands, for its protection and perpetuation, a system of policy which is utterly incompatible with the principles upon which the organization of free labor society rests. There is the antagonism. There is the essence of the 'irrepressible conflict.' It is a conflict of principles underlying interests, always the same, whether appearing as a moral, economic, or political question. Mr. Douglas boasted that he could repress it with police measures; he might as well try to fetter the winds with a rope. The South means to repress it with decisions of the Supreme Court; they might as well, like Xerxes, try to subdue the waves of the ocean by throwing chains into the water. (*Applause.*)

"The conflict of constitutional construction is indeed a 'mere incident of the great struggle, a mere symptom of the crisis. Long before the slavery question in the form of an abstract constitutional controversy agitated the public mind, the conflict of interests raged in our national councils. What mattered it that the struggle about the encouragement of home industry and internal improvements was not ostensibly carried on under the form of pro and antislavery? What mattered it that your new-fangled constitutional doctrines were not yet invented, when slavery tried to expand by the annexation of foreign countries? that no Dred

Scott decision was yet cooked up, when the right of petition was curtailed, when attempts were made to arrest the discussion of the slavery question all over the Union, and when the trial by jury and the writ of habeas corpus were overridden by the fugitive slave law? And even lately, when the slave power, with one gigantic grasp, attempted to seize the whole of our national domain, what else was and is your new constitutional doctrine but an ill-disguised attempt to clothe a long-cherished design with the color of law?

"Read your history with an impartial eye, and you will find that the construction of the constitution always shaped itself according to the prevailing moral impulses or the predominance of the material over political interests. The logic of our minds is but too apt to follow in the track of our sympathies and aspirations. It was when the South had control of the government that acts were passed for the raising of duties on imports, for the creation of a national bank, and in aid of the American shipping interest. It was under the lead of the South that the systems of internal improvements and of the protection of home industry were inaugurated; it was the South no less than the North that insisted upon and exercised the power of Congress to exclude slavery from the territories. So long as these measures seemed to agree with the predominant interest there seemed to be no question about their constitutionality. Even Mr. Calhoun himself said in one of his most celebrated speeches, delivered in the session of 1815–1816, 'That it was the duty of the government, as a means of defense, to encourage the domestic industry of the country.' But as soon as it was found out that this policy redounded more to the benefit of free labor than that of the unenterprising South, then the same men who had inaugurated it worked its overthrow, on the plea that it was at war with the principles of the Constitution. The constitutionality of the Ordinance of 1787 was never questioned as long as the prevailing sentiment in the South ran against the perpetuation of slavery. The Missouri Compromise was held as sacred as the Constitution itself, so long as it served to introduce slave states into the Union; but no sooner, by virtue of its provisions, were free territories to be organized, than its unconstitutionality was discovered.

"The predominance of interests determines the construction of the Constitution. So it was and it will ever be. Only those who remained true to the original program of the fathers, remained true to the original construction. Decide the contest of principles underlying interests, and the conflict of constitutional construction will settle itself. This may seem a dangerous political theory. It is not an article of my creed, not a matter of principles, but a matter of experience; not a doctrine, but a fact.

"Thus the all-pervading antagonism stands before us, gigantic in its dimensions, growing every day in the awful proportions of its problems, involving the character of our institutions; involving our relations with the world abroad; involving our peace, our rights, our liberties at home; involving our growth and prosperity; involving our moral and political existence as a nation.

"How shortsighted, how childish are those who find its origin in artificial agitation! As though we could produce a tempest by blowing our noses, or cause an earthquake by stamping our puny feet upon the ground. (*Laughter.*) But how to solve, how to decide it? Let us pass in review our political parties and the remedies they propose. There we encounter the so-called Union party, with Bell and Everett, who tell us the best way to settle the controversy is to ignore it. (*Laughter.*)

"Ignore it! Ignore it, when attempts are made to plunge the country into war and disgrace, for the purpose of slavery extension! Ignore it, when slavery and free labor wage their fierce war about the possession of the national domain! Ignore it, when the liberties of speech and of the press are attacked! Ignore it, when the actual settler claims the virgin soil, and the slaveholding capitalists claim it also! Ignore it, when the planting interest seeks to establish and maintain its exclusive supremacy in our economical policy. Ignore it, indeed! Ignore the fire that consumes the corner posts of your house! Ignore the storm that breaks the rudder and tears to tatters the sails of your ship! Conjure the revolted elements with a meek Mt. Vernon lecture! Pour upon the furious waves the placid oil of a quotation from Washington's farewell address! (*Cheers and laughter.*)

"It is true that they tell us that they will enforce the laws and the constitution well enough! But what laws? Those that free labor demand or those that slavery give us? what constitution? That of Washington and Madison, or that of Slidell, Douglas, and Taney? (*Loud and long-continued cheering.*)

"The conflict stands there with the stubborn brute force of reality. However severely it may disturb the nerves of timid gentlemen, there it stands and speaks the hard stern language of fact. I understand well that great problems and responsibilities should be approached with care and caution. But times like these demand the firm action of men who know what they will, and will do it, not that eunuch policy, which, conscious of its own unproductiveness, invites us blandly to settle down into the imbecile contentment of general impotency. They cannot ignore the conflict if they would, but have not nerve enough to decide it if they could.

"The next party that claims our attention is the so-called Democracy. As it is my object to discuss the practical, not the constitutional aspects of the problems before us, I might pass over the divisions existing in that organization. In fact, the point that separates Mr. Douglas from Mr. Breckenridge is but a mere quibble, a mere matter of etiquette. Mr. Douglas is unwilling to admit in words what he has a hundred times admitted in fact, for, can you tell me, what practical difference there is in the world between direct and indirect intervention by Congress in favor of slavery and that kind of nonintervention by Congress which merely consists in making room for direct intervention by the Supreme Court? And besides, in nearly all practical measures of policy Mr. Douglas is regularly to be found on the side of the extreme South. Like that great statesman of yours (I beg your pardon, gentlemen, for alluding to him in decent political company), he always votes against measures for the encouragement of home industry, perhaps because he does not understand them. (*Laughter.*) He is one of the firmest supporters of the ascendency of the planters' interests in our economical questions, and as to the extension of slavery by conquest and annexation, the wildest fillibusters may always count upon his tenderest sympathies.

"So I say that I might have ignored him, if he had not succeeded in creating the most deafening of noises with the hollowest of drums. (*Loud cheers.*)

s

"He proposes to repress the 'irrepressible conflict' with what he emphatically styles 'his great principle.' At first he defined it as 'self-government of the people in the territories'; but it became soon apparent that under his great principle the people of the territories were governed by anybody but self, and he called it 'popular sovereignty.' It soon turned out that this kind of sovereignty was not very popular after all, and he called it 'nonintervention.' (*Laughter.*) Methinks something will intervene pretty soon and he will strain his imagination for another name, if it be worth while at all to christen a thing which never had any tangible existence.

"But if we may believe him, his 'great principle,' and nothing but his 'great principle,' will settle the 'irrepressible conflict,' and restore peace and harmony to the nation; and, in fact, Mr. Douglas is about the only one of the presidential candidates who insists that there is an immediate necessity of saving that ancient institution.

"Let us judge the merits of the great principle by its results. Has it secured to the inhabitants of the territories the right of self-government? Never were the people of a territory subject to a despotism more arbitrary, and to violence more lawless and atrocious than were the people of Kansas after the enactment of the Nebraska bill. Has it removed the slavery question from the Halls of Congress? The fight has never raged with greater fierceness, and Congress hardly ever came so near debating with bowie knives and revolvers, as about the questions raised by the Nebraska bill. Has it established safe and uniform rules for the construction of the Constitution? It has set aside the construction of the Constitution by those who framed it; and for the rest, let Mr. Douglas give you his opinion of the Dred Scott decision. Has it given peace and harmony to the country by repressing the 'irrepressible conflict'? Alas! poor great principle! this harangue of peace and harmony inflamed the 'irrepressible conflict,' even inside the Democratic party, and rent into two sections an organization that claimed the exclusive privilege of nationality.

"These were its immediate results. It is true, Mr. Douglas accuses his adversaries of having created the disturbance. Certainly; if the whole American nation had bowed their heads in silent obedience before Mr. Douglas' mandates, there would have

been no strife.   Mr. Slidell, Mr. Buchanan, and Mr. Breckenridge may say the same; so may the Emperor of Austria and the
King of Naples.   Such men are apt to be disturbed by opponents,
and Mr. Douglas need not be surprised if he has a few !

"The source of the difficulty was this: The Kansas-Nebraska
bill was thrown, as an ambiguous, illogical measure, between two
antagonistic interests, each of which construed it to its own advantage.   It brought the contesting forces together, face to face,
without offering a clear ground upon which to settle the conflict.
Thus it quickened and intensified the struggle, instead of allaying
it.   Hence its total failure as a harmonizing measure.

"What, then, is the positive result?   As to its practical importance in the conflict between free and slave labor, Mr. Douglas
himself enlightens us as follows : —

"'Has the South been excluded from all the territory acquired
from Mexico?   What says the bill from the House of Representatives now on your table, repealing the slave code in New Mexico
established by the people themselves?   It is part of the history
of the country that under this doctrine of non-intervention, this
doctrine that you delight to call squatter sovereignty, the people of
New Mexico have introduced and protected slavery in the whole
of that territory.   Under this doctrine they have converted a tract
of free territory into slave territory, more than five times the size
of the state of New York.   Under this doctrine slavery has been
extended from the Rio Grande to the Gulf of California, and from
the line of the Republic of Mexico, not only up to 36° 30' but up
to 38° — giving you a degree and a half more territory than you
ever claimed.   In 1848 and 1849 and 1850 you only asked to have
the line of 36° 30'.   The Nashville convention fixed that as its
ultimatum.   I offered it in the Senate in August, 1848, and it was
adopted here but rejected in the House of Representatives.   You
asked only up to 36° 30' and nonintervention has given you up
to 38°, a degree and a half more than you asked; and yet you say
that this is a sacrifice of Southern rights.

"'These are the fruits of this principle which the Senator from
Mississippi regards as hostile to the rights of the South.   Where
did you ever get any more fruits that were more palatable to your
tastes or more refreshing to your strength?   What other inch of

free territory has been converted into slave territory on the American continent since the revolution, except in New Mexico and Arizona under the principle of nonintervention affirmed at Charleston? If it is true that this principle of nonintervention has conferred upon you all that immense territory; has protected slavery in that comparatively Northern and cold region where you did not expect it to go, cannot you trust the same principle further South when you come to acquire additional territory from Mexico? If it be true that this principle of nonintervention has given to slavery all New Mexico, which was surrounded on nearly every side by free territory, will not the same principle protect you in the Northern states of Mexico, when they are acquired, since they are now surrounded by slave territory?'

"Indeed! This, then, is the practical solution of the difficulty which Mr. Douglas proposes: 'The great principle of nonintervention' which, according to his own testimony, strengthens slavery by increasing the number of slave states, and their representation and power in the general government; to which is to be added the annexation of Cuba and the Northern states of Mexico, out of which an additional number of slave states is to be carved. But his Northern friends say that he is the champion of free labor — and they are honorable men.

"Oh! what a deep-seated overweening confidence Mr. Douglas, when he made this statement, must have had in the unfathomable, desperate, incorrigible stupidity of those Northern Democrats who support him for the purpose of baffling and punishing the fire-eaters of the South. Good, innocent souls, do they not see that by supporting Mr. Douglas' policy which throws into the lap of slavery territory after territory, they will strengthen and render more overbearing the very same slave power they mean to baffle and punish? Do they not see that they were preparing a lash for their own backs? It is true, when they feel it, and they deserve to feel it, they may console themselves that it is a whip of their own manufacture.

"At last we arrive at the program of the slave power in its open and undisguised forms, of which Mr. Breckenridge is the representative and Mr. Douglas the servant, although he does not wear its livery except on occasions of state.

"This program is as follows: The agitation of the slavery question, North and South, is to be arrested; the Fugitive Slave Law, in its present form, is to be strictly carried out, and all state legislation impeding its execution, to be repealed; the constitutional right of slavery to occupy the territories of the United States and to be protected there, is to be acknowledged; all measures tending to impede the ingress of slavery, and its establishment in the territories, are to be abandoned; the opposition to the conquest and annexation of foreign countries, out of which more slave states can be formed, is to be given up; the economic policy of the planting interest, to the exclusion of the encouragement of home industry, is to become the ruling policy of the country.

"This is the Southern solution of the 'irrepressible conflict.'

"This program possesses at least the merit of logic, the logic of slavery despotism against the logic of free labor and liberty. The issue is plainly made up. Free labor is summoned to submit to the measures which slavery deems necessary for its perpetuation. We are called upon to adapt our laws and systems of policy, and the whole development of our social organization, to the necessities and interests of slavery. We are summoned to surrender. Let us for a moment judge the people of the free states by the meanest criterion we can think of; let us apply suppositions to them, which, if applied to ourselves, we would consider an insult.

"If the people of the free states were so devoid of moral sense as not to distinguish between right and wrong; so devoid of generous impulses as not to sympathize with the downtrodden and the degraded, so devoid of manly pride as to be naturally inclined to submit to everybody who is impudent enough to assume the command; tell me, even in this worst, this most disgusting of all contingencies, could free labor quietly submit to the demands of the slave power so long as it has a just appreciation of its own interests? If we did not care, neither for other people's rights nor for our own dignity, can we submit as long as we are for our own pockets? Surrender the privilege of discussing our social problems without restraint! Be narrowed down to a given circle of ideas, which we shall not transgress! Do we not owe our growth, prosperity, and power to that freedom of inquiry which is the source of all progress and improvement?

"Surrender the national domain to slavery! Do we not owe our growth and prosperity to the successful labor of our neighbors just as well as our own? Shall we consent to be surrounded and hemmed in with thriftless communities, whose institutions retard our own? Abandon all laws like the homestead bill, tending to establish free labor on our national domain! Shall we thus give up the rights of labor, and destroy the inheritance of our children?

"Give up our opposition to the extension of slavery by the conquest of foreign countries! Shall we squander the blood of our sons and the marrow of the land in destructive wars, for the profit of the enemies of free labor, while it is a peaceful development to which we owe our power in the world? Adopt the exclusive economic policy of the planting interest! Shall our mineral wealth sleep undeveloped in the soil? Shall our water powers run idle, and the bustle of our factories cease? Shall the immense laboring force in our immense population be deprived of the advantage of a harmonious development of all the branches of human labor? Shall we give up our industrial and commercial independence from the world abroad? Impossible! It cannot be thought of! Even the most debased and submissive of our dough-faces cannot submit to it as soon as the matter comes to a practical test; and therefore the success of the Southern program will never bring about a final decision of the conflict. Suppose we were beaten in the present electoral contest, would that decide the conflict of interests forever? No! Thanks to the noble instincts of human nature, our consciences would not let us sleep; thanks to the good sense of the people, their progressive interests would not suffer them to give up the struggle. The power of resistance, the elasticity of free society, cannot be exhausted by one, cannot be annihilated by a hundred defeats. Why? Because it receives new impulses, new inspirations from every day's work; it marches on in harmony with the spirit of the age.

"There is but one way of settling the 'irrepressible conflict.' It is not by resisting the spirit of the times, and by trying to neutralize its impelling power; for you attempt that in vain; but it is by neutralizing the obstacles which have thrown themselves in the path. There is no other. The 'irrepressible conflict' will rage with unabated fury until our social and political development is harmonized with the irrepressible tendency of the age.

"That is the solution which the Republicans propose. Their program is simple and consistent.

"Protection of our natural and constitutional rights. Noninterference with the social and political institutions existing by the legislation of sovereign states. Exclusion of slavery from the national territories; they must be free because they are national. (*Immense cheering.*)

"Promotion and expansion of free labor by the homestead bill and the encouragement of home industry. (*Cheering renewed.*)

"Will this effect a settlement of the conflict? Let the fathers of this republic answer the question, and I will give you the Southern construction of their policy. In a debate which occurred in the Senate of the United States, on the 23d of January, Mr. Mason of Virginia, said: 'Now, as far as concerns our ancestry, I am satisfied of this — they were not abolitionists. On the contrary, I believe this was their opinion — their prejudice was aimed against the foreign slave trade, the African slave trade, and their belief was, that cutting that off, slavery would die out of itself, without any act of abolition. I attempted at one time to show, by the recorded opinions of Mr. Madison, that the famous Ordinance of 1787, so far as it prohibited slavery in the territory northwest of the Ohio River, was aimed at the African slave trade, and at that alone; the idea being that if they would restrict the area into which slaves would be introduced from abroad, they would, to that extent, prevent the importation of slaves, and that, when it was altogether prevented, the condition of slavery would die out of itself; but they were not abolitionists, far less within the meaning and spirit of the abolitionists of the present day.'

"Well, I am willing to accept this as it stands, and Mr. Mason may certainly be considered good Southern authority. I will not stop to investigate the depth and extent of the antislavery sentiments of such men as Franklin, who was father of an abolitionist society, and of Washington, who expressed his desire 'to see slavery abolished by law'; I am satisfied with Mr. Mason's admission.

"This, then, is what the fathers intended to effect; to bring about a state of things by which slavery would die out of itself. What else do we want? 'You mean, then,' I am asked, 'to adopt a policy which will work the peaceable and gradual extinction of slavery?' And I answer, 'Yes; for if we do not, we shall have to submit to a policy which will work the gradual extinction of liberty.' There is the dilemma. Our answer is understood. If Washington, Madison, and Jefferson were abolitionists, we are; Mr. Mason says they were not; well, then, we are not, for our policy has been theirs, and theirs has become ours. (*Loud cheers.*)

"Will this policy effect a solution of the conflict? It will; because it will harmonize our social and political development with the tendency of our age, by neutralizing the obstacles that stand in its way.

"But I am told that these obstacles refuse to be neutralized. They will resist. Resist by what? By dissolving the Union! This specter has so long haunted the imaginations of superstitious people, that it is time at last to anatomize the bloodless body.

"They threaten to dissolve the Union. Why? First, because we do not stop the agitation of the slavery question. It is true, we do discuss every social problem that presents itself to our consideration; we agitate it, and we do not mean to stop. And, therefore, slaveholders, you will dissolve the Union? Do you think we shall make haste to stop the agitation, to muzzle our mouths and our press after you have dissolved it? United as we are with you at present, we certainly are not devoid of fraternal sympathy; but let the acrimonious feelings arising from a divorce embitter our relations, will not the agitation, which annoys you now, be a hundred times more dangerous to you then? (*Cheers.*)

"Second, you threaten to dissolve the Union because we do not show sufficient alacrity in the catching of fugitive slaves. True, we are not much inclined to perform for the slaveholder a menial, dirty service, which he would hardly stoop to do for himself. (*Enthusiastic cheering.*) And, therefore, you will dissolve the Union! Do you not see that, while now, indeed, a great many slaves escape, the North would, after a dissolution, scorn to surrender a single one? Would not what is now the Canada line be removed right to the banks of the Ohio?

"Third, you threaten the dissolution of the Union because we do not mean to surrender the territories to slavery. True, we mean to use every constitutional means within our reach to save them to free labor. And, therefore, you will dissolve the Union! Do you think that after a dissolution we shall courteously invite slavery to make itself comfortable on our national domain? As things are now, 'champions of free labor,' such as Douglas, may occasionally offer you a chance to acquire for slavery a territory 'five times as large as the state of New York,' but will that be possible after the Union has been dissolved? Mark well what position the North will take, if, by a revolutionary act against our national government, you should attempt to cut loose from the Union. The territories are the property of the Union as such; those who in a revolutionary way desert the Union, give up their right to the property of the Union. That property, the territories, will remain where the Union remains, and the slave power would do well first to consider how much blood it can spare, before it attempts to strip the Union of a single square foot of ground. (*Tremendous cheering.*) Thus, while according to Judge Douglas, you now have a chance to acquire slave territory by the operation of his 'great principle,' that chance will be entirely gone as soon as by a secession you give up the least shadow of a right to the property of the Union.

"Lastly, you threaten to dissolve the Union, if the North refuses to submit to the exclusive economic policy of the planting interest. You want to establish the commercial and industrial independence of the slaveholding states. For years you have held Southern conventions and passed resolutions to that effect. You resolved not to purchase any longer the products of Northern industrial labor, but to build your own factories; not to carry on your exporting and importing trade any longer by Northern ships, but to establish steamship lines and commercial connections of your own. Well, enough. Why did you not do it, after having resolved it? Was it want of money? You have an abundance of it. Was it want of determination? Your resolutions displayed the fiercest zeal. What was it, then? And, indeed, the failure is magnificently complete. Senator Mason's homespun coat, sewn with Yankee thread and needle, adorned with Yankee buttons, hangs in the closet, a lone star in solitary splendor.

(*Loud laughter*.) After trying to establish a large shoe factory for the South, you came after a while to the irresistible conclusion that you must wear Massachusetts shoes and boots or go barefooted. And even your Norfolk steamships are not launched yet from the dry-docks of Southern imagination. (*Laughter*.) How is this? I will tell you. The very same institution for the protection and perpetuation of which you want to establish your commercial and industrial independence, is incompatible with commercial and industrial labor and enterprise.

"For this there are several excellent reasons. First, that class of your society which rules and wants to perpetuate its rule, does not consist of workingmen. The inspiration of regular activity is foreign to their minds. Living upon the forced labor of others, they find their pride in being gentlemen of leisure. But it requires men of a superior organization to make leisure productive; men of the ordinary stamp, who have the leisure for doing something, will in most cases do nothing. But it requires active labor to make us understand and appreciate labor in order to be able to direct labor. Hence the slaveholders cannot take the lead in such a commercial and industrial movement without changing the nature of their condition. But you may object, that they can at least encourage commerce and industry, and leave the execution of their plans and wishes to others. Indeed! But you must not forget that in modern times the most active and enterprising class of society as soon as it becomes numerous, will inevitably become the ruling class. How can, therefore, the slaveholders do as you say, without undermining the foundation of their own ascendency! But it is just that ascendency by which they mean not to weaken, but to fortify. Do not bring forward this city of St. Louis as proof to the contrary. Your commerce and your industry are indeed largely developed, although Missouri is a slave state, but do you not see that in the same measure as they rise, the ascendency of the slave power disappears? (*Repeated cheering*.) Thus this has become a free city on slave soil.

"But this is not all. Not only are the slaveholders, as a class, unfit to direct the commercial and industrial movement, but their system of labor is unfit to carry it out. Commerce and industry, in order to become independent, need intelligent labor. In the

North, every laborer thinks, and is required to think. In the South the laborer is forbidden to think, lest he think too much, for thought engenders aspirations. (*Laughter and applause.*) With us progress and enterprise derive their main support, their strongest impulses, from the intellectual development of the laboring classes. We do not dread the aspirations from it; it is the source of our prosperity, and, at the same time, of our safety. Our laboring man must be a free man, in order to be what he ought to be, an intelligent laborer. Therefore, we educate him for liberty by our system of public instruction. In the South, the intellectual development of the laboring classes necessary for intelligent labor, would create aspirations dangerous to your domestic institutions. Your laboring man must be a brute in order to remain what you want him to be, a slave. Therefore, you withhold from him all means of intellectual development. Among our farms and workshops there stands an institution from which our system of labor derives its inspirations; that is, our schoolhouse, where our free laborers are educated. On your plantation fields there stands another institution, from which your system of labor derives its inspirations; and that is your schoolhouse, where your slaves are flogged. And you speak of establishing the commercial and industrial independence of the slaveholding states! Do you not see, that, in order to do this, you must adapt your system of labor to that purpose, by making the laborer intelligent, respectable, and at the same time aspiring? But if by making the laborer intelligent, respectable, and aspiring, you attempt to force industrial enterprise, in a large measure, upon the slave states, do you not see that your system of slave labor must yield? To foster commerce and industry in the slave states, for the purpose of protecting slavery, would it not be like letting the sunlight into a room which you want to keep dark? Hence the slave states can never become commercially and industrially independent as long as they remain slave states. They will always be obliged to buy from others, and others will do their carrying trade. At present they do their business with friends, who are united with them by the bonds of the Union. They speak of dissolving that Union; then, as now, they will be obliged to transact the same business with us, their nearest neighbors, for if they could do otherwise, they would have done so long ago. Would they prefer by the dissolution of the Union to make enemies of those upon whom they will always be commercially and industrially dependent?

"Thus, you see, the dissolution of the Union would in all points of dispute defeat the very object for which the South might feel inclined to attempt it. It would effect just the contrary of what it was intended for, and indeed, if there is a party that can logically and consistently advocate the dissolution of the Union, it is the party of extreme abolitionists who desire to extinguish slavery and punish the South by a sudden and violent crisis. But as to the slave states, as long as they have sense enough to understand their interests, and to appreciate their situation, they may thank their good fortune, if they are suffered to stay in the Union with confederates, who are, indeed, not willing to sacrifice their own principles and interests to slavery, but by the radiating influence of their own growth and energy will, at least, draw the Southern states, also, upon the road of progressive development.

"But we are told that the people of the slave states are a warlike race, and that they will gain by force what we are unwilling peacefully to concede. War! What a charm there is in that word for a people of colonels and generals! Well, since that old German monk invented that insignificant black powder, which blew the strongholds of feudalism into the air, war falls more and more under the head of the mathematical sciences. Don Quixote, who, undoubtedly, would have been a hero in the seventh century, would certainly be the most egregious fool in the nineteenth. I have nothing to say about the bravery of the Southern people, for aught I care they may be braver than they pretend to be; but I invite them candidly to open their eyes.

"I will not compare the resources of the South, in men and money, to those of the North, although statistical statements would demonstrate the overwhelming superiority of the latter. We can afford to be liberal, and for argument's sake, admit that the South will equal the North in numbers; and if they insist upon it, excel us in martial spirit. But it requires very little knowledge of military matters to understand that aside from numbers, equipment, courage, and discipline, the strength of an army consists in its ability to concentrate its forces, at all times, upon the decisive point. 'Providence is on the side of the big battalions,' said Napoleon. That means not that victory will always be with the most numerous army, but with that which is always able to appear in strength where the decisive blow is to be struck. An army that is always scattered over a large surface is, properly speaking, no army at all. Even by a much less numerous but concentrated enemy, it will be beaten in detail, division after division; it is defeated before having lost a man. This is plain.

"The South thinks of going to war for the benefit and protection of slavery. But slavery is not merely an abstract principle; slavery consists materially in the individual slaves, in so and so many millions of human chattels scattered over so and so many thousands of square miles. In order to protect slavery, it is essential that the slaveholders be protected in the possession of their slaves.

"I say, therefore, that slavery cannot expect to be protected in general without being protected in detail. But how can you protect it in detail? By guarding fifteen hundred miles of Northern frontier and two thousand miles of seacoast against an enemy who is perfectly free in his movements, and aided by an extensive railroad system always able to concentrate his forces wherever he pleases? It is impossible; the dullest understanding sees it. It may be said that it will not be necessary; indeed, for the free states it would not; they may, in order to concentrate their forces, expose their territory; for the damage done by an invasion is easily repaired. The retreating invader cannot carry the liberties of the invaded country away with him. (*Cheers.*) Not so with slavery. A Northern antislavery army, or even a small flying corps invading a slaveholding state, would perhaps not systematically liberate the slaves, but at all events it would not squander much time and health in catching the runaway. The probability, therefore, is that wherever a Northern army appears, the slaves disappear, and slavery with them — at least for the time being. Invade a free state and the restoration of liberty, after the attack is repulsed, requires only the presence of freemen. But the restoration of slavery will require capital; that capital consisted principally in slaves; the slaves have run away, and with them the capital necessary for the restoration of slavery.

"The slave states, therefore, cannot expose their territory without leaving unprotected the institution, for the protection of which the war was undertaken. They have to cover thousands and thousands of vulnerable points, for every plantation is an open wound, every negro cabin a sore. Every border or seaboard slave state will need her own soldiers, and more, too, for her own protection; and where will be the material for the concentrated army? Scattered over thousands of miles without the possibility of concentration.

"Besides, the slave states harbor a dangerous enemy within their own boundaries, and that is slavery itself. Imagine they are at war with an antislavery people, whom they have exasperated by their own hostility. What will be the effect upon the slaves? The question is not whether the North will instigate a slave rebellion, for I suppose they will not; the question is, whether they can prevent it, and I think they cannot. But the mere anticipation of a negro insurrection (and the heated imagination of the slaveholder will discover symptoms of a rebellious spirit in every trifle) will paralyze the whole South. Do you remember the effect of John Brown's attempt? The severest blow he struck at the slave power was not that he disturbed a town and killed several citizens, but that he revealed the weakness of the whole South. Let Governor Wise of Virginia carry out his threatened invasion of the free states, not with twenty-three, but with two thousand and three hundred followers at his heels; what will be the result? As long as they behave themselves we shall let them alone; but as soon as they create any disturbance they will be put into the station house; and the next day we shall read in the newspapers of some Northern city, among the reports of the police court: Henry A. Wise and others, for disorderly conduct, fined $5 (*loud laughter and applause*); or, if he has made an attempt on any man's life, or against our institutions, he will most certainly find a Northern jury proud enough to acquit him on the ground of incorrigible mental derangement. (*Continued laughter and applause.*) Our pictorial prints will have material for caricatures for two issues, and a burst of laughter will ring to the skies from Maine to California. And there is the end of it.[1] But behold

[1] See pp. 187–189 for the humorous treatment of secession by the Republicans.

John Brown with twenty-three men raising a row at Harper's Ferry; the whole South frantic with terror; the whole state of Virginia in arms; troops marching and countermarching, as if the battle of Austerlitz was to be fought over again; innocent cows shot at as bloodthirsty invaders, and even the evening song of the peaceful whippoorwills mistaken for the battle cry of rebellion; (*incessant laughter*), and those are the men who will expose themselves to the chances of a war with an antislavery people? Will they not look upon every captain as a John Brown, and every sergeant and private as a Coppoc or a Stephens? They will not have men enough to quiet their fears at home; what will they have to oppose to the enemy? Every township will want its home regiment, every plantation its garrison; and what will be left for the field army? No sooner will a movement of concentration be attempted than the merest panic will undo it and frustrate it forever. Themistocles might say that Greece was on his ships; a French general might say that the Republic was in his camp; but slavery will be neither on the ships nor in the camp; it will be spread defenseless over thousands of square miles. This will be their situation; either they concentrate their forces and slavery will be exposed everywhere; or they do not concentrate them and their strength will be nowhere. They want war? Let them try it! They will try it but once. And thus it turns out that the very same thing that would be the cause of the war, would at the same time disable them to carry on the war. The same institution that wants protection will at the same time disarm its protectors. Yes, slavery which can no longer be defended with arguments, can no longer be defended with arms.

"There is your dissolution of the Union. The Southern states cannot desire it, for it would defeat the very objects for which it might be undertaken; they cannot attempt it, for slavery would lay them helpless at the feet of the North. Slavery, which makes it uncomfortable to stay in the Union, makes it impossible for them to go out of it. What, then, will the South do in the case of a Republican victory? I answer that question with another one, what can the South do in the case of a Republican victory? Will there be a disturbance? The people of the South themselves will have to put it down. Will they submit? Not to Northern dictation, but to their own good sense. They have considered us their enemies as long as they ruled us; they will find out that we are their friends as soon as we cease to be their subjects. They have dreamed so long of the blessings of slavery; they will open their eyes again to the blessings of liberty. They will discover that they are not conquered, but liberated. Will slavery die out? As surely as freedom will not die out.

"Slaveholders of America, I appeal to you. Are you really in earnest when you speak of perpetuating slavery? Shall it never cease? Never? Stop and consider where you are and in what days you live.

This is the nineteenth century. Never since mankind has a recollection of times gone by, has the human mind disclosed such wonderful powers. The hidden forces of nature we have torn from their mysterious concealment and yoked them into the harness of usefulness; they carry our thoughts over slender wires to distant nations; they draw our wagons over the highways of trade; they pull the gigantic oars of our ships; they set in motion the iron fingers of our machinery; they will soon plow our fields and gather our crops. The labor of the brain has exalted to a mere bridling and controlling of natural forces the labor of the hand; and you think you can perpetuate a system which reduces man, however degraded, yet capable of development, to the level of a soulless machine?

"This is the world of the nineteenth century. The last remnants of feudalism in the old world are fast disappearing. The Czar of Russia, in the fulness of imperial power, is forced to yield to the irresistible march of human progress, and abolishes serfdom. Even the Sultan of Turkey can no longer maintain the barbarous customs of the Moslem against the pressure of the century, and slavery disappears. And you, citizens of a Republic, you think you can arrest the wheel of progress with your Dred Scott decisions and Democratic platforms? (*Enthusiastic cheers.*)

"Look around you and see how lonesome you are in this wide world of ours. As far as modern civilization throws its rays, what people, what class of society is there like you? Cry out into the world your wild and guilty fantasy of property in man, and every echo responds with a cry of horror or contempt; every breeze, from whatever point of the compass it may come, brings you a verdict of condemnation. There is no human heart that sympathizes with your cause, unless it sympathizes with the cause of despotism in every form. There is no human voice to cheer you on in your struggle; there is no human eye that has a tear for your reverses; no link of sympathy between the common cause of the great human brotherhood and you. You hear of emancipation in Russia and wish it would fail. You hear of Italy rising, and fear the spirit of liberty should become contagious. Where all mankind rejoices, you tremble. Where all mankind love, you hate. Where all mankind curses, you sympathize.

"And in this appalling solitude you stand alone against a powerful world, alone against a great century fighting, hopeless as the struggle of the Indians against the onward march of civilization. Use all the devices which the inventive genius of despotism may suggest, and yet how can you resist? In every little village schoolhouse, the little children who learn to read and write, are plotting against you; in every laboratory of science, in every machine shop, the human mind is working the destruction of your idol. You cannot make an attempt to keep pace with the general progress of mankind, without plotting against yourselves. Every steam whistle, every puffing locomotive is sounding the shriek of liberty into your ears. From the noblest instincts of our hearts down to sordid greediness of gain every impulse of human nature is engaged in this universal conspiracy. How can you resist? Where are your friends in the North? Your ever ready supporters are scattered to the winds as by enchantment, never to unite again. Hear them trying to save their own fortunes, swear with treacherous eagerness that they have nothing in common with you. And your opponent? Your boasts have lost their charm, your threats have lost their terrors upon them. The attempt is idle to cloak the sores of Lazarus with the lion skin of Hercules. We know you. Every one of your boasts is understood as a disguised form of weakness; every shout of defiance as a disguised cry for mercy. That game is played out. Do not deceive yourselves. This means not only the destruction of a party, this means the defeat of a cause. Be shrewder than the shrewdest, braver than the bravest; it is all in vain; your cause is doomed.

T

"And in the face of all this you insist upon hugging, with dogged stubbornness, your fatal infatuation? Why not with manly boldness, swing round into the grand march of progressive humanity? You say it cannot be done to-day. Can it be done to-morrow? Will it be easier twenty, fifty years hence, when the fearful increase of the negro population will have aggravated the evils of slavery an hundred fold, and with it the different ties of its extinction? Did you ever think of this? The final crisis will come with the inexorable certainty of fate, the more terrible, the longer it is delayed. Will you content yourself with the criminal words, 'after me the deluge'? Is that the inheritance you mean to leave to coming generations? an inheritance of disgrace, crime, blood, destruction? Hear me, slaveholders of America. If you have no sense of right, no appreciation of your own interests, I entreat, I implore you, have at least pity on your children.

"I hear the silly objection that your sense of honor forbids you to desert your cause. Imagine a future generation standing around the tombstone of the bravest of you, and reading the inscription, 'Here lies a gallant man who lived and died true to the cause — of human slavery.' What will the verdict be? His very progeny will disown him, and exclaim, 'He must have been either a knave or a fool.' There is not one of you, who if he could rise from the dead a century hence, would not gladly exchange his epitaph for that of the meanest of those who hung at Charleston.

"Sense of honor! Since when has it become dishonorable to give up the errors of yesterday for the truths of to-day? to prevent future disasters by timely reforms? Since when has it ceased to be the highest glory to sacrifice one's prejudices and momentary advantages upon the altar of the common weal? But those who seek their glory in stubbornly resisting what is glorious, must find their end in inglorious misery.

"I turn to you, Republicans of Missouri! Your countrymen owe you a debt of admiration and gratitude to which my poor voice can give but a feeble expression. You have undertaken the noble task of showing the people of the North that the slaveholding states themselves contain the elements of regeneration; and of demonstrating to the South how that regeneration can be effected. You have inspired the wavering masses with confidence in the practicability of your ideas. To the North you have given encouragement; to the South you have set an example. Let me entreat you not to underrate your noble vocation. Struggle on, brave men! The anxious wishes of millions are hovering around you. Struggle on until the banner of emancipation is planted upon the capitol of your state, and one of the proudest chapters of our history will read — Missouri led the van and the nation followed!"

APPENDIX C

DOUGLAS DEMOCRATIC SPEECH BY STEPHEN A. DOUGLAS, RALEIGH, NORTH CAROLINA, AUGUST 30, 1860 [1]

"MR. PRESIDENT, I am conscious that you have, in the enthusiasm produced by the circumstances with which you are surrounded to-day, done me more than justice in your presentation to this audience. I thank you, sir, sincerely for the kind terms in which you have been pleased to speak of me. It is a matter of pride and pleasure to be presented to the people of the Old North State, by a representative of Mecklenburg. (*Cheers.*) History will always preserve the fact that in North Carolina the first Declaration of Independence was declared to the world, and that Mecklenburg has the honor of being the county where that glorious deed was done. Carolinians have a right to be proud of that great event in her history, but while you pride yourselves upon it, you must remember, that the sacred obligation rests upon you and your children to maintain inviolate the principles which the Declaration was intended to perpetuate.

"What was the grievance of which North Carolina complained, when she proclaimed to the world her separation from the British Crown? what the grievance of which all the colonies complained? and what were the objects they intended to accomplish by that Declaration? Independence was not their motive. They did not desire separation from England. On the contrary the first Continental Congress that assembled, and each succeeding one, until the Declaration was put forth, adopted an address to the Crown, and to the people, and to the Parliament of England, affirming their devotion to the British people, their devotion to

[1] *The Newbern Daily Progress*, Newbern, North Carolina, September 5, 1860.

the British constitution, and their loyalty to the Crown of England. They did not desire separation from the mother country. They demanded a redress of grievances under the British constitution, and while they remained a part of the British Empire. What were these grievances? You will find them in the Bill of Rights, put forth by the first Continental Congress, which assembled in 1774.

"In that bill of rights the colonies proclaimed to the world their desire to remain a part of the British Empire; they acknowledged the right of Great Britain in Parliament to make all laws which affected the general welfare of the Empire, without interfering with the local and internal concerns of the colonies; they acknowledged the right of the British government to regulate foreign affairs, to make war and peace, to regulate commerce, and to do those things that affected the general welfare of the Empire of Britain; but they declared in that Bill of Rights that the colonies possessed the sole and exclusive power of legislating in their colonial legislatures over their domestic policy. That was the point on which they were prepared to sacrifice life if necessary, the right of self-government in each colony so far as affected their local and domestic concerns; Great Britain refused to recognize that right, and before our fathers would surrender it, they determined that they would resort to force and even carry force to the point of separation from, and an entire independence of Great Britain.

"It is important to bear this fact in mind, in order to determine precisely the principles on which our government is founded. The British Parliament denied the right of the colonies to regulate their internal affairs, because they said that those colonies possessed no other rights than those that the Prince of England had granted to them in their charters. Washington, Jefferson, and Hancock, and the heroes of that day told the king that they did not get their rights from the Crown, and they denied the power of the king or of Parliament to take those rights away. The colonies claimed that the right of local self-government was inherent in the people, derived from the Ruler of the Universe, the only power and jurisdiction of kings and Parliaments. Upon this point the Revolution turned. This right of local self-government as being inherent in the people was affirmed by the American Revolution.

The Constitution, under which we live, was made for the purpose of confirming and perpetuating the liberties achieved by the Revolution.   The question now arises whether we will maintain at this day those principles for which our fathers fought and which were secured to us by the sacrifices of the Revolution.

"The abolitionist party at the North, some years ago, attempted to violate this great principle of self-government in the territories of the United States by the application of the Wilmot Proviso. They introduced into Congress a law for the purpose of prohibiting slavery everywhere in the territories of the United States, whether the people wanted it or not.   The whole South, with a large portion of the Northern Democracy, resisted the Wilmot Proviso as a violation of the right of self-government, at the same time that it was a usurpation of power by the Federal government.   In the discussion which took place, we who opposed the Wilmot Proviso appealed to the Revolutionary struggle as furnishing the grounds on which we ought to resist the interference by Congress with the domestic affairs of the people of the territories.   We reminded the people then that the first serious point of controversy which ever arose between the American colonies and the British government was upon the slavery question.

"For more than seventy years previous to the Declaration of Independence the colony of Virginia asserted her right to control the question of slavery through her colonial legislature.   During the early portion of that period the Virginians passed laws to encourage the introduction of slaves and protect slavery in the colonies, but after a while they found the number of slaves increasing in a greater ratio than the white people, and being surrounded by large bands of hostile Indians, they became alarmed lest the savage Africans just introduced should unite with the savage Indians surrounding the settlement, and exterminate the whites.   In order to prevent a calamity so fearful, the colony of Virginia passed laws adverse to the further introduction of slaves into that colony.   The British merchants engaged in the African slave trade then appealed to the king to annul the legislation of these few adventurers in the colony of Virginia.   They set forth that they had a right as British subjects to move from England, and carry with them their slaves as well as all other property, and hold them in the colonies without reference to the legislation of the colonial legislatures. The king in council sustained that claim, annulled the local legislation of Virginia, and instructed its governor not to allow any more laws to be passed in the colony adverse to the slave trade; but as late as 1772, only four years before the Declaration of Independence, the legislature of Virginia adopted a memorial to his Majesty, telling him that unless he granted to the colony of Virginia the right to control this question according to the interest of their own people, he would lose his dominions in America.

"Thus we find that the controversy on the slave question in the territories began seventy years before the Revolutionary War, reached down to the beginning of the war itself, and led into the very contest that produced the final separation. Each of the other colonies passed laws also regulating the question of slavery. You did it in North Carolina. Some of your laws protected it, some encouraged it, and others discouraged it, just as you believed, or rather your ancestors, that the interests of this colony required at the time. So it was with each of the New England colonies. Some protected it, some invited it, others excluded it altogether, and others regulated it with a tendency rather against its encouragement; but the principle involved in that whole contest was the exclusive right of the people in each colony in their colonial legislature to regulate all their domestic affairs to suit themselves, without the interference of the British government. I presume that no person present will controvert the correctness of ·this historical proposition.

"I have resisted the Wilmot Proviso from the time of its first introduction in Congress down to the present day, upon the ground that it violated the principles upon which our fathers fought the Revolutionary War. (*Applause.*) If British subjects in the colonies before the Revolutionary War were entitled to the inherent right of self-government over their domestic affairs, I cannot see why the same right should not be guaranteed to the people of our territories since the Revolution. (*Applause.*) I have never claimed for the people of the territories any other right, or higher right, than our fathers maintained at the point of the bayonet for the colonies prior to the Revolution. (*Ap-*

plause.)   If an American citizen of North Carolina moving to a territory of the United States, is not entitled to as many rights of self-government there as a British subject before the Revolution, let me ask, what did you gain by the sacrifices of the Revolution? (*Applause.*)

"Who are the people of the territories that they are not capable of self-government?   You do not doubt that you people of North Carolina are entirely competent to make laws for your own government.   You do not doubt but that the right of self-government is an inherent right in North Carolina.   If it be an inherent right in this state, let me ask you, when you emigrate to Kansas, at what point of time do you lose that right?   Do you lose all the sense, all the intelligence, all the virtue you had on the wayside, while emigrating to a territory of the United States?   No man doubts your capability while you stay at home to decide for yourselves what kind of laws you will have in respect to negroes, as well as to white men.   Are you any less capable after you have left your native land and gone to a territory?

"Is there anything in the character of the men who emigrate from their native valleys to the plains and prairies of the West that renders them less fit for self-government than those who remain where they were born?   Those of us who in early life left the old states, who penetrated into the wilderness, secured our homes, made our own farms, erected schoolhouses and churches, made our fences and split our own rails (*laughter*), think that we know what kind of laws and institutions will suit our interests quite as well as you who never saw the country.   (*Applause.*) We have quite as much interest in the laws under which we are to live as you have, who never expect to go to that country, and therefore have no concern about our laws.   These are the opinions of a Northwestern man, a man who has spent his whole life on the frontier.   You cannot convince us that we are not as good as our brothers who remain in the old states.   I know there is something in the human mind that leads every one to suppose that his own birthplace is the very center of civilization, and that there is nothing good beyond the range of his infant vision.   When I was a child I thought that the mountains that surrounded the valley in which I was born were the confines of civilization; and my vision was limited by them; and I fancied that beyond their boundaries there was nothing but border ruffians and outside barbarians. When, however, I crossed them and went into the next valley, I found there were just as good people there as I had left behind me, and so with the next and every step I took, from the East toward the setting sun, I unloosened and shook off unjust prejudice.

"Ignorance has fixed around other people prejudices similar to those I then had. We in the Northwest have much more respect for you than you for us. We love you better than you do us. We love this Union better than you do, in consequence of the circumstances that surround us. You go into one of our settlements, in Kansas, Nebraska, Illinois, or any of them, and there you will find that a North Carolinian has settled down by the side of a Connecticut farmer, with a Virginian next to him, a New Yorker, a South Carolinian and representatives from every state around him, the whole Union being represented on the prairies by the farmers who have settled on it. In the course of time the young people of this society begin to visit, and in a little while the North Carolinian boy sees a Yankee girl he likes, and his prejudices against her people begin to soften. (*Laughter.*) In a few years the North Carolina and the Connecticut people are united, the Virginian and the Pennsylvanian, the Yankee and the slaveholder, are united by the ties of marriage, blood, friendship, and social intercourse; and when their children grow up, the child of the same parents has a grandfather in North Carolina and another in Vermont; and that child does not like to have either of those states abused. That child has a reverence for the graves of his grandfather and his grandmother in the good old North state and he has the same reverence for the graves of his grandfather and his grandmother in the valleys of Vermont; and he will never consent that this Union shall be dissolved so that he will be compelled to obtain a passport and get it viséed to enter a foreign land to visit the graves of his ancestors. You cannot sever this Union unless you cut the heartstrings that bind father to son, daughter to mother, and brother to sister in all our new states and territories. (*Cheers.*)

"Besides the ties of blood and affection that bind us to each of the states, we have commercial intercourse and pecuniary interests that we are not willing to surrender. Do you think that a citizen of Illinois will ever consent to pay duties at the Custom House when he ships his commerce down the Mississippi to supply the people below? Never on earth. We shall say to the custom-house gatekeepers of the Mississippi River that we furnish the water that makes that great river, and we will follow it throughout its whole course to the ocean, no matter who or what may stand before us. (*"Good."*) So with the East; we are bound to the people of the East by the same ties of blood and kindred, and you cannot sever this Union without blasting every hope and prospect that a Western man has on this earth.

"Then, having so deep a stake in the Union, we are determined to maintain it, and we know but one mode by which it can be maintained; that is, to enforce rigidly and in faith every clause, every line, every syllable of the Constitution as our fathers made it and bequeathed it to us. (*Cheers.*) We do not stop to inquire whether you here in Raleigh or the Abolitionists in Maine like every provision of that Constitution or not. It is enough for me that our fathers made it. Every man that holds office under the Constitution is sworn to protect it. Our children are brought up and educated under it, and they are early impressed by the injunction that they shall at all times yield a ready obedience to it. I am in favor of executing in good faith every clause and provision of the Constitution (*loud cheers*) and of protecting every right under it (*cheers*) and then hanging every man who takes up arms against it. (*Cheers.*) Yes, my friends, I would hang every man higher than Haman who would attempt by force to resist the execution of any provision of the Constitution which our fathers made and bequeathed to us. (*Loud cheers and cries, "That is Southern enough for us," etc.*) A gentleman behind me says that that sentiment is Southern enough for him and for you. I do not go for the Constitution because it is Southern or Northern, nor because it is Eastern or Western, but I go for it because my allegiance to the Constitution, my oath and my duty, my love for my children, and my hope of salvation in the future, makes it my sacred and bounden duty to vote for it and maintain it. (*Cheers and cries of "Hurrah for Douglas."*)

"I claim no rights for my state that I will not concede to you and defend for you and the whole South (*cheers*) ; I will accept no privileges for Illinois that I will not permit to North Carolina, and I claim no right in the territories for my citizens or for my property that I will not guarantee for every other state in the Union. I believe in the absolute and unconditional equality of all the states of the Confederacy. (*Applause.*) But I claim that I have the right to go to the territories and carry my property with me and hold it there and to have it protected on the same terms that you have in the slave holding states. ("*Good.*") But upon what terms, I ask, can I carry my property into the territories?

" I carry it there subject to the local law. If I am a dealer in cattle, in horses, in sheep, in stock of any kind, I carry my property subject to the local law. If I am a dealer in dry goods, I go to the territories subject to the local law. If I find the local tax heavier on the peddlers than on the local merchants, I must either pay the tax or quit peddling. ("*Good.*") If I am a dealer in groceries or liquors, I must carry my liquors there subject to the local law, and I had better inquire what that local law is before I start, and if on inquiry I ascertain that the Maine liquor law is in force there, I think that I had better carry my liquors somewhere else and seek a better market for it. (*Cheers.*) The Northern man goes into the territories with his property subject to the local laws of the territory as the people may have made those laws through their local legislatures. Are you not willing to go upon the same terms? (*Cries, "We are as willing," "We never asked more."*) Do you claim more than is granted to us? ("*No*") You may go there also and carry your slaves with you subject to the local laws, in the same way that I can carry my goods. Equality of rights is the principle, and obedience to the local law is the only condition on which any man can go into the territories of the United States with safety.

"I know that there is a class of politicians who are in the habit of telling you that Congress will not grant you protection for your slave property in the territories, and Congress will not. When did Congress ever pass a law to protect any particular kind of property in the territories? Congress never yet passed a criminal code for an organized territory on the American continent.

Murder is a crime in the territories, not under any act of Congress, but under the territorial law. Horse-stealing is a crime not by an act of Congress, but by the territorial law. And so with every crime against the person or the property of a citizen, no matter where. You are told that this is squatter sovereignty. Just such squatter sovereignty was established in North Carolina by the men who put forth the Declaration of Independence, and drove the agents of George III from the continent. It is the simple right of every people to make their own laws, and establish their own constitutions according to their own interests, without any interference of any person outside their own borders. That is all it is.

"Is not that a sound principle? Why, there are two classes of politicians who tell you that it is very unsound. Who are they? First, the Northern abolitionists and the Black Republicans think it very unsound. They assert that it is the duty of Congress to prohibit slavery wherever the people want it. That is the doctrine of the Abolitionists. They are in favor of Congress prohibiting it wherever it is necessary, and they say that wherever it is not necessary, the people do not want it, and that the people will exclude it themselves. Here it is only necessary to say they are for Congress to prohibit and exclude slavery wherever the people do want it. There is another class of politicians who are in favor of Congress interfering in favor of slavery wherever necessary. They are not interventionists, however, except when necessary. When do they hold that intervention is necessary? Why, it is clear that it is unnecessary to interfere to protect slavery where the people are in favor of it, for in that case they will pass laws to protect it themselves. For instance, New Mexico was in favor of slavery, and hence the people, two years ago, passed a law in their local legislature establishing a very efficient slave code, protecting slavery in the territory. Hence it is not necessary in the estimation of the Southern Secessionists to protect it there, for the people wanting it will have it and protect themselves. It is only necessary for Congress to interfere, they say, and protect slavery where the people do not want it, and therefore will not protect it themselves. Thus you find that in this country there are two parties in favor of Federal intervention. The Black Republicans of the North and the Secessionists and Disunionists of the South agree in respect to the power and duty of Congress to control the slavery question in the territories. They agree that Congress may control it and that the people of the territory ought not to be allowed to do so. Agreeing thus far, they differ on this point, as to what way Congress ought to control it. While the Northern fanatics say that Congress ought to control the question as against the South, the Southern Secessionists say that it must be controlled as against the North. Each party appeals to the passions, prejudices, the ambitions of his own section, against the peace and harmony of the whole country.

"Now, suppose you acquiesced in the demands of this Southern Secessionist party and allowed them to rally all the people of all the Southern states under a Southern intervention banner, and suppose we Democrats of the North would be craven-spirited enough to yield to the demands of a dominant majority in our own section, and join the cry of Northern intervention against slavery, and rally every Northern man under that banner. Then you have two sections of this Union separated, with a broad line between them, every Southern man on one side, and every Northern man on the other, both abusing each other. Now, what is your Union worth after that is accomplished? Remember that the Union cannot survive the affections of the people on whom it rests. Whenever you have alienated Northern and Southern men, whenever you have separated them so far that they cannot belong to the same political party, and the same church, and cannot commune in the House of God at the same communion table, your Union is very nearly dissolved. This sectionalism has reached this point. It has reached the House of God and separated the members of the same church. That good old church in which I was born and reared, the old church in which my father and my mother, my grandfather and my grandmother and my ancestors for many generations were in the habit of communing, separated into a church North and South, and when we travel from one side of the line to the other, we are not permitted to go to the same table. And what has produced this estrangement? It is the agitation of the slavery question in the Halls of Congress. What good has been accomplished for anybody by the agitation? What benefit has been conferred on the white man? what benefit has been conferred on the black man by this agitation? It has alienated friend from friend; you have rallied section against section by it; you have spread mischief and dissensions and heartburnings, without any redeeming or corresponding advantage. What is the remedy for this state of things? I answer, the remedy is to banish the slavery question from the Halls of Congress; remand it to the people of the territories and of the states.

" Let the people make just such laws as they choose, so that they do not violate the Constitution of the country. If they should pass a law in violation of the Constitution, the Supreme Court is the only tribunal on earth that can ascertain and decide that fact. (*Applause.*) If you go to a territory, and when you get there you do not like their laws, and you think that a particular statute is unconstitutional, all you have to do is to make out a case under the law so as to have the question tried in the territorial courts, appeal to the Supreme Court of the United States, and there get your case decided, and if that court decides that the law is unconstitutional, there is an end of it — it cannot be enforced. On the contrary, if it be decided that the statute complained of is constitutional, it must stand till the people of the territory get tired of it, and have sense enough to change it. If the people of the territory make bad laws, let them suffer under them till they are wise enough to make good ones. If they make good laws, let them enjoy all the advantages of their good laws. Let us act upon this principle, and there will be peace between the North and the South.

"I affirm to you that the Democratic party is pledged by its honor, its organization, its platform, and its principles, to this doctrine of the nonintervention of Congress with slavery in the territories. (*Applause.*) What man will be bold enough to deny that every Democrat in America up to the present hour was pledged to the doctrine of nonintervention? Read the platform of the party that nominated Cass in 1848, Pierce in 1852, and Buchanan in 1856. There you find the doctrine of the nonintervention of Congress with slavery in the territories of the United States. Is not this so? What, then, has produced this sudden change? Nonintervention was a good doctrine four years ago, intervention is necessary now. Four years ago there was no intervention with the slavery question in America, except among the Black Republicans of the North. I appeal to you, my fellow-citizens of North Carolina, without distinction of party to tell me whether every Democratic speaker in the state did not tell you that your rights, your honor, your equality in the Union, depended upon maintaining the doctrine of nonintervention by Congress with the question of slavery as affirmed by the Democratic platform? Now they tell you, that this doctrine which they taught you to believe, and making you to believe, to carry the state by a large majority for Buchanan, they now tell you that this doctrine, taught and preached four years ago, is little better than Black Republicanism. I stand to-day where I stood when the Secessionists eulogized me as the best friend that the South ever had. (*Cries of "That's so."*)

"I defy them to show where I have changed a hair's breadth, and when I have heretofore defied them face to face to show it, the only answer they could make was, that I was constant and would not change. (*Laughter and applause.*) No. I would not change merely because presidents and caucuses, backed by extensive patronage, said I must. (*Cries of "Good," "That's right."*) It is as much my right and duty to think for myself as it is for the President to do it for himself. (*Cries of "Right."*) I do not recognize the right of the Executive Department to interfere with the action or speech of any member of the Senate of the House of Representatives. (*Applause.*) So long as the President chooses to confine himself to the performance of his duties in obedience to the Constitution, I will sustain him to the utmost in the right to free and independent action. But whenever the President is permitted to say to the Senator or Representative of a sovereign state, 'Abandon your convictions, betray your constituents, do as I say, or I will remove you from office and behead every friend you have in office throughout the land'; whenever it is permitted to him to do that with impunity, then the Republic is but a sham and a mockery. (*Applause.*) There is no freedom, there can be no liberty, when the representative of the people is not responsible to his constituents instead of to the Executive power. (*"It is despotism."*) Yes, the worst of all despotisms is when the Executive can say to a man, 'Violate your conscience, betray your constituents, and follow me, or I will remove from office every friend you have got, and defeat you at home through the Executive power.' I speak with some feeling on this subject. (*Applause.*)

"I have had some experience. I have been under the necessity in my lifetime of fighting Abolitionists and Black Republicans, aided and supported by a Democratic administration with all its patronage and power. For three years every Federal officeholder in Illinois has been required to oppose the Democratic and support the Republican ticket, as a condition to holding office, and even yet in the Northern states, and from one end of the land to the other, every officeholder is removed unless he works against the regular organization of the Democratic party. You are told now that there is a danger of Mr. Lincoln being elected President and that his election would be such a calamity that it would become your duty to dissolve the Union rather than submit to his domination. What hope of an election has Mr. Lincoln? None on earth, except through the assistance of the seceders at Baltimore. (*Cheers.*) After I was nominated there according to the usages of the party by two-thirds of all the votes cast, there being present two-thirds of the electoral college not objecting, these men bolted and got up a new convention. Now, let me ask you, is there a man in America who doubts that I would have beaten Lincoln, if the Breckenridge men had acquiesced in my nomination? (*Applause.*) Nobody doubts that Lincoln could never have carried but two states in the Union, Vermont and Massachusetts, but for that secession. What was their object in bolting? Was it not to beat me? (*Cries of "Yes."*) If it was, did they not know that the only way to do it was to divide the Democratic party in the North and the South and allow Lincoln to carry each one of these states by a minority vote? The secession took place for the purpose of defeating me, and by the division of the party electing Lincoln. There was not a man engaged in the scheme who did not expect that his act was to elect Lincoln. There could be no other expectation, no other motive, no other hope, and I never have seen a man yet who would risk his reputation by denying that Lincoln would have been beaten but for this division, and that the danger of his election grows out of it. Then how do they justify their course? Why, they say that it is better to have Lincoln elected than Douglas. Why? Why, they do not like Douglas. They do not like his platform. Why do they not like the platform? Because I stand now on the very platform on which they stood four years ago. And what confidence can you have in the integrity, in the truthfulness, in the honor of a man who will abuse the Charleston platform now, after he supported it four years ago? Were they cheating you then? Were they cheating you at that time to get your votes? If they were, how much confidence should you place in them now? (*Cheers.*) If they were honest then, it does not become them to abuse those of us who do not change quite as rapidly as they have done. (*Applause.*)

"I stand now where I stood then. I stand now where I stood when I brought forward the bill to repeal the Missouri restriction and organize the territories of Kansas and Nebraska. They cannot and do not pretend that I have changed. But they have started a story I learn since I got down here, that I went home and explained the Nebraska bill in a different way from what I had South, and said that it was the best abolition bill ever got up to prohibit slavery everywhere. I have tried to find out where I ever made such a speech, but those who made the charge do not name the place. I now say that no honest man will ever make the charge. (*Cheers.*) It is an invention of the enemy, and has been circulated by the mean author who knew it to be false or had no reason for believing it to be true. (*Applause.*)

"I will tell you what explanation I have made in every Northern state of my motive for passing the Nebraska bill, and repealing the Missouri Compromise. I have sustained that act, by the argument that if slavery was right South, it was right North, and if it was right to leave the people to do as they pleased South of the Missouri Compromise line, it was right North of the line. The object was to allow the people to do just as they pleased both sides of 36° 30.' I assert that if the people of a territory want slavery, they have a right to have it, and if they do not want it, no power on earth should force it upon them. I go farther and say that whether the people will want it or not, depends solely

U

upon the climate, the soil, the productions, and self-interest of the people where it exists. In the hot climate where the people cannot work in the open sun, where rice, the cotton plant, and sugarcane flourish, you must have negro slaves to work there or you must abandon the country to the crocodile. In a cold climate where you have almost perpetual snow, and where the negro could not produce by his labor half as much as would feed and clothe him and furnish him wood enough to bake his hoe cake at night, you cannot force slavery to exist, because it will not pay for itself. Slavery, therefore, does not depend on the law. It is governed by climate, soil, and productions, by political economy, and you might as well attempt to pass laws by Congress compelling cotton to grow on the summit of the Rocky Mountains or rice to flourish on the granite hills of New Hampshire (*laughter and applause*) as slavery to exist where it cannot possibly exist. (*Applause.*) I tell you that wherever climate renders slavery necessary, there it will go, and furthermore, the people of a territory will be the first to introduce it and pass all laws for its protection, but wherever climate renders it unprofitable and no money can be made out of it, there you cannot force it to go. I care not how many laws you have, or how many armies to enforce these laws. Hence I said in my Freeport speech that no matter how the court might decide the abstract question, that practically slavery would not go where the people do not want it, for it would not be practicable. That is what I said and that is all I said and that has been tortured into a declaration that I would not obey the decision of the Supreme Court of the United States. I like to be charitable, but I have not sufficient charity to believe that he, let him be who he may, who has represented me as saying I would not obey the Dred Scott decision, or any other decision of the Supreme Court, did not know that he was perverting and misrepresenting my whole idea.[1] (*Applause.*)

"I have made more speeches than any living man in defense of the Dred Scott decision as pronounced by the court, and I am as ready as any man to enforce the decrees of the court and to put the halter around the neck of all men who wish to resist the constituted authorities of the land. (*Applause, and "Hurrah for Doug-*

[1] For Douglas' words at Freeport, see pp. 97–98.

las.") I do not desire to be misunderstood on these questions. I am being hunted down by a body of men who four years ago endorsed me, every man of them, knowing that I held the same opinions then that I do now. There is not a living man with intelligence enough to venture away from home alone who does not know that I have held these sentiments for years. (*"Good," laughter and applause.*) I have come down here now to meet you face to face and to utter these opinions just as I uttered them in the Northern states; and in order to prevent them from misrepresenting me any more I have invited a friend of mine to take down every word and syllable as it falls from my lips and without any revision or my seeing it to hand it over to your papers here, if they will publish it, in order that the people of the North and the South may see whether I do not explain my doctrines in the South precisely as I have explained them in the North."

A voice. "We have no organ here but one."

Douglas. "It is stated that my friends have no organ here but one.

"I do not care how often I may make speeches in the Senate correcting the misapprehensions, they are never published here. Why? Certain gentlemen have made charges to the contrary and it would convict them if it acquitted me. I hold no opinions of these public questions that I wish to conceal anywhere, for I hold that so long as we live under a constitution, which is common to all the states of the Union, any political creed is radically wrong that cannot be avowed alike in all the states of the Union.

"Why cannot you of the South and of the North live in peace together under this Constitution, as our fathers made it? The only reason is that there is an attempt to create uniformity through the action of the Federal government in the local and domestic institutions of the states. Mr. Abraham Lincoln, now the Black Republican candidate for the presidency, when some two years ago a candidate for the United States Senate against me, commenced his opening speech with this proposition. I will try to give his precise language or as near as I can from recollection, and I believe I have quoted the passage a thousand times. He said that 'a house divided against itself cannot stand, this government divided into free and slave states cannot permanently endure, that either slavery must be extended to all the states, or it must be placed in the course of ultimate extinction in all the states; they must become all free or all slave.'

"Now that was his proposition. I replied to that speech the moment I got home. I took bold issue with him and made the canvass of Illinois on that proposition and one other. The other was, he assailed the Supreme Court decision in the Dred Scott case, and I defended it. These were the two issues upon which we fought that battle. Mr. Seward made his celebrated Rochester speech four months afterwards, in which he put forth his doctrine of the irrepressible conflict, borrowing it from Lincoln, who was the author and the enunciator of that principle, that the Union cannot exist divided into free and slave states, but must become all free or all slave. The Black Republican party is based upon the principle of making them all free states; the Secession party is based on the theory that the territories and consequently the states must be all slave, whether the people want them so or not. I hold to the doctrine that uniformity in domestic institutions of the different states is neither possible nor desirable. Slavery must be good in one place and bad in another; it may be necessary in one state and unnecessary in another. And so with every other domestic institution. Our fathers knew when they made this government that in a country as broad as this, with such a variety of soil, of climate, and of productions, there must necessarily be a corresponding variety of interests, requiring separate and different laws in each locality. They knew that the laws which would suit the granite hills of New Hampshire would be unsuited to the rice and tobacco plantations of the Carolinas. They knew that the regulations necessary in a mining district like California would be unsuited to the wheat and corn fields of Illinois. Hence they provided that each state should retain its own sovereignty, in order that each might have just such laws as it chose. This right, therefore, of each state to have different laws from every other one, lies at the very foundation of our government. Uniformity, regardless of the wants and the conditions of the people, is the worst possible despotism you can inflict on any people.

"Well, the Abolitionists of the North and the Secessionists of the South admit that this doctrine of the right of each state to regulate and decide for itself is a good doctrine in the states, but will not do in the territories. They admit that in the states you have an inherent right to govern yourselves, but lose it when you go to the territories. Why not allow a territory to do it as well as a state? Why, they tell you that a territory is not a sovereign power, and therefore cannot do it; that none but sovereign powers have a right of self-government. Our fathers of the Revolution did not think so. The Revolutionary struggle began in the defense of the right of the dependent colonies, dependent territories, dependent provinces, to exercise this right of self-government as well as sovereign states. None of the Tories of the Revolution ever contended before that the right of self-government was to be restricted to sovereign states. George III and Lord North, his minister, and his Tory friends, on the continent, all denied the right of the people of these colonies to regulate their own domestic affairs. They all said that the people of the colonies had no rights except those the king granted them in the charters. The same old doctrine. Our fathers of the Revolution told the king that they did not get their rights from the king, but they got them from God Almighty. And the people of the territories will be likely to tell you that they do not get their rights from Congress, they get them from a purer source. (*Laughter.*) From what I have said you will see that unless I am right in maintaining this principle of self-government for the people of the territories, our fathers in the Revolution must have been wrong in that struggle. There is no other argument used against squatter sovereignty, as they term it, that they have not copied from the Tories of the Revolution, in almost its identical language. (*Applause.*) But of course these gentlemen are very sincere in denouncing this doctrine of the noninterference of Congress. I wish they had been frank enough to denounce it before they had joined me in helping to sustain it. They knew when they adopted the Cincinnati platform that this was the doctrine. Read the platform. It declares in so many words, no interference by Congress with slavery in the states and territories.

"At Charleston every friend I had from the Northwest offered to take the Cincinnati platform, word for word, as it read. They said it was not good Democracy. How came that platform to be adopted in 1856, if it was not sound? You know it was adopted at the suggestion of the Alabama legislature, on four propositions drawn by Mr. Yancey, and when introduced into the Cincinnati convention received the vote of every delegate from every state in the Union, free and slave. They proposed it and we of the North said it was fair and just, and we took it. It was adopted by a unanimous vote, and four years after you are told that a man is a traitor to the South who stands by the pledge we all made at Cincinnati. There is something strange about this. I cannot change as rapidly as that. (*Applause.*)

"If the Democratic party would stand now where they did then, there would be no trouble. In order to get out of the scrape, these men have turned round and charged me with having said I would not stand by the Dred Scott decision. I tell them now that any man who makes that charge hereafter will know that he is falsifying the truth. Then where is the cause of the trouble in the Democratic party? It is an attempt to introduce a new article of faith into the Democratic creed, in direct violation of the former creed of the party. It is an attempt again to introduce this slavery question into the Halls of Congress, and have Congress decide it. So long as that question remains in Congress, there will never be peace; and if we expect to live together, we must agree to banish this whole subject from Congress, remand it to the people interested in it, and let the Supreme Court explain the Constitution in reference to each case as it arises; then we will have peace."

A gentleman. "There is in the minds of a large portion of the people of the Southern states an apprehension that the purpose of a certain class of extinct politicians of the South, is to provoke a division of the Democratic party upon this question of the platform for the purpose of electing Lincoln, and thereby without any overt act on his part, effect a dissolution of the Union. I desire to ask Judge Douglas respectfully to give to the audience all the evidence he has in reference to the purposes of these parties, and as we have heard that he was called out at Norfolk, by an elector on the seceders' ticket, to give his opinions as to his course as a Senator in the event of such dissolution, we desire him to repeat it here, as we intend to ask Mr. Breckenridge what his course would be also, being a Senator of the United States after the 4th of March, 1861." [1]

Mr. Douglas. "Upon the point presented in the first suggestion : I have no evidence in respect to the designs and purposes of the seceders, which I am at liberty to use, except that which is known to the whole world. I know that Lincoln has no shadow of a chance of being elected, unless the Breckenridge men succeed in dividing the Democratic party, and thereby electing him through a minority vote. (*Cries of " That's so."*) Supposing that I should decline to-day, no man believes that Breckenridge could be elected. Supposing on the other hand, that Breckenridge declines to-day, no man doubts but I would be elected. Why, then, is he keeping the track, unless it is that Lincoln may be elected ? Then the first time I place my foot on Virginia soil in this canvass, I am asked by the head man on the electoral ticket, the man who leads the ticket, whether in the event of Lincoln being elected, the Southern states would be justified in a dissolution of the Union ; and whether I would go in for enforcing the law in the event of the Southern states seceding ? A good many present at the time said that I ought not to answer the question, because the gentleman was opposed to me, and that under the circumstances it was discourteous for him to propound such a question. I told them I was ready to answer it. I told them that in my opinion, the election of any man according to the forms and provisions of the Constitution, is no excuse for dissolving this glorious Union. (*Applause.*) I would regard the election of Lincoln as a great calamity, to be avoided by all honorable means by patriotic men, North and South. But I will not consent that the mere act of the election of an unworthy man, or a worthy one either, by the people, according to the forms of the Constitution, is any excuse or justification for breaking up this Union of states. (*Applause.*) On the other hand, I said then what I say to you now, that I am in favor of the enforcement of the law, under all circumstances and in every contingency. (*Applause.*) If Lincoln should be elected President for the United States, or Breckenridge, and any man, after such election, should attempt to violate the Constitution of the country, or infringe on any law or right under it, I would hang him higher

[1] For the Norfolk questions, see pp. 180–181.

than Haman, according to law. (*Great applause.*) I would have no more hesitation in hanging such a man than Virginia felt on hanging John Brown when he invaded her dominion. (*Applause.*) I do not think it would do the country any harm to try an experiment of the kind. (*Laughter.*) We have already demonstrated to the world that we are the greatest nation in the world in many respects; we grow faster than any other people, we spread wider and more rapidly, and we annexed all countries adjoining to us with greater speed than can be done by any other people; besides we can whip all we come in contact with. We are become a model for the friends of liberty throughout the world, and we are the admiration of all who love free institutions, while we are the terror of all tyrants. (*Applause.*) We have demonstrated our great national wealth, our military power and progress. We have proved our commercial power and productive capacity; but there is one thing remaining to be done to prove us capable of meeting any emergency, whenever any emergency arises. I trust that the government will show that it is strong enough to execute that final act, that is, to hang all traitors before it thinks of dissolving this glorious Union. (*Applause.*) If a bad man, or a dangerous man, or a fanatic should be made President of the United States, sustain the government, preserve the Union, stand by the enforcement of the laws, see that they are submitted to and obeyed; and hang the man who refuses. (*Applause.*)

"It will not do for these gentlemen to get up a program, if not designedly, yet knowingly leading inevitably to the election of Lincoln, and then to come and ask me to help them dissolve the Union because they elected him. If Lincoln is elected and does not give the seceders all the fat offices in the government, I say that he will be the most ungrateful wretch that ever lived. (*Laughter and applause; the repetition of the sentence was called for, and when given, was received with fresh applause.*) I never would receive such support from a body of men without acknowledging it afterwards. (*Laughter.*) I hope my friend is satisfied on this point.

"I have been talking at random, taking up these topics as they occurred, changing the threads of my discourse as suggestions were made or questions proposed; for my object has been to answer frankly all the points on which my enemies have been attacking me. I did not come here to solicit your votes. I have nothing to say for myself or my claims personally. I am one of those who think that it would not be a favor to me to be made President at this time. Not that I underrate the honor and the dignity of that high office, but I believe that I can render my country as much service while I am in the Senate of the United States for the next four years. I can there make as much reputation for myself as in the presidential chair, and if any attempt be made at disunion, leave a record to my children of which they will be more proud than they would be of my election to the Chief Magistracy of this glorious Republic. (*Applause.*) And hence my object in visiting the South is to explain how it is that these feelings of fraternity and kindness and brotherly love have been severed, and hostile, sectional parties organized in their places. I desire to know if there is not some common ground on which all constitution-loving men may rally and unite in putting down Northern Abolitionists and Southern Secessionists. (*A voice, "There is."*) I desire to know whether the old Democratic masses are not content to stand by their time-honored organization, by their time-honored platform, by their time-honored principles, to save the Union now as we have saved it on so many occasions before. (*Applause.*) I tell you that intervention by Congress means disunion, I care not whence it comes, whether from the North or from the South. (*Applause.*) I have too much respect for the intellect of all the interventionists, to believe that any one of them thinks that the Union could exist unless through the doctrine of nonintervention.

"In 1850 the agitators of the North and the agitators of the South got up similar trouble to the one that now threatens us. The Northern free soilers demanded the Wilmot Proviso prohibiting slavery wherever the people wanted it. Yancey at the head of the fire eaters of the South demanded that Congress should protect slavery wherever the people did not want it. The issue then is precisely the issue now. The issue was pushed then as it is now, pertinaciously pushed till the best men in the country became alarmed, lest this glorious Union should fall a sacrifice to faction. Even the great Clay who had performed his glorious mission on earth, and who had retired to the shades of Ashland to prepare for another world, in his retirement heard the harsh and discordant notes of discord and sectional strife, and rousing himself, came forth from his retirement and resumed his seat in the Senate, that great theater of his great deeds, to see if he could not do something to restore peace to a distracted country. Union Whigs and Union Democrats assembled together every morning with Clay in the chair, Cass upon his right, and Webster upon his left, to see if by united council we could not devise some scheme to put down the Southern sectionalism and the Northern abolitionism, and restore peace to the country. Now you are all aware that the Compromise measures of 1850 were the results of the councils. They were the joint work of the Union men of the country, without reference to politics. The measures adopted passed despite the joint efforts of all the disunionists and other patriotic men who had hoped something better than compromise might be adopted. But you all know that the compromise measures were adopted, and that they were based on the principle of the nonintervention by Congress with slavery in the territories. The Compromise measures of 1850, rejecting the Wilmot Proviso on the one hand, and intervention on the other, rejected both, and banished the slavery question from the Halls of Congress, and referred it to the people to do as they pleased. In 1852, when the Whigs assembled in national convention for the last time, and nominated Scott for the presidency, they affirmed the same principles of nonintervention. When the Democrats assembled at the same place and nominated Pierce, we affirmed the same principle of nonintervention by Congress with slavery in the territories. But when we got to Baltimore in convention, we found there all the seceders, who with Seward and Sumner, had attempted to defeat the Compromise measures. They came and asked us to receive them back into the Democratic party. We told them that we would attempt to take them back on the condition that they renounce their opposition to the doctrine of nonintervention and stand by the principle in the future. They agreed to do it, and we received them back, and the convention unanimously affirmed the Compromise measures. Hence every Democrat in America in 1852 by his vote for Pierce affirmed the doctrine of nonintervention just as we hold it and understand it now, and every Whig in America meant the same thing by his platform.

"In 1856 the same principle was affirmed again. Buchanan accepted the office on that principle. In his letter of acceptance he went the full length of squatter sovereignty. He said that the people of a territory, like those of a state, should decide for themselves whether slavery should be or should not be excluded within their limits. Breckenridge pledged himself to the same thing in his Lexington speech accepting the nomination to the vice presidency. Every Democrat should know that the party was pledged to that doctrine then. Now you find that the old Secessionists of 1850 are trying to play the same game over again, under the same leader for demanding intervention. Yancey was the leader then as he is now, with the same object in view now that he had then. The question is, Are we going to permit them, permit these interventionists, North and South, to alienate the people and break up the Union? I tell you it never shall be done if I can prevent it. (*Applause.*) I love my children but I do not desire to see them survive this Union. I know of but one mode of preserving the Union. That is to fight against all disunionists. Beat them for the legislature; beat them for Congress; beat them for governor; beat them for President (*cheers*) and teach them to love the Union at the same time that they say the Lord's Prayer. (*Applause.*) Then we will have peace. The only mistake we Democrats made was in tolerating disunionist sentiments in our bosoms so long. We never ought to have received them back when they went into the disunionist movement of 1850. Being back, some of them have become good citizens. We shall stand by them, but we shall apply the rigor of the law against every man that raises his hand against the peace and harmony of the country. Why should we not live together now as our fathers did when they made the government? At the time of the Revolution Southern men were led to battle by Northern generals, and North Carolina bore bloody evidences of her gallantry at such times, and, on the other hand, Northern troops were led to battle by Southern generals. There was no sectional strife in Washington's camp. Then Northern men and Southern men shed their blood in a common cause on the same battlefield in order that they might transmit to their posterity a glorious inheritance. (*Applause.*) Now when you tell me that you are going to divide the Union, I ask where you will run your line? Will you run it between the graves of your ancestors? Are you going to separate the father from the son? the brother from the sister? the daughter from the mother? What are you going to do with the glories of Bunker Hill, Yorktown, Saratoga, and King's Mountain? Are you going to divide them, too? It is a sacrilege to talk about disunion. (*Applause.*) Let us obey the law, obey the Constitution, perform our duties under it, and then compel every man to yield obedience to it.

"I thank you very kindly for the attention with which you have listened to me. I appreciate the compliment which this large concourse of people, assembled under such circumstances, implies. I shall depart from North Carolina as I did on many occasions before, with my heart full of gratitude for your kindness and for the favors you have bestowed upon me. I shall anxiously desire to return at some future time and renew my acquaintance with you."

APPENDIX D

BRECKENRIDGE CAMPAIGN SPEECH BY WILLIAM L. YANCEY, NEW YORK, NEW YORK, OCTOBER 10, 1860 [1]

"FELLOW-CITIZENS of New York, I trust that an Alabamian may yet speak to the citizens of New York in the language of fellowship. I trust that the hour is not yet arrived in which, when an Alabamian speaks to his brothers of the city and the state of New York as brothers it will be a subject of jeering and hissing. We ought to be brothers, if we are not. There ought to be a brotherhood of citizenship throughout this vast country which would knit together its social and business relations in bonds so strong that the fanatics of the whole world could not burst them. (*Loud cheers.*)

"I am not unaware, gentlemen, of the delicate position which a speaker from the far South occupies, who in this hour of an excited political canvass, undertakes to speak in one of the Northern states, words of truth and justice for his section. (*Cheers.*) But I believe, my countrymen, that truth and frankness will win their way at all times to hearts that are swayed by truth, by generosity and by justice. (*Applause.*) I do not disguise from you — I would not have it otherwise — that I speak to you here to-night as a Southern man. I speak to you here to-night for the home that I love better than any other home, for the state that I love better than any other state, for the section that I love better than any other section (*cheers*), my own, and surely it may not be amiss to speak these words in this spirit to a brave people who love their own homes and their own state, and their own section better than they do others. But I trust they have, and I desire to-night to inculcate in their bosoms that they shall

[1] The *New York Herald*, October 11, 1860.

have a respect and a loyalty and an allegiance to the common law and bond that binds us together in one Union. (*Applause*.) I feel, too, the difficulty in addressing a popular audience in this canvass in any other strains than as the advocate of the election of Breckenridge and Lane, whose friend I am. (*Cheers*.) But, my countrymen, events have happened, the wires are bringing to us the news now that the great state of Pennsylvania, to which good and conservative men have looked for safety in this canvass, has given way, and is about to cast its vote for a sectional candidate on a great issue, a candidate all of whose sentiments are at war with the Constitution of the country.[1] I therefore feel it my duty to-night to try to rise above any party aspects of these questions. These aspects, great and interesting as they are at all times, sink into insignificance beside that other question that has arisen yesterday and to-day, if it did not exist before, our loyalty to an endangered Union under the Constitution. Therefore, passing aside the mere claims of men, passing aside these mere questions of party politics, and endeavoring to rise to the dignity of this great question, the safety of the country under the Constitution, I address you to-night in behalf of that union of good men which was inaugurated here in the City of New York, and whose influence will, I trust, extend wider over this vast state, till it produces a conservative majority in favor of the Constitution and the Union. (*Cheers*.) In speaking, my countrymen, in behalf of this great issue, I shall necessarily have to deal with the fate of my section. I shall necessarily have to deal with her position in this Union, past, present, and prospective. I shall necessarily have to deal with her relations to the Constitution and the Union, and her relations and connections with you in this section of the country.

"It is another mistake that is made by some men — good men, doubtless, indulge in it but it is no less a mistake — that the South, on the great issue that divides the North and the South, has been on the aggressive. Far, very far from it. The readings of history, the teachings of your own age and your own experience, all disprove it. The South asks from this government but simple protection from wrong. (*Cheers*.) She claims and she must have it, and she will have it. (*Tumultuous cheers*.) She must have

[1] Pennsylvania goes Republican in a state election.

and she will have a recognized equality in the Union, or she will take it out of it. (*Cheers.*) We desire, my countrymen, the Union of the Constitution. We know no other. Convince us, as very possibly it might be done, — and I am very far from thinking it cannot be done — that we can be a more prosperous people outside of the Union and the Constitution, and the Southern mind will reject it. The South is loyal to the compact which her fathers made with your fathers, and that compact she means to defend against all comers, whether in a majority or in a minority. She claims only equality within the Union, not asking of this government one single act that will aggress on any right that you have. Ready at all times now, as she has been in the past — and it is a part of her glory to refer to it — to defend your rights when assailed, whether from abroad or from within, the South has occupied in this canvass and in times past, on all issues, affecting her peculiar institution, slavery, a defensive position.

"I defy the astutest declaimer of those who attack her, to point to one historical act of legislation which she has asked that is aggressive on the rights of this favored section. (*Cheers.*) It is quite common here to say that the South was aggressive in repealing the Missouri Compromise. It was my lot to be in the public councils when that compromise was proposed three different times to be applied to the territories of Oregon and New Mexico, the territories acquired from Mexico. Three different times was that compromise proposed by Southern men." (*Here there were demonstrations of hostility to the speaker, and cries of "Put him out."*)

Yancey. "No, let him alone, gentlemen, I want him to hear some truth. (*Cheers.*) Three different times did Southern men propose this compromise and three different times, while I was in the councils of the country, did Northern men vote it down. Up to the final admission of Oregon, in 1848, was that compromise proposed again and again, and again and again was it rejected by the House by the Northern men. They claimed the Wilmot Proviso to be the law applicable to the territory. They claimed that they should have all. The South, while recognizing the injustice done her under the Missouri Compromise, was willing to stand by and adhere to the idea which appeared to be the settled policy of the country. The convention which was thought to be a convention of ultra men, the Nashville convention, proposed again the Missouri Compromise as the measure by which the South would stand. But finding that this compromise repeatedly proposed by her was rejected by those who had control of legislation in one of the branches of the government, the South threw herself on her constitutional position in the government, on the principle in the Constitution which made them equal in the territories; she demanded an equal showing in the territories and she never demanded more. (*Applause.*) It does not lie in the mouth of men who propose to take all the territories, and to exclude the owners of four millions of slaves from settling in these territories, to say that the South is aggressive, when they take from the South the privilege of forming more slave states out of the vast and magnificent domain of our common country. (*Cheers.*)

"Now, friends, we do not stand upon compromise. We stand upon something far higher than compromise, something more sacred than compromise. (*Applause.*) We stand upon the constitutional compact made by our fathers with your fathers, and we take that compact as it was interpretated by them and by the Supreme Court of the United States; and with this faith the South takes her position, and from that position she will not recede, nor will she be driven so long as there is a Union worthy of being preserved. (*Loud applause.*) What is that constitutional position? It is this: we are the owners of four million slaves. How did we get them? We have inherited them from the men of the Revolution, who fought the battles and wrote the Declaration of Independence, and maintained their principles by the spilling of their blood and the sacrifice of life, courage, and personal welfare. We have received this system of labor as an inheritance from those men who, after the Declaration of Independence, wrote the Constitution. Now, in that instrument provision was made, not only for the increase, but for the safety and protection of the slave as property. But at this day it is propounded in high quarters, that there is an irrepressible conflict in the Constitution between free labor and the slave labor, and that that conflict must go on till Southern institutions and Southern citizens are all destroyed. Gentlemen, there is an irrepressible conflict between that gentleman and his policy and the writings of our fathers and the compact which they left us. (*Applause.*)   In that irrepressible conflict all these good men who love the Union and the Constitution, and love justice, truth, and their neighbors at the South, must stand by the Constitution or else they will be recreant to the principles of constitutional loyalty.   (*Applause.*)

"Now, what has the Constitution done for us?   Our fathers were not only slave owners, but they bought slaves in Africa and brought them into this country.   When the framers of the Constitution were drawing it up, Virginia desired to get rid of slaves but Massachusetts and several other states desired that it should be carried on (*laughter and applause*), and Massachusetts and the other states that joined with her succeeded in engrafting into the Constitution the provision that the slave statute should not be abrogated by the act of Congress, nor any amendment made to the Constitution, before the year 1808.   (*Applause.*)   Under the Constitution all other clauses but those relating to the slaves could be amended, if the people desired it; but the friends of the slave traffic were so strenuous in regard to it that there is a distinct provision of the Constitution that the clause relating thereto shall not be amended.   In fact, it was beyond the reach of constitutional amendment.   It was a fundamental provision made by our fathers, one with the others, that it should not be altered or amended till 1808.   How does that stand with the doctrine of the irrepressible conflict?   To me it appears that there is so little agreement between the two things that the Constitution knocks the irrepressible conflict on the head.   That our fathers provided for the increase of the institution is beyond all doubt.   They were not satisfied with the four hundred thousand slaves that existed at the commencement of the Revolution, but demanded that the number should be increased by importation until the year 1808, and in that year no less than one hundred thousand slaves were imported into the country under the authority of the Constitution, and it is the descendants of these slaves who are now scattered throughout the Southern states.   And these are the slaves, guaranteed to us by the Constitution, whom Mr. Seward and Mr. Lincoln propose to take away from us by infamous legislation.   (*Applause.*)   Now, gentlemen, what our fathers deemed a thing so sacred that

x

they demanded a constitutional guarantee for its increase, continuance and protection as property, should certainly be no less so to their sons, and they, therefore, hold that they shall not be robbed of their slaves under any form of law. (*Applause.*)

"Not only did our fathers provide for the increase of this species of property, but for its safety against attacks that are made against it to this day. It has often been said that the Constitution of the United States is inspired with something almost divine. These great men who framed it for the common good seem to have known what would be the ultimate fate of the negroes in the North; they seem to have foreseen that they would die out in the colder states of the North, and that, as a consequence, they would seek to locate themselves in the more genial regions of the South. Such has been the fact. And our fathers were not ignorant either that there would always be men along the borders and near the slave states seeking to mislead the slaves; and therefore they took the precaution of inserting into the Constitution the provision that all fugitive slaves should be given up, and made it incumbent on the states that they should aid in the execution of the laws, and that they should cause all escaping slaves to be surrendered. Therefore, while there were provisions for the increase and the spread of the institution, its protection was also amply provided for. Now, the law is given to government for carrying out its great mission, the protection of life, liberty, and property. Our fathers increased the power of protection and this was done by the Constitution.

"It was further given to the slaveholding states to have representation for three-fifths of their slave property. Although the slaves are not citizens under the form of our government, yet our fathers had a three-fifths representation by virtue of their possessing these slaves. But then they were organized property for taxation, and under the Constitution direct taxation is to be imposed in proportion of three-fifths of the slave population. Here, then, is the constitutional increase of the institution of slavery; also the safety guaranteed to it under the provisions of the Fugitive Slave Act. It is an acknowledgment of property to be taxed as such when the nation chooses to derive a revenue from it.

"Under this compact the South has existed and prospered, and you in the North, in conjunction with the South, have derived much benefit from slavery. It has been said that the South is not prosperous owing to this institution, and they undertake to compare the North and the South in a very invidious manner. I do not desire to make any such invidious comparisons. I rejoice in the prosperity of this nation. I rejoice that the North is a great, a prosperous, an intelligent, and a happy people; also that my section is not behindhand in any of those qualities in a nation which make up a true and great manhood. (*Applause.*) When the Revolution commenced, the South possessed a population of 812,000 whites and 450,000 slaves. The North, on the other hand, had 1,900,000 whites and 47,000 slaves, making in the aggregate about a half million slaves in the two sections. How is it now? According to the best statistical statement, taken from official sources, there are now in the Northern states 18,000,000 whites, and in the South 8,000,000 whites and 4,000,000 slaves. Now, this will show that population in the North and in the South has kept pace very well together. In fact, the North has not kept quite up to the Southern ratio in increase of population; and this, notwithstanding the great advantages in this respect which you have had from 4,000,000 foreigners, a benefit which does not extend to the South. The natural increase of the South surpasses the natural increase of the North, and it is remarkable that the natural increase of the slaves is equal to their masters, considering that they are in a sickly country exposed to noonday heat of a Southern sun, and the masters are protected by exemption from real manual labor. Yet the black population, notwithstanding all the difficulties under which they labor, and which are incident to their condition, have kept pace with those who are in happier circumstances of life. It proves that our institution is well calculated to improve their condition. They are not treated with cruelty or tyranny as a general thing, although in all communities there will be found hard men. I have no doubt it is so in New York, but not greater than it is in the South, though to an equal extent. Now, these facts about the census cannot be denied. Figures, they say, when properly arranged and calculated, cannot lie, although I believe they can very often be located in such a manner as to tell very big lies. (*Laughter.*)

"Look, now, at our industry, and it will favorably compare with yours, although you in the North are peculiarly an industrious people. But the men of the South, like those of the North, have not been wasting the time that God has given them. Look at the exports of 1848 and 1849. There has been a large amount of surplus production in the two sections, which we do not require for our own uses, but export to foreign countries, and it is well known that a nation is generally judged by the quantity of surplus products which it exports to other parts of the world. There was exported last year for the whole country products to the value of $353,894,000; $57,000,000 of which was in specie, leaving as the result of produce and actual labor, $278,292,000 for the year ending June, 1859.[1] Now, of this vast quantity of property, it will not be uninteresting to inquire how much has come from the greatly despised Southern section, where it is said that labor meets with no reward and that everything is demoralized with the white and black men. What is it? Let the agitators and political speculators look at the actual figures. The North exported $5,281,000 exclusively, with produce amounting to $650,000,000, and $150,000 in ice. There was exported in that year, $84,417,000 of mixed productions common to both sections of the country, as to North Carolina, Tennessee, Mississippi, and Illinois, Ohio, and other states. Now, it is deemed a fair calculation that the North has one-third of that. The whole product then is $188,692,000; of this the following is the proportion of the articles exported: cotton, $161,434,000; tobacco, $21,074,000; rosin and turpentine, $3,554,000; rice, $2,207,000; tar and pitch, $141,000; brown sugar, $96,000; molasses, $5000; hemp, $9000, (*A voice, "Hemp is still growing, I hope."*) A gentleman says he hopes hemp is still growing. I am glad that hemp yet grows, and I am only sorry that there is not more of it. (*Laughter and applause.*) What is the result of these figures? They show that the South in the fiscal year alluded to exported $217,000,000, and the North exported only about seventy, no, not seventy, but about sixty-one millions of dollars, exclusive of the amount of specie

[1] The figures given in this paragraph either were intentionally garbled by Yancey, or the reporter in taking down the speech made mistakes; as given, the figures are meaningless.

shipped from California, which adds about one hundred and ten or one hundred and twelve million, and the exports of the South, therefore, are nearly double. Now the agitators, speculators, and others would do well to think of this, and it would be right for these philosophers to study the figures before they undertake to abuse my section of the Union.

"In the present year the results are much larger in the favor of the South, as $195,000,000 is the increase of the cotton crop. It will be found that this is not an isolated case. The cotton crop is more extensive generally than in previous years. But no matter how far this may go, the results will show that there have been large increases in the production of tobacco, rice, etc. On the whole, the South produces more than the North, including the specie from California. This shows that this institution is valuable, not only to the South, but to the North. The prosperity we have derived is great, and you have legitimate share in it."

Mr. Yancey then proceeded to speak at length concerning the differences between the climate of the North and of the South and of the capacity for active labor possessed by the Northern men, and the beneficial results following from those fraternal relations. "This labor is the means of producing much wealth from the South, and while the white people of the North can undergo continuous labor, those of the South, exposed as they are to the heat of the climate, cannot do so. No white man can work at laborious occupation under the fervid heat of the South. The consequence is that every one works in the North. The merchants here in the counting house works as well and as hard as his clerk to whom he pays $1000 or $1500 annually, and with a far greater sense of responsibility.

"The commerce of the North and of the South in its rapid development has also been the means of producing wealth to both sections, in the friendly competition with other countries in carrying merchandise abroad. New York is the great heart of the whole commerce of the country. Commerce has its seat here, large-headed and large-hearted commerce, and here it takes these products and disperses them, two-thirds through this part of the country and then over the world. (*Applause.*) The prosperity of the whole country depends on the advancement of New York. (*Applause.*) Now, then, look at your coasting trade. Look at it and you will find that it is a most gratifying spectacle. Then see what are the demands of the South. The South asks nothing from there but that you will not allow any one to steal away her niggers. (*Laughter and applause.*) Enlarge your jails and penitentiaries, reënforce and strengthen your police force, and keep the irrepressible conflict fellows from stealing our niggers, and we are satisfied. (*Applause.*) Now, is there anything unreasonable in that? (*"No! no!"*) It is the voice of reason; it is the voice of loyalty; it is the voice of common sense, which those speculating theorists do not have. (*Applause.*) Now I say that we ask nothing else.

"When has the South come and asked you to protect her cotton? Gentlemen, we defy the world. England, with her acknowledged power in the world, is seeking a spot in which to make cotton, an aggression probably for the very reason of conquering nation after nation, whose fertile soil and climate are fitted for trying the experiment. England, after all her efforts has raised cotton at the cost of fifty cents per pound, which she has sold in the market in competition with American cotton at ten to fifteen cents per pound. We ask no premium against competition with the cultivation of rice and tobacco. The peculiar products of Southern labor defy the competition of the civilized world. The South in that respect is independent of the world. (*Applause.*)

"Now, how is it with you? I know you will bear with me when in a friendly way I undertake to trace the history of legislation as regards Northern labor. How often has New England beseeched Congress for protection to her cotton and woolen manufactures? How often has protection been asked for your iron manufactures? And you, gentlemen, here in New York, Boston, and Philadelphia, have got protection to your shipping interests. Just think of it a moment. Nobody can compete with you for our carrying trade. Let the English or French ships anchor by the side of a Yankee skipper in the harbor of Mobile Bay. I take to them my one hundred and fifty bales of cotton and I say to the English captain, 'What will you take this to New York for?' 'For a dollar a bale,' says he. Can I send it by him? The

Yankee alongside says, 'I will take it for two dollars a bale.'
What am I bound to do? To give it to the Yankee skipper because our coasting laws protect the shipping of the Northern
states to the exclusion of all others. Consequently your shipping
is encouraged. The carrying trade is almost exclusively confined to the products of the South. England, France, and Hol-
land cannot compete with you, owing to our laws. Now we have
no such law protecting our industry. We cannot deal in shipping;
you do. And yet we do not complain.

"Now, how is it with you? There is a tariff of from twenty to
thirty per cent on your iron manufactures. To be sure we derive
a revenue from this, but you derive also a premium to your labor,
and consequently the labor of the North, that I have been comparing to the labor of the South, has the benefit of a premium
given to it by this tariff. The South has no such benefit; she asks
none. She can afford to let you have all that. (*Applause.*) I
know that some of our Southern friends complain of this, and say
that it is not exactly right. South Carolina, you know, once
brought us very near the verge of dissolution in consequence of
what she believed a discrimination between the industries of the
country. But this has passed away; there is comparative mutual
understanding now. We have come somewhere near a substantial
agreement about these matters. Less protection is demanded
now than formerly. You can compete much easier with foreign
industry than formerly, and by and by, perhaps, you will be able
to throw it off in the coastwise trade. But the fact remains that
your Northern labor demands and receives from the government
a premium, and that Southern labor receives none; and yet it
outstrips the labor of the North in a fair contest. (*Applause.*)
Now this protection is very valuable to you, and it is also valuable to us. It is valuable to the whole country; and I do not mention these facts for the purpose of producing any fear. I trust
that you are not on that level in which your loyalty can only be
measured by the amount of money you make out of this government. (*Laughter and applause.*)

"Now, if this is the result, then comes up another question.
This mutual interchange of commodities throughout our vast
country, the gold of California, the grain of the West, the manu-

factures, the commerce; what more? What a sound, magnificent basis is presented in these states for a prosperous Union under our glorious Constitution. (*Applause.*) We aid each other with a proper sense of brotherhood, a proper sense that we are citizens of the same country, that we have a like common protection, and should deal out justice to each section with an equal hand, not raising up this section at the expense of any other, knowing no section, but dealing with them all in the same spirit of justice. That spirit should exist throughout the land. But this cry of the assailant that now resounds throughout your borders, from the rock-bound coast of Maine to the golden sands of Oregon, this cry of the assailant, which, it is said, is made by a majority of your people, that this great institution, in itself worth $2,800,-000,000 — worth incalculably more than that when all its social relations which are interwoven with it and which must go down if that institution is destroyed — this cry of the assailant of this great and valuable institution, now presents an issue. I ask you, gentlemen of New York and of this Northern section; I ask you, an integral part of the eighteen millions that have been held up *in terrorem* by one unwise braggart son of your section as able to conquer eight million (*sensation*); I ask you, my countrymen, what benefit will it be to you to have all this vast industrial and social relation of the South destroyed? (*Applause.*) But it is not to be destroyed.

It is said that cotton, which is so valuable, which builds up the South and the North, which keeps the world going, out of which nations make their profit, derive their comfort, that this incomparable article can be raised by white labor. How utterly absurd to any one who knows anything of our climate, of our system of labor, and of the necessities of the cotton crop. We have a temperature in the summer ranging in the open air from one hundred and ten to one hundred and thirty degrees Fahrenheit. No white man can stand labor under that burning sun, and they do not. The owners of the slaves seek your genial climate. They fill all your watering places, they fill the hotels of this vast metropolis; they travel all over your rivers and lakes, and stop at your places of resort, seeking not for recreation, but to get rid of the miasma, the fever, the hazards of life that are incurred in the hot summer

climate in the summer months. And how do the overseers avoid
these things? They protect themselves with all the care that a
man can who does not labor. They often go to the fields with
umbrellas over their heads, or seek the shade of a friendly tree,
while they see the slaves working in the broiling sun without a
hat or anything to protect their heads. Why, the negro can almost, like the eagle, look the sun in the eye. (*Laughter and
applause.*)

"These glorious sons of toil, who are satisfied with their condition, love their masters, contribute to the wealth of the world,
and are the best population under the sun, if these philosophers
will only let them alone. (*Great laughter and applause.*) Billious
fevers and congestive chills are things peculiar to a climate where
heat and moisture prevail; and great heat and moisture are necessary to the cultivation of the cotton crop. But the diseases which
heat and moisture generate do not affect the black man. He
moves among them perfectly unharmed. He is fitted for such a
climate. Hard labor and the privations incident thereto do not
destroy the negro. Of course, they are under the commands of
a master, who gives them their food and their clothing, and from
the natural selfishness which is common to all men, they are occasionally kept at work longer than they ought to be. We do not
pretend to deny these things. But the census shows that these
people increase as fast as the whites. Take the rate of their increase since the Revolutionary War and compare it with that of
the whites, and see if this is not so. This shows that the climate
is fitted to them and they to the climate.

"Not so with the white race. I have lived at the South. Several years ago I passed over a road leading to Tuscaloosa, in Alabama, called the Old Line Creek Road. It is a level cotton region.
When I went to Alabama in 1836, what do you think that was
called? It was called the Widows' Road. There was not a male
head of a family living there. The women lived because they
were not exposed to the noonday's sun nor to the night air. Being
engaged in household duties they escaped the mortality that carried off nearly every man living on that road. I mention this to
show you the nature of the Southern climate. No man exposes
himself to the heat of the sun without great danger, and we have

to take great care of ourselves. The white man cannot stand the climate; the negro can.

"But even admitting that the white man can stand it, he cannot make the cotton crop. It is planted about the first of April — the last week in March and the first week or ten days in April — and from that time until the crop is gathered, which is not before the first of January if there is a fair crop, there is not one week of intermission, not one week that the laborer can be spared without danger and loss. Continuous labor is absolutely necessary for the safety and preservation of that plant all through the heat of the summer. The cultivation of cotton is remarkable. I have seen a field of five or six hundred acres in some of our fine cotton-growing counties in which there was not a spear of grass to be seen. The cultivation requires more care and attention than any of your garden products, and demands regular, continuous, persistent labor. Now, don't you know that white labor is not continuous and persistent during the whole season? Look at your strike. What do you think the effect of one like that that took place in the town of Lynn amongst the shoemakers, would be among the cotton crops of the South? Why, a hundred millions would be lost to the world; possibly a revolution in England, and in all the civilized world, owing to the want of this cotton. (*Applause.*) Therefore, I say in view of the independence of white labor, striking off when it pleases for better wages, seeking for more genial employment, going off, it may be, to some more inviting region, that with the white labor the cotton crop of the South could not be raised; such labor could not be depended upon. Instead of having four and one-half million cotton bales as now, if we depended upon white labor, in my opinion the product would not amount to two million bales. How could the civilized world spare two and one-half million bales, merely to gratify these speculating philosophers? (*Laughter.*)

"So, then, gentlemen, this institution is necessary to the civilization of the world, is necessary to your prosperity as well as to ours. It is an institution, too, that doesn't harm you, for we don't let our niggers run about to injure anybody (*laughter*); we keep them; they never steal from you; they don't trouble you even with that peculiar stench, which is very good in the nose of the Southern

man, but intolerable in the nose of a Northerner. (*Laughter.*)
None of these things trouble you.   The police force that we require troubles only ourselves; the expense of maintaining it is
ours, and by the bye, that reminds me of an interesting item that
you ought to consider.   The masters have to take care of the slaves.
Now, what do you suppose is the cost of the clothing of these four
million of negroes, which the North furnishes?   The cost is some
twenty million of dollars.   Twenty million dollars worth of cotton
and woolen goods are bought at the North; but five millions in
the shape of axes, hoes, chains, iron castings, etc., are paid to the
North for the purpose of carrying on your industry.   The South
does not choose to devote her labor to these things.   She is willing
to raise what she can and sell it at a fair price, and then to go to
you and buy that which you can raise cheaper than herself.   They
spend in the Northern states on an average $10 per annum for each
slave, which would be $40,000,000.

"And these $40,000,000 Mr. Seward sneers at and thinks it
folly to regard the trade as an important one.   He would not
legislate of course in relation to it, and Lincoln I presume would
never think of making it a material subject of consideration in the
way of legislation.   They want to carry out their peculiar theo-
retical views in relation to religion and morals. (*Laughter.*)   Well,
I hope, gentlemen, as you are said to be a very conscientious
people, descended from the Puritans and also the Dutch (*laughter*),
who are a conscientious people, I hope that you will intrust the
legislation on morals and religion to the Great Ruler of the Universe
and won't let Lincoln and Seward have anything to do with it.
(*Great laughter.*)   Now these gentlemen, who are disposed to legislate for material interests, are not going of course to consider this
institution one of that class, no matter how much you suffer.
They scoff at the merchants who talk about fusion for the purpose
of saving the country and its industry.   I may be mistaken, but
I am ready to sit at the feet of philosophers who will teach me
better; but my idea is that the government was instituted to protect material interests alone; that it is not a school for ethical
theories; that we are all to worship as we think proper; and that
our morals are in no ways meddled with except that we shall be
required to act with decency and order.   All these things are left

to the individual consciences and to the consciences of public opinion governing the states. Government deals alone with the material interests of life, and is designed for the protection of the liberty of our own citizens and of their property. It sets up no school of morals or religion, touching the right of one man to hold in bondage another man which our fathers settled.

"Our fathers settled the right to hold the negro in bondage for his labor; not, of course, to hold property in man. I do not hold property in any black man as a man; as a man he belongs to my state and is protected by it. My state says: ' You shall not give him an unusual or cruel whipping; if you do, I will fine you and imprison you, one or both, at the discretion of the judge or the jury. As a man you shall feed him and shall not starve him; if you do not give him a fair allowance, you will be indicted. It is a misdemeanor and you shall be punished for it.' As a man I may work him and exact a proper degree of labor, and no further. I cannot take his life or injure his limbs; if I do, I am liable to the same penalties as if it were a white man."

A voice. "Suppose, as a man, he runs away." (*Laughter.*)

Yancey. "Then I recover him, because the Constitution says that he shall be delivered up. (*Great cheering.*) Gentlemen, the negro has got legs, you may be certain, and when any of these speculating philosophers go down South, they make him think that he is one of the worst-used people in the world, and he runs away, and after being half-starved in the brambles and briars, he comes home hungry and ragged, and is glad to go to work again. (*Laughter.*) Running away negroes is a common thing. Now we have horses that run away. (*Laughter.*) Does that deprive them of being property? If any man takes a runaway horse and appropriates him, the law calls it theft. So with a negro. Now, I wish you to enforce that law when my negroes run away. (*Applause.*)

"Now I say that this institution is assailed, and I will give you a Southern man's view which we as defendants occupy, and the position in which our assailants stand, as we conceive. They say that there shall be no more slave trade; that that is in accordance with the spirit of the Constitution and the teaching of the fathers. All the vast territory, that belongs to the government and which the Supreme Court has said the government holds in trust for the people of the various states, for Alabama as well as for New York, shall be kept free of slavery. There is an area of territory belonging to the United States large enough to form twenty states equal to New Jersey or Maryland, and even, I believe, South Carolina. In all this territory the South is to have no share whatever in settling with its property. The South wants the advantage of a community of young and sister states around her to sustain her against the conflict of sectional passion; she wants the advantage of a spread of her institution which the figures show you is as much for your prosperity as for hers. In other words, if there are to be no more new slave states, the general prosperity is to be curtailed in precisely that proportion. (*Applause.*) I will consider hereafter what is the teaching of the fathers on this question. I am now making a statement of what I consider to be the point of assault which the South is undergoing. Again, they say that the slave trade between the states is to be abolished; that they have a right to do so under the Constitution. Now, that slave trade between the states is incident to its life and prosperity. Confine a man to one spot and say that you must make a show right there and nowhere else, and would that man prosper and thrive and be a benefit to the community and to himself? You know it is not so. Trade must be allowed to seek its own mart and level. Otherwise you are interfering unconstitutionally and improperly and pursuing a bad policy as to trade. It needs to be entirely unshackled. The great idea of the world at this time is for free trade. Now, take away the right to sell our slaves and you destroy the value of our property to that extent. It is so in regard to any property. Again, they endeavor to nullify the Fugitive Slave Law, and twelve states have passed laws to that end. They mean to abolish slavery in the District of Columbia, and in the arsenals and dockyards."

A voice. "Who says so?"

Yancey. "The abolitionists and Black Republicans say so. (*Loud applause.*) I know no distinction. Seward says so. Lincoln says so. Lincoln first enunciated the irrepressible conflict. (*Applause.*) Put him in power and he will build up an abolitionist party in every Southern state; there is no doubt about it. There are men there who will take office and will come to sympathize with his views in time, and so we shall have a demoralized public opinion among our own people. Marshals, postmasters, and other federal officers will sympathize with Lincoln and this irrepressible conflict notion.

"With the election of a Black Republican all the South will be menaced. Emissaries will percolate between master and slave as water between the crevices of the rocks underground. They will be found everywhere, with strychnine to put in our wells, as is the case now in Texas. (*Laughter, hisses, and long applause.*) Gentlemen, there are various modes in which ideas are expressed. Men have tongues and they speak reason; adders have tongues and they hiss. (*Laughter and cries of "Put the strychnine fellow out."*) As I was saying, that in Texas it was proved beyond all doubt that men were taken there prowling about, some of whom were called levellers, upon whom were found all the means and appliances of exciting the slaves there to insurrection. Pistols and bowie knives and boxes of ammunition were found in buggies, and various things in different places, and such quantities of strychnine were found also as to excite wonder as to where in the world it all came from, and where on earth it could have been manufactured. But there those things were found, and for what purpose do you think? Of carrying on the irrepressible conflict in the underground way they have of doing these things; and carrying on the irrepressible conflict not in the open face of day, not meeting the Southern men face to face, but carrying it on in the darkness of the night, with the torch lighted to burn and destroy, with the springs and wells poisoned, and the slaves secretly incited to insurrection. At this moment we have the slave in insurrection in Alabama and Virginia, and in various other states. In many places the thing is showing itself, and it will spread, too, under the action of these marauding bands who are scattered over the country, and who are so fanatical as to think that they are doing a good and just thing in carrying on the irrepressible conflict between the sentiment of freedom and the sentiment of slavery. So that you see that the South is in a dangerous position, and that the torch when applied will come in contact with a very inflammable article, and it will be a wonder if the institution be not blown up by the torch of the incendiary.

"Thus we are attacked in every relation of life by men of power and sense enough to do incalculable injury to us. Our property destroyed; our social relations unsafe; our slaves incited to insurrection; and our persons and property unsafe. Do you tell us to get rid of the cause of this state of things? No sooner do we get rid of it than we destroy the prosperity of the South.

"Then comes the question, what will the South do under these circumstances? Will the South submit? Some men imagine that she will. I do not. (*Applause.*) But, gentlemen, suppose for a moment that the South will submit. Granted that the South does submit. Granted that she thinks that the mere form of the Constitution is enough for her, even while the spirit of it is fled, even while property is unprotected and the lives of her people unsafe — although her property becomes a desolation, her wealth wrested from her, her fields burned up, her industry destroyed; what will be the result? We become like St. Domingo or another Jamaica. We can expect but the same result as the English have experienced from her attempt to set her slaves free, and to endeavor and expect to insure the same degree of prosperity with these slaves free as when they were slaves in bonds. The experience of England and of all the countries on the face of the earth is that if you free the slaves, you can get no work from them. All the evidences of history show that to tamper with these slaves is to open a path for bloodshed, civil war, and desolation. (*Applause.*) If these results follow to us, what results follow to you? Desolation, also, to a great extent. The employment of your shipping gone to the extent of three-fourths, your warehouses desolated and empty to the same extent, and your merchants destroyed. Take away, in fact, $200,000,000 from the $300,-000,000, and New York will feel the effect; so will Boston and Philadelphia and every manufacturing city in the country, with all their great interests, — all will share the desolation of the South. You will also feel the desolating effects of these things, though perhaps not to so great an extent as we of the South.

"But it is not the destruction of property alone that is to be considered. That is the least of the evils we would have to deplore, which will follow the march of the irrepressible conflict. There is the terrible war of races. It is the terrible conflict between four million of blacks and eight million of whites. It is the conflict that destroys civilization, and which will make us the enemies of that race until we drench our fields with the blood of our unfortunate people. One or the other of us must go to the wall. That, indeed, would be an irrepressible conflict. (*Applause.*)

"Therefore, I say that even if the South did submit to these things, you will share in the evils that must follow. We may be destroyed, but you will be less powerful, less happy, and less prosperous. And thus I presume this irrepressible conflict, this great scheme of destruction and desolation, will affect you as well as us. You may master us, you may outvote us, and take away from us our social relations, and leave us desolate, but you yourselves will be in part vanquished by the very means you employ to vanquish us. Turn loose your hordes of a majority, your minions to trample upon the rights of property and the sacred relations of society; turn them loose, but beware you do not meet the fate of Acteon, who was devoured by his own dogs. (*Applause.*) You have a society that needs to be actuated by loyalty to law, that needs to be imbued with the fundamental principles of government, that needs the restraints of the law to keep them observers of the law and obeyers of it as self-working machines. But allow the elements of destruction which underlie your whole social system to be disturbed, loose the bonds which bind them, withdraw the restraints which control them at present, impair in their minds all reverence to law and the constitutional authority, and no power on earth can save you from destruction. Then, I tell you that there would be such an upheaving of society as was never heard of before. It would be like the terrible bursting forth of a volcano, whose fiery lava would overthrow and destroy you. (*Applause.*)

"But I have said that the South would not submit. I have said that the South would not and ought not to submit to any curtailment of her constitutional rights and equality (*applause*), to any denial of her rights in the government. (*Continued applause.*) It is true she is in the minority. Under the forms of law you could do as you pleased with her interests. But was the Constitution made for you to exercise your will at pleasure? Was it made only that the majority might oppress the minority? (*"No!"*) What

was the Constitution made for but as the express assurance that
the strong should not oppress the weak and trample them down?
(*Applause.*) The Constitution was an assurance to the man who
had property that he would not be robbed of it, an assurance to
the minority that the majority would in all things be governed
by the written law and not by the higher law. (*Applause.*) Now,
you at the North think that you can do without the Constitution
in one particular. So far as your relations with the South are
concerned you do without the Constitution. Why? Because
you have the strength and power of the government at your back.
Because you have 183 electoral votes to 120. If you set section
against section, you have sixty-three per cent, a majority over us.
You have more votes than we have, and therefore you have more
votes than we have in the Senate. You have more votes than we
have, and therefore you have a majority over us in the House.
Having more votes than we have, you can elect the President,
you can reform the legislature and the judiciary. You have power
in all the branches of the government to pass such laws as you like.
If you are actuated by passion or prejudice or by the desire of self-
aggrandizement, it is within your power as far as physical power
goes to outnumber us and commit aggression upon us, and therefore I say you can do without the Constitution. Then with a
majority in every part of the government, what have we to look
to for protection? Not to numbers; there we are weak.

"But have we not rights, or have we no rights but such as are
subject to your will, but such as you may chance to give us? If
so, then I say that this is a most despotic and tyrannical government of ours, a despotism of the millions; and for my part I would
deem it better and prefer to live under the despotism of an enlightened king than under the despotism of the millions. (*Applause.*)

"Then the South has but one thing to look to for protection;
that is the Constitution. (*Applause.*) The Constitution was made
for her protection. The Constitution was a compact entered into
on the understanding that the majority should legislate and govern
according to certain laid-down laws, by the laws as received from
the hands of Washington and the other patriots of the Revolution,
by laws specified in the Constitution. (*Applause.*) Will the South
permit you to trench upon the Constitution as given to the country

Y

by the patriot fathers, the Constitution which is to-day as it was
then? Your fathers then agreed to allow that our fathers should,
in all time to come, be governed by the provisions of the Constitution. You may alter it, you may change it, because you have
a superior physical force to us; but there is a certain feeling within
the breast of every Southern man; that feeling is loyalty to the
fundamental institutions of the land; loyalty is the pride of the
Southern heart; to this very hour and to that loyalty and these
fundamental principles of government and the Constitution she
now appeals. (*Applause.*) Mind you, the South asks for nothing
that is not her right. She claims nothing from you that is not her
due. She stands upon the platform of the Constitution where you
stand, your peer, your equal. (*Applause.*)

"Whenever you propose by a system of hocus-pocus legislation
indirectly to undermine or get rid of the Constitution, or to carry
it out according to the mere will of the majority, the South will
hold up that instrument to you and say to you by this you must
be guided, and will further say to you, that as long as you are
loyal defenders and observers of the Constitution, you are our
brethren. But attempt to set it aside, to trample it under your
feet, then I tell you that by that first act of aggression, of invasion
upon our rights, we are free and independent. (*Applause.*)
Gentlemen, God has given that instinct to the poor worm that when
it is trodden upon it will turn upon the foot that tramples it. We,
thank God, are men, sentient, intelligent men, who know our rights
and who dare to maintain them. (*Applause.*) In the advocacy
of our rights we do not assail, nor do we in any way trench upon,
your rights. In our advocacy of our rights we simply ask of you,
gentlemen, to curb your will, restrain that passionate desire for
the advancement of power, let not a mere feeling of pride create
and force an enmity against us. Rise to the high elevation of
good and wise men, who would do unto others as they would have
others do unto them. (*Applause.*)

"I have been asked here to-night certain questions, which I
deem it right to answer now, at the present. One of the questions
is, 'Would you consider the election of Abraham Lincoln as President a sufficient cause to warrant the South in seceding from the
Union?' The second is, 'Whether, in the case of Mr. Lincoln

being elected, and any of the states attempted to secede, you would support the general government and the other states in maintaining the integrity of the Union?' The first question is a speculation, a political speculation at that. It has nothing to do with the canvass. I am here, however, aiding you to prevent such a calamity. I am honestly endeavoring to maintain the integrity of the government and the safety of the Union at the ballot box. (*Applause.*) I am here to aid you in trying to prevent the election of Abraham Lincoln, the author of the irrepressible conflict; and if others as faithfully do their duty, he will never be elected. (*Applause.*) I am asked, and have been asked before, whether I consider that the election would be a just cause for the secession of the Southern states. That is a matter to come after the ballot box. (*Cheers and derisive laughter, and cries, "Answer the question."*) Be quiet, gentlemen. Hear me, hear me. (*Great excitement and tumult and cries of "Order, order," from the platform.*) Don't be impatient, gentlemen. (*Increasing disorder.*) Don't be impatient, and above all things keep your temper. (*Laughter and applause.*) This is not the time to fight, certainly. (*Laughter.*) This is the time to vote and to consider how to vote."

A voice. "Let us have an answer to the question."

Yancey. "You are impatient, my friend. What is the matter with you?"

Excited man on the platform. "Put him out."

Yancey. "If the gentlemen are so desirous of knowing my opinions, they ought to abide by my decisions when uttered. (*Cheers.*) This thing of asking advice of a man, and then not taking his advice, is a monstrous poor way of getting along. Now, I am going to say this about it. This question that is put to me is a speculation as to the future. It is what I consider in the event of something else happening. I hope to God that that will never happen, and that the speculation will never come to a head. (*Applause.*) I am no candidate for the presidency, my friends who wrote these questions, though some of you seem to have thought so, judging from the manner in which you have treated me and Mr. Breckenridge. I am no candidate for office, and I don't want your vote. But I would like to advise with you and get you to vote for a good man — for any man, I do not care who it is, excepting one of the irrepressible conflict men. (*Great applause.*) In the first place, there is no such thing as the South seceding. I do not know how you would go about it. (*"Good" and cheers.*) There is such a thing as a state seceding; but the South seceding is a thing that I cannot comprehend. I do not know how the South would go about it. I do not think that it would ever happen; and, therefore, I have no answer as to what the South should do.

"Now, then, I am a citizen of Alabama. I am what is called a states' rights man. (*Cheers.*) I believe in the rights of my state. The Constitution of my country tells me that certain powers were given to the general government, and that those which were not expressly given or were not necessary to carry out the powers granted, were reserved to the states and to the people of the states. My state has reserved powers and reserved rights, and I believe in the right of secession. (*"Good."*) Virginia and New York were parties to that contract. When the question was presented, the state of Virginia expressed her willingness to join under the compact. The state of New York also did so through her convention. It was provided that if nine states assented, it would be a government for these nine and for all the states that would sign the compact. Therefore the compact was a compact between the states mutually assenting. If any dissented, there was no proposition to force them into the Union. Therefore, I believe in the right of a state to go out of the Union, if she thinks proper. The state of Alabama in her last General Assembly passed a law requiring the governor in the event of a Black Republican being elected President of the United States, to convene, within so many days after he ascertained that fact, a convention of the people of the state, for the purpose of considering the question which is here presented to me. It is a question for the decision of my state; I cannot decide it. As one of the citizens of Alabama, I shall abide by the decision of my state. If she goes out, I go with her. If she remains in, I remain with her. I could not do otherwise. (*Laughter and applause.*)

"It is a grave question for any citizen to consider whether he will dissolve, or aid in dissolving, the bonds which connect his state with the government. It is a grave question, but one which

I hope God in his providence will keep me from considering by the safety of this government in the election of some man opposed to this irrepressible conflict party. (*Cheers.*) But when the time comes for me to make up my mind, I will have deliberate consultation with my fellow-citizens in Alabama. You in New York have nothing to do with it; nothing. Whatever deliberations you choose to have, as citizens of New York, on the fate of your state, will be for yourselves. I have no interest in the question except incidentally, and have no right to advise with you or to say anything to you about it. But upon this presidential question I have a common interest with you, because it is the election of one to administer the government for the next four years for my state as well as for yours. Therefore it is a common question about which I can consult with you. But whether my state or any other state shall go out of the Union is a question which it will be for that state to determine. It is not to be determined by arguing it before election. It would be a grave matter for me to commit myself here, to a crowd in New York, to any policy that might be influenced by after events, by surrounding circumstances, by the expressed sympathies of large majorities of the people of New York or other states with the South. For me here, merely to gratify some personal antagonist, to express any opinion on that point would be folly; it is the wildest folly to expect that I will. That opinion will be rendered to my state whenever they ask for it. ("*Three cheers for the answer.*") [1]

"Now, I am asked one other question. I am asked, whether if any portion of the South secedes, I will aid the government in maintaining the integrity of the Union. Yes, my friends, the integrity of the Union. (*Cheers.*) I am now struggling for it and shall struggle for it to the day of election. The integrity of the Union I shall struggle for with my life's blood, if required. (*Enthusiastic cheers.*) But if this questioner meant by the integrity of the Union the preservation of any administration that shall trample on any portion of the rights of the South, I tell him that I will aid my state in resisting it to blood. (*Great cheering.*) The common rights of resistance to wrong that belong to the worm, those

[1] For his answer in Baltimore, see p. 215; see Breckenridge's answer, pp. 174–175, and Douglas', pp. 180–181.

rights are not the rights that were meant to be secured by our fathers in the Declaration of Independence, when they cut themselves loose from the despotism and the despotic ties of the old world. The serf of Russia has got the right of revolution. The hog has got the right to resist if you try to put a knife to his throat. (*Cheers and laughter.*) The right of revolution is the poor serf's right. It is no right at all. It is only the last expiring throw of oppressed nationality. (*Tumultuous cheering.*) Yes, gentlemen, there is the poor degraded people that for centuries have groaned under the armed head of a powerful despotism, that knows no rights in the masses save the privilege of rendering up their hard-earned earnings in order that the masters might revel in infamous and criminal luxury and wealth. Poor Italy is trying to raise up her bleeding and bruised body, and is now perchance on one knee, and with manacled hands is yet struggling for the great right of revolution. (*Cheers.*)

"Have our fathers provided no better fate for us? Yes, they have. They have made this a government existing on the will of sovereign states, a compact between sovereign states, not made states by force, not made consolidated masses by the conquering march of a hero, with his army at his back and his sword thrown into the scale, where the will of the conquered is not considered. That is not our form of government. Ours is a form of government that the people have willed. It is self-government. It is government where states have willed to make a compact with each other ; and whenever that compact is violated, who is there higher than the states? Who is there more sovereign than the parties to the compact who have the reserved rights guaranteed to them? There are rights reserved to these states; the Constitution itself guarantees them; and there is the great right that rises above revolution — because it is the right of humanity, the right of civilization, the right of an intelligent public opinion, the right of freemen — and that is, that when governments become oppressive and subversive of the objects for which they were formed, then, in the language of our fathers, they have the right to form a new government. (*Cheers.*)

"Governments should not be changed for light and transient causes, but whenever the whole property of an entire community

is swept away by a policy that undermines it or deals it a deathblow directly; when the social relations of an enlightened, virtuous
and Christian people shall be utterly destroyed by a policy that
invidiously undermines them, and produces inevitably a contest
between castes and races; when these rights are touched upon and
the people see that the attack is coming, they will not wait until
the policy is clinched upon them. The very moment their equality
is destroyed in the government under the Constitution, then, in
my opinion, it becomes the duty of the state to protect its people
by interposing its reserved rights between the acts of the general
government and its people. And when it does that, if Abraham
Lincoln or any other man who aids Abraham Lincoln or any
other man in the presidential office shall undertake to use Federal
bayonets to coerce free and sovereign states in this Union (I answer that question as an individual because it does not involve
my state), I shall fly to the standard of that state and give it the
best assistance in my power. (*Great cheers.*)

"But consider for a moment where we would be. Suppose
Georgia should determine to secede in the event of the refusal to
admit a slave state into the Union. Georgia has deliberately
resolved by her ordinance in convention — and it is a fact of her
constitution and irrepealable, save as the constitution is repealable
— that in the event of the refusal to admit a state into the Union
because it is a slave state (and that is a part of the irrepressible
policy), it shall be the duty of her government to call a convention
of her people together, and it is made their duty to go out of the
Union. That is the law of Georgia and she will resist to the utmost, and sever the last tie that binds her to the Union. Now,
suppose Georgia does that, that she goes out of the Union. She
does not hurt you. She does not trespass upon your rights. She
takes nothing with her that belongs to you. She takes nothing
but what belongs to her. She merely withdraws from the government. Suppose that the Federal army was told to march against
her, and the navy told to blockade her ports, and suppose that
Georgia should be conquered by these eighteen million; is she,
then, a free and sovereign state in the Union? The Constitution
says that she is. But will she be so? She will be a conquered
province of the Union. Would the Union then be a Union of the

states, a Union under the Constitution, a Union of states free and
equal, based on the mutual assent of the people? No; it would
be a military despotism. The very moment such a thing occurred,
the whole character of the government would be revolutionized,
and the Cabinet itself would do what Georgia had not done by
withdrawing. Georgia, by withdrawing, leaves you free and
sovereign and independent states in the Union, and she herself
free and sovereign and independent out of it. But to force that
state into submission, to keep her a conquered province, dissolves
your constitutional government, provides for a standing army
and entails the evils that follow in the train of a standing army.[1]

"But, gentlemen, this is the time, this is the place, this is almost
the hour for you to decide — what? That your Constitution and
your government shall not be put to such desperate straits. This
is the day and the hour almost for you to decide that, as men,
you will not bring about a course of events where you will have
to protect your Union by bayonets, but that you will, as wise men,
protect it at the ballot box. That is the genius of the country.
And how are you to do it? Vote for some party or for some
candidate that acknowledges that the Southern states are equal
in this Confederacy; that they are entitled at least to protection
in this Confederacy; that they shall not be trampled upon; that
no rights shall be torn from them; that they shall have equal
rights in forming new states and in the admission of new states;
that they shall have free and equal chance given to their industry
and civilization; that the civilization and industry of the North
shall march side by side with the civilization and industry of the
South, in a generous, noble, enlightened spirit of emulation; and
that the bayonet shall not be thrown into the scale of the North,
as the sword of Brennus was when the fate of Rome hung in the
scale. (*Applause.*) Give us a fair showing. It is all we ask.
Give us an equal chance with you. It is all we ask. Trammel not
our civilization and industry with your schemes of emancipation,
your schemes of abolition, your schemes to encourage raids upon
us. Give us the showing we give you. Hands off! Meet us in
generous rivalry, and he who conquers in the strife is a conqueror

---

[1] For Douglas' answer, see pp. 180–182.

indeed, because the victory will be given to him as the just meed of superior sagacity, superior intelligence, and superior virtue; and whenever you get to be superior to the South in these things, gentlemen, we will bow in reverence before you. (*Applause.*) "And now, my friends, let me close. ("*Go on.*") The events of yesterday press heavily upon me. I acknowledge that I have no exultation.[1] I feel none. I can feel none. I feel that the Constitution is weighed down beneath these heavy majorities. I feel, gentlemen, that the hour progresses in which these tests must be applied, which tests may be attended with the rending of the ties that bind us, in the dissolution of the government that has made us happy and prosperous, and in the destruction of that general prosperity which is the admiration of the civilized and Christian world. I feel it, gentlemen. The keystone of the arch of the Union is already crumbling, and the great fabric rests upon the shoulders of New York. (*Cheers.*) In the hands of New York is the decision of the question. A more weighty question was never before you. One freighted with the fate of societies and of nationalities is on your mind. Peace, prosperity, Union, the Constitution, the blessings of Christian liberty, may depend upon the vote of New York. That vote may crush all these things. That vote may perpetuate these blessings. That you may be equal, gentlemen, to the great responsibilities of this occasion, is the prayer of him who addresses you, and who now bids you respectfully farewell." (*Great cheering.*)

[1] Pennsylvania goes Republican in a state election.

APPENDIX E

CONSTITUTIONAL UNION SPEECH, BY W. G. BROWN-LOW, KNOXVILLE, TENNESSEE, OCTOBER, 1861 [1]

"GENTLEMEN OF THE BELL AND EVERETT CLUB, AND FELLOW-CITIZENS: The Bible tells, in reference to a high and holy theme, that 'day unto day uttereth speech, and night unto night showeth knowledge.' This is emphatically true in regard to the presidential election. The developments of every day and night add strength to the conviction that the presidential contest has narrowed down to a choice between John Bell and Abraham Lincoln. Breckenridge has been distanced at the start; he let down the first heat; and it is the very madness of folly to talk about electing him. The leaders of the Democratic party, who procured his nomination by a rebellious faction at Baltimore, took that method of accomplishing a long-cherished object, the dissolution of this Union and the 'precipitating of the cotton states into a revolution.'

"Douglas, too, is out of the question, really not in the race. He may carry a few of the Northern states, and, I think, will do so; but his election is impossible. His friends desire the defeat of Lincoln, first, because he is a sectional candidate, as they say, running upon the nigger issue alone; and next, because he holds the position of a candidate for the presidency by virtue of the prominence given to him by Buchanan, Breckenridge, and the other members of the cabinet, who ran him against Douglas for the United States Senate, and brought the whole patronage of the government to bear in his favor. Intelligent Douglas men see that Bell is the only man who can now defeat Lincoln. They see that Bell will carry nearly all the Southern states, if the Breck-

---

[1] *Sketches of the Rise, Progress, and Decline of Secession*, by W. G. Brownlow, Philadelphia and Cincinnati, 1862, p. 191.

enridge party are not bent upon the dissolution of the Union, and
their conservatism and devotion to the Union will finally lead them
to the support of Bell.

"With these preliminary remarks I will proceed to address you
on the subject, not of Mr. Bell's record, but of the record of
Breckenridge and Lane, and of the merits of the party putting them
forth as candidates.

"I charge, first of all, that Buchanan's is the most corrupt
and profligate administration ever known to this government
since its organization; nay, that ours is the most corrupt
government in the civilized world, and that this corruption
and profligacy have grown up under Democratic rule; for, with
the exception of four years under Taylor and Fillmore, the
Democrats have had the control of the government for the
last twenty-four years.

"In 1856, when out of power, Buchanan denounced the expenditures of $40,000,000 under Fillmore as an outrage, in an
electioneering letter he put forth, and said that an honest
people ought not to submit to it. In power, when clothed with
authority to correct these abuses, he expended double the
amount; for in one year after he was inaugurated, he increased
the public expenditures to $80,000,000. Here was economy with
a vengeance! Nay, he found a surplus of $20,000,000 in the
treasury, but has borrowed until the outstanding debt is the rise
of $100,000,000.

"But, it may be inquired, what has all this to do with voting
for or against Breckenridge and Lane? Much, every way. Breckenridge is the tail end of this miserable administration, has been
connected with its cabinet councils from the beginning, and is now
its pet candidate for the presidency. Old Joe Lane has stood
upon the floor of the Senate for the last three years and defended
its villainous measures, however monstrous they have been.
Both of these men, if elected, will seek to hide its revolting de-
formities, if, indeed, they do not carry out the same lying and
thieving policy. We need a change. I am sick of seeing it paraded
in foreign journals that the President of the United States is a
thief and a liar. Mr. Buchanan has been convicted of lying and
hiding for thieves, as well as of advising them to steal from the

government, by the sworn testimony of various men of his own party before the Covode Committee.

"As a general thing, the Breckenridge speakers pass all this over as unworthy of notice. Whilthom, the state elector, does meet it, it is true, by charging that John Bell and Judge Douglas voted for the appropriations, and thereby placed money within the reach of Buchanan and his dishonest officeholders. This is a defense with a vengeance.

"But it will be said that these are mere assertions. Let us, then, have the proof. Here it is; and it is high Democratic authority and will not be called in question.

" ' When I first entered Congress, in 1843, the expenses of the government were only thirty million per annum. The country had gone through the expensive Mexican War, with sixty-three thousand soldiers in the field, for thirty millions, and now, in the time of peace, the estimates are seventy-three millions! He believed forty millions an abundance for the national expense.' — HON. A. H. STEPHENS.

" 'This government, sixty-nine years of age, scarcely out of its swaddling clothes, is making more corrupt use of money in proportion to the amount collected from the people, as I honestly believe, than any other government on the habitable globe.' — HON. ANDREW JOHNSON, of Tennessee.

" 'I think it is not saying too much to declare that this country has gone faster and further in ten years, in extravagance, than most other countries have gone in centuries.' — GENERAL SHIELDS.

" 'Before God, I believe this to be the most corrupt government on earth.' — SENATOR TOOMBS.

" 'From the byways and highways of the government the rottenness of corruption sends forth an insufferable stench. Why are the people so patient? Why slumbers the indignation of the Democracy?' — ROGER A. PRYOR.[1]

"But, gentlemen, I object to Breckenridge on account of his antislavery record; and, as a Southern man, I would not vote for him even if John Bell were not a candidate, and the race were between him and Lincoln! I, therefore, ask of you the privilege of exhibiting this record.

[1] See pp. 132–141 for further treatment of the corruption of Buchanan.

BRECKENRIDGE ON INTERVENTION

"'The whole theory of Congressional intervention is a libel on our institutions.' — *The Congressional Globe*, Vol. XXIX, p. 442. "John C. Breckenridge is the nominee of a party claiming Congressional protection.

BRECKENRIDGE'S IDEA OF THE EFFECT ON THE COUNTRY OF THE PASSAGE OF THE KANSAS BILL

"'No, sir, if we reject this bill, we open up the waters of bitterness, which will be sealed again in time, but not until these agitators shall have rioted awhile in the confusions of the country. We blow high the flames to furnish habitations for these political salamanders who can exist only in the fires of domestic strife. But if it passes, the question will be forever removed from the Halls of Congress, and deposited with the people, who can settle it in a manner answerable to their own views of interest and happiness.' — *The Congressional Globe*, Vol. XXIX.

BRECKENRIDGE'S IDEA OF THE OBJECT OF THE KANSAS BILL

"'Then, sir, neither the purpose nor the effect of the bill is to legislate slavery into Nebraska and Kansas; but its effect is to sweep away this vestige of Congressional dictation on this subject, to allow the free citizens of this Union to enter the common territory with the Constitution and the bill alone in their hands, and to remit the decision of their rights under both to the courts of the country.' — *The Congressional Globe*, Vol. XXIX.

BRECKENRIDGE ON SLAVERY IN KANSAS

"'Among the many misrepresentations of the Kansas-Nebraska Bill perhaps none is more flagrant than the charge that it proposes to legislate slavery into Kansas and Nebraska. Sir, if the bill contained such a feature, it could not receive my vote. The right to establish involves the right to prohibit; and, denying both, I would vote for neither.' — *The Congressional Globe*.

J. C. Breckenridge on the Kansas Bill

"'Did not the non-slaveholding states (generally) insist that the true policy was the prohibition of slavery in the territories of the Union by act of Congress, and, by consequence, insist upon applying this principle to Utah and New Mexico? Did not the slaveholding states, on the contrary, planting themselves on the ground of Federal non-intervention, resist this policy, and, by consequence, its adoption and application to those territories? And, after a long and fearful struggle, did not the latter doctrine prevail? and was it not carried into law in the Utah and New Mexico acts? Did not the public, the press, conventions, and states hail the result as a final settlement, in principle and substance of the subject of slavery?' — *The Congressional Globe*, Vol. XXIX, p. 441.

"If this is not sufficient to establish the antislavery proclivities of Breckenridge, I will add a few brief extracts from his celebrated Tippecanoe speech in 1856, delivered before ten thousand Freesoilers, whose votes he solicited for himself and Buchanan.

"'I am connected with no party that has for its object the extension of slavery, nor with any to prevent the people of a state or territory from deciding the question of its existence with them for themselves.'

"'I happened to be in Congress when the Nebraska bill passed, and gave it my voice and vote, and because it did what it did, viz.: it acknowledged the right of the people of the territory to settle the question for themselves, and not because I supposed, what I do not now believe, that it legislated slavery into the territory. The Democratic party is not a proslavery party.'

"Now, the Southern wing of the Democratic party indignantly rejected Douglas, seceded at Baltimore, and nominated Breckenridge, because Douglas held the very doctrines herein avowed by Breckenridge! That you may see them in a still more ridiculous light, here is the resolution adopted by the Douglas Democratic state convention of Illinois, declaring: 'Slavery, if it exists in a territory, does not derive its validity from the Constitution of the United States, but is a mere municipal institution, existing in such territory under the laws thereof.'

"In 1850, while Breckenridge was a member of the Kentucky legislature, he declared, by resolution : —

"'*Resolved*, By the General Assembly of the Commonwealth of Kentucky, that the question of slavery in the territories, being wholly local and domestic, belongs to the people who inhabit them.'

"Will some one of the Breckenridge speakers traveling through this country, quoting garbled extracts from Bell's record, and misrepresenting that able and experienced statesman's legislative course, show a shade of difference in the squatter sovereignty principles set forth in these two resolutions? They both declared slavery in the territories to be local, and only subject to the laws thereof.

"But 'Old Joe Lane,' as he is familiarly called, holds the same doctrine, and said in one of his speeches : —

"'The question of slavery is a most perplexing one, and ought not to be agitated. We should leave it with the states where it constitutionally rests, and to the people of the territories, to prohibit or establish, as to them may seem right and proper.'

"Here, then, are two rank and straight-out squatters, who have outsquatted Douglas, taken up by these Baltimore disunionists and seceders and run for the presidency and vice presidency, and Douglas unceremoniously thrust aside because he was a squatter.[1]

"Will some Breckenridge orator explain why it was that Douglas was set aside for heresy, and two other gentlemen selected, holding the same heresy and hugging it closer? The answer will be, 'Because we wanted our rights under the Constitution.' What rights? The right to secede from the Union and to form a Southern Confederacy. Of this right and this unholy purpose I shall have something to say before I close.

"I inquire again, why was Douglas rejected and Breckenridge

[1] For Douglas' treatment of the popular sovereignty record of the Breckenridgeites, see pp. 95–96.

selected by the intense Southern wing of the party? I have the
true answer to this question, given on the floor of the Senate on the
24th of last May by a distinguished politician. I want you to
hear it, and when you hear it ask me who he was: —

"'It is the fault of the Democratic party, in dodging truth,
in dodging the Constitution itself, that has brought the trouble
upon the country and the party that is experienced to-day.'

"Who said that last May on the floor of the Senate, and is
thus reported in the *Congressional Globe?* It was 'Old Joe Lane';
and I am glad that he said it, in lieu of some opposition man;
for the latter would have been charged with abusing the Democratic party!

"Well might Herschel V. Johnson of Georgia exclaim in a public
speech at Macon but the other day: —

"'This whole secession movement is without justification. It
is not dignified by devotion to principle. It is scarcely redeemed
from the odiousness of faction. Its highest attribute is that of
sheer, naked, and ungenerous warfare against a great and distinguished Democrat. Let its authors bear the responsibility
and reap the coming retribution. It will come when the popular
mind shall be awakened to its legitimate tendencies.'

"But I come now to the subject of disunion. This is a sore
subject with the Breckenridge party, and they are the more sen-
sitive when it is named and prone to denunciation when it is
charged, because they know and feel that they are justly liable to
the charge. The Breckenridge men are not all disunionists, but
the unsophisticated disunionists are Breckinridge men. The
states that seceded from the regular Democratic convention had
expressed themselves as favorable to disunion before the national
convention met even at Charleston. In the debates at Charleston
and Baltimore they showed that that was their cherished project.

"Many of the leading men who supported Breckenridge, in
different states, openly avow that they are in favor of disunion
in the event of the election of Lincoln, though he might be legally
and constitutionally elected, and by a majority of the American
voters. Here are a few of their names: —

Hon. Jefferson Davis of Mississippi

Hon. L. M. Keitt of South Carolina

Hon. Mr. Curry of Alabama

Hon. J. T. Morgan of Alabama

Hon. J. L. Orr of South Carolina

Hon. R. B. Rhett of South Carolina

Hon. Wm. L. Yancey of Alabama

Gov. J. J. Pettus of Mississippi

Ex-Governor McRae of Mississippi

Governor Perry of Florida

Ex-Governor McWillie of Mississippi

Mr. Dejarnette of Virginia

Hon. L. P. Walker of Alabama

Hon. Sydenham Moore of Alabama

Hon. Mr. Pugh of Alabama

Hon. D. Hubbard of Alabama

Hon. Mr. Gartrell of Georgia

Hon. Mr. Crawford of Georgia

Hon. Mr. Bonham of South Carolina

Hon. Mr. Singleton of Mississippi

Hon. R. Davis of Mississippi

Hon. R. A. Pryor of Virginia

Hon. H. S. Bennett of Mississippi

Governor Gist of South Carolina

Hon. Mr. Boyce of South Carolina

Hon. A. Burt of South Carolina

"Now, hear what two of these ardent Breckenridge men have said. It will be remembered that Hon. Barnwell Rhett said, 'The Richmond convention is not national; a national convention is one based on principles common to all portions of the United States.' The Hon. A. Burt said: 'I have not an element of a national Democrat in me. I was raised a nullifier, and should be recreant to principle if I were to apostatize and find myself in the ranks of the national democracy.'

"Yancey's scheme for 'precipitating' the cotton states into a revolution you are all familiar with.

"Major Polk, Douglas elector for the state at large, in speaking with Haynes and Peyton, at Fayetteville, August 31, stated that he was prepared to prove by a telegraphic dispatch that Breckenridge and Lane were nominated by the Richmond seceding convention one hour before they were at Baltimore! This plot explains why the letter of the Richmond seceding convention, notifying Breckenridge of his nomination, was never published, though his letter of acceptance was.

z

" The *St. Louis Republican*, good democratic authority, positively asserts, 'The rupture at Charleston and Baltimore is seen
to have been a preconcerted part of the disunion program, con-
cocted in the secret lodges of the disunion leagues; that the plot
was deliberately hatched there for the disruption of the only national party organization, as an essential preliminary to 'precipitating the cotton states into a revolution,' and that by a division
of the Democrats of the North, and consequent election of Lincoln,
the disunionists hoped to "fire the Southern heart" to the work
of overthrowing the Constitution and the Union.'

"A recent issue of the *Huntsville Democrat*, a Breckenridge
organ, edited by a brother of Senator Clay, says : —

"'If we wait till our enemies get control of the power of the
Federal government, as they now have of the Northern state
governments, and have possession of the purse and the sword, the
treasury, army and navy, then we white men of the South, who
wield the power of slavery, will be in the course of ultimate extinction. The war of extermination, as Douglas called the irrepressible conflict, predicted by Lincoln — already declared — will
then have been waged.'

"Hon. Eli S. Shorter, Breckenridge elector in Alabama, recently said in a speech in Pike County, which speech is reported
in the *States Rights Advocate* : —

"'He took the position boldly, that upon the election of a Black
Republican, upon a sectional platform and by a sectional vote,
he was for a dissolution of the Union.'

"The *Columbia South Carolinian*, a Breckenridge organ of
recent date, says : —

"'The Republicans will push forward in their work and elect
their President, and, when too late to reflect or retreat, will find
themselves face to face with an indignant and outraged people,
with the flag of revolution unfurled.'

"The *Columbus Times*, Columbus, Georgia, a Breckenridge-
Yancey paper, thus unfurls the flag of disunion : —

"'We have not postponed the issue indefinitely. We are not

going to wait for an overt act of aggression before resisting a Black Republican President. We repeat, there is no issue of dissolution in the platform of any party now before the country. We repeat that when Lincoln is declared elected we shall appeal to the "people to redress their grievance." We repeat all that we have ever said that means resistance to Black Republican rule, from first to last.'

"Hon. John Driver, of Russell County, Alabama, an ardent Breckenridge man, and a member of the Charleston and Baltimore conventions, says in a published card over his signature, July 23, 1860, in defense of a dissolution of the Union : 'To effect this object, we, the disunion party, disrupted the Democratic convention at Charleston, and at Baltimore induced others to join us by our agreeing to support men not entirely of our sentiments.'

"James D. Thomas, the Breckenridge elector for the Knox district, said at Maynardsville, on the 28th ultimo, that if the judiciary, legislative, and executive departments refuse protection to slave property, he and his party were for secession. He said that thing, and I presume he represents his party in Tennessee. Governor Harris is committed to the same odious and revolutionary doctrine. So are all the disunion leaders in this state.

"The Bell and Everett elector in the state of Georgia, Colonel S. C. Elam, has renounced the Union ticket and come out in a card for Breckenridge; Colonel Elam gives his reasons for the change; and I beg you to hear those reasons.

"He says that Breckenridge and Lane stand even a slimmer chance than Bell and Everett. Then why does Colonel Elam leave us ? He says that his 'controlling reason' is that 'the Breckenridge party is pledged to dissolve the Union if Lincoln is elected,' and that 'Breckenridge's running renders Lincoln's election certain.' He thinks that 'Douglas might be elected if Breckenridge was out of the way,' but 'Breckenridge couldn't beat Lincoln if Douglas was out of the way.'

"So here is the whole game of the Yanceyites. Colonel Elam has let the disunion cat out of the bag. The Breckenridge party is pledged to dissolve the Union in a certain contingency, the election of Lincoln. To make that contingency certain, they are running Breckenridge.[1]

"Mr. Bell owns eighty-three slaves in his own right, and his wife owns just an equal number, making in all one hundred and sixty-six, and still he is sneeringly pointed at as unsound on the slavery question! Mr. Douglas owns no slaves, and never did in his own right, and is a Northern man; and he has an electoral ticket in almost all of the Southern states. Mr. Breckenridge and family live in Lexington, and board at the Phœnix Hotel, and he votes in that city, regarding it as his home. For several years past he has returned no property for taxation, either real or personal, as appears from the tax book, and for the best reason in the world — he has none. He has a free colored woman as a nurse, and this is all the connection he has with slavery; and yet he is the proslavery candidate for the presidency, and is supported by the slave code, slave trade, disunion party, as the only man prepared to do justice to the South upon the question of the everlasting nigger!

"Now, gentlemen and members of the club, I am about through with the remarks I intended to submit to you on this occasion. Candor requires me, as the contest is rapidly drawing to a close, to admit that the chances are that Mr. Lincoln will be elected. If so, the entire Breckenridge party in the South will go in for a Southern Confederacy. If I am living, — and I hope I may be, — I shall stand by the Union as long as there are five states that adhere to it. I will say more; I will go out of the Confederacy if the rebellious party sustains itself. Nay, I will say still more; I will sustain Lincoln if he will go to work to put down the great Southern mob that leads off in such a rebellion!

"These are my sentiments, and these are my purposes; and I am no abolitionist, but a Southern man. I expect to stand by this Union, and battle to sustain it, though Whiggery and Democracy, Slavery and Abolitionism, Southern rights and Northern wrongs, are all blown to the devil! I will never join in the outcry against the American Union in order to build up a corrupt Democratic party in the South, and to create offices in a new govern-

[1] See pp. 175–178 for further treatment of the secession proclivities of the Breckenridgeites.

ment for an unprincipled pack of broken-down politicians, who have justly rendered themselves odious by stealing the public money. I may stand alone in the South; but I believe thousands and tens of thousands will stand by me, and, if need be, perish with me in the same cause.

"I will conclude, fellow-citizens, by reading the following document, which ought to be published once a year in every newspaper in America, and read out as often from every pulpit in the land, that the real people may see who signed it, and what they pledged themselves to stand by : —

"'The undersigned, members of the thirty-first Congress of the United States, believing that a renewal of sectional controversy upon the subject of slavery would be both dangerous to the Union and destructive of its objects, and seeing no mode by which such controversy can be avoided except by a strict adherence to the settlement thereof effected by the Compromise acts passed at the last session of Congress, do hereby declare their intention to maintain the said settlement inviolate, and to resist all attempts to repeal or alter the acts aforesaid, unless by the general consent of the friends of the measure, and to remedy such evils, if any, as time and experience may develop.

"'And for the purpose of making this resolution effective, they further declare that they will not support for the office of president or vice president, or of senator or representative in Congress, or as a member of the state legislature, any man, of whatever party, who is not known to be opposed to the disturbance of the settlement aforesaid, and to the renewal in any form, of the agitation upon the subject of slavery.

' Henry Clay	H. A. Bullard
Howell Cobb	C. H. Williams
C. S. Morehead	T. S. Haymond
William Duer	J. Phillips Phœnix
Robert L. Rose	A. H. Sheppard
H. S. Foote	A. M. Schermerhorn
William C. Dawson	David Breck
James Brooks	John R. Thurman
Thomas J. Rusk	James L. Johnson

Alexander H. Stephens
Jeremiah Clemens
Robert Toombs
James Cooper
M. P. Gentry
Thomas G. Pratt
Henry W. Hilliard
William M. Gwin
F. E. McLean
Samuel Eliot
A. G. Watkins
David Outlaw
Alexander Evans

D. A. Bokee
J. B. Thompson
George R. Andrews
J. M. Anderson
W. P. Mangum
John B. Kerr
Jeremiah Morton
J. P. Caldwell
R. I. Bowie
Edmund Deberry
E. C. Cabell
Humphrey Marshall
Allen F. Owen'"

INDEX

343